ACEP Master Level Sport Science Courses

ACEP Master Level sport science courses are available to accompany the following texts.

Coaches Guide to Sport Law by Gary Nygaard and Thomas H. Boone. The authors explain a coach's legal responsibilities in easy to understand terms and give practical advice for improving standards of care and safety for athletes.

Coaches Guide to Time Management by Charles Kozoll. This innovative text shows coaches how to improve their self-organization and how to avoid the harmful effects of stress by controlling the pressures inherent in many coaching programs.

Coaches Guide to Sport Physiology by Brian Sharkey leads coaches step-by-step through the development of fitness-training programs suitable for their sport and for the athletes they coach.

Coaches Guide to Sport Injuries by David Bergeron and Holly Wilson gives coaches information on injury prevention and on the immediate treatment and follow-up care for common athletic injuries.

Coaches Guide to Teaching Sport Skills by Robert W. Christina and Daniel M. Corcos uses practical coaching examples to take coaches through the teaching/learning process and offers coaches valuable advice for improving their teaching effectiveness.

Coaches Guide to Sport Psychology by Rainer Martens presents information on motivation, communication, stress management, the use of mental imagery, and other fascinating topics for enhancing coach-athlete relationships and for stimulating improved sport performances.

Each course consists of a *Coaches Guide*, a *Study Guide*, and a *Workbook*. ACEP certification is awarded for successful course completion. For more information about these courses, write to:

ACEP Level 2
P.O. Box 5076
Champaign, IL 61825-5076
1-800-747-5698

COACHES GUIDE TO SPORT PSYCHOLOGY

A publication for the
American Coaching Effectiveness Program
Master Level Sport Science Curriculum

Rainer Martens, PhD
President, Human Kinetics Publishers

HUMAN KINETICS PUBLISHERS
Champaign, Illinois

Library of Congress Cataloging-in-Publication Data

Martens, Rainer, 1942-
    Coaches guide to sport psychology.

    "A publication for the American Coaching Effectiveness
Program, level 2 sport science curriculum."
        Bibliography: p.
        Includes index.
        ISBN 0-87322-022-6
        1. Coaching (Athletics).   2. Sports--Psychological
aspects.   3. School sports.   I. American Coaching
Effectiveness Program.   II. Title.
GV711.M35   1987   796'.07'7   87-16814

ISBN: 0-87322-022-6

Developmental Editor: Linda Anne Bump, PhD.; **Copyeditor**: Lise Rodgers; **Assistant Editor**: Janet Beals; **Production Director**: Ernie Noa; **Text Design**: Keith Blomberg; **Typesetter**: Sandra Meier; **Text Layout**: Gordon Cohen; **Interior Art**: Craig Ronto; **Cartoon Illustrations**: Jerry Barrett; **Cover Design and Layout**: Jack W. Davis; **Printed By**: Versa Press

Printed in the United States of America   15   14   13

Human Kinetics
Web site: www.humankinetics.com

United States: Human Kinetics, P.O. Box 5076, Champaign, IL 61825-5076
800-747-4457
e-mail: humank@hkusa.com

Canada: Human Kinetics, 475 Devonshire Road, Unit 100, Windsor, ON N8Y 2L5
800-465-7301 (in Canada only)
e-mail: hkcan@mnsi.net

Europe: Human Kinetics, P.O. Box IW14, Leeds LS16 6TR, United Kingdom
+44 (0) 113 278 1708
e-mail: humank@hkeurope.com

Australia: Human Kinetics, 57A Price Avenue, Lower Mitcham, South Australia 5062
08 8277 1555
e-mail: liahka@senet.com.au

New Zealand: Human Kinetics, P.O. Box 105-231, Auckland Central
09-309-1890
e-mail: hkp@ihug.co.nz

Dedication

To Marilyn,
my courageous and
vivacious wife.

Acknowledgments

I wish to give special thanks to Damon Burton, Dave Feigley, Dean Ryan, and Robin Vealey for critiquing an earlier draft of this book. I especially want to acknowledge Damon Burton's contribution. As a former student and colleague of mine, Damon made numerous and significant contributions to the development of the Psychological Skills Training (PST) program presented in part III. Damon and I had intended to write a book on PST for athletes, but just never got it done. Thus Damon graciously permitted me to use many of his ideas in this book.

Linda Bump served two vital roles in the development of this book. As a sport psychologist, she too critiqued the manuscript, making many helpful suggestions. She also was the developmental editor at Human Kinetics who masterfully guided this book through the editorial and production stages. My sincere thanks, Linda, for all your help.

I am also indebted to all my staff at Human Kinetics for granting me three sabbatical leaves to disappear to the coast of Maine in the autumn and the Florida sunshine in the winter to write this book. I am indeed fortunate to have so many dedicated professionals at HKP who manage the business well during my absence.

I owe more than I can put into words to my wife Marilyn, the inspiration in my life. Her support has been extraordinary even while she has battled numerous health problems. The book is dedicated to her as my twenty-fifth wedding anniversary gift.

Contents

Preface

This book should be required reading for every coach. That may sound terribly boastful coming from the author, but it is not intended to be. My confidence in this book is not rooted in my writing it, but in the subject matter about which I am writing. I encourage you to read this book carefully because I know the content will help you be a better coach—but only if you put the information to use. It will also help you enjoy coaching more.

Last year I sat next to an elderly man and his wife as we were flying from Boston to Orlando, Florida. As we came to know each other, he told me of his interest in poetry and he recited these words:

> All that I know
> Has been given by other souls.

How true. My task as the author of this book has been relatively simple—to compile the information for you. The difficult task was acquiring the knowledge that makes it possible to write this book. So the real credit for this book goes to the psychologists, especially those who call themselves sport psychologists, for conducting the thousands of studies that provide the knowledge base for this book.

As I began to write this book I stared at another quote I jotted down when visiting with an elderly potato farmer from Maine. He said:

> Thoughts are pollen of the mind,
> and words are but the wind
> to hasten their departure.

What a beautiful way to envision the process of writing a book. I hope you will be receptive to the pollen and that it will germinate in your mind.

I believe coaching is one of the most difficult professions in the world. The effective coach must possess extraordinary skill and knowledge to produce skillful athletes. And yet coaches are expected to do even more—they are expected to produce decent human beings. And all this must be done with unique and diverse human beings, under intense pressure and close public scrutiny. A successful coach must not only be knowledgeable about the skills and strategies of the sport, the successful coach must indeed be a skillful psychologist.

Sport psychologists have learned much that can be beneficial to coaches, but few coaches are aware of what is known. This knowledge is a combination of scientific research and practical experience of veteran coaches and athletes. But why are coaches unaware of this useful knowledge? Because the scientific research is written in a technical language unfamiliar to them, and because one needs to read thousands of scientific studies to gain a complete picture. Furthermore, academe emphasizes producing scientific research rather than interpreting it to potential consumers. Thus little attention has been given to the dissemination of sport psychology knowledge. From my experience, coaches are not uninterested in sport psychology. Rather, they are enthusiastic about this field when the information is understandable and relevant to their coaching. The major problem is not lack of interest; it is the lack of a delivery system for making this information available. The American Coaching Effectiveness Program, of which this book is a part, is one effort to establish such a delivery system.

A few ultraconservative research sport psychologists say we do not yet have the definitive scientific evidence needed to be offering advice to coaches about how athletes can acquire psychological skills. I agree that we do not have definitive research on how to teach these skills, just as we do not have complete scientific evidence on how to rear children properly, teach English effectively, or rehabilitate chemically dependent people. Yet we must bring up our children, teach them English, and rehabilitate people in the best way we know how. Athletes need assistance in developing psychological skills today, and we have considerable knowledge that can be helpful. There is little risk that teaching these skills will cause psychological damage. Indeed, greater damage is likely if coaches fail to provide the assistance recommended in this book.

North American coaches and sport administrators sometimes credit the Soviet Union and Eastern Block countries with having superior knowledge in the sport sciences, believing this knowledge is the reason athletes from these countries are so successful. That is *not* true, at least for the field of sport psychology where I have monitored the research from these countries. The Soviets and Eastern Block allies are at least ten years behind North America in knowing how to prepare athletes psychologically, and most of what we know has been discovered in the last ten years. The Soviets and Eastern Block countries, however, are perhaps ten years ahead of us in their elaborate national delivery system that disseminates the information they have.

Coaches Guide to Sport Psychology and its companion *Study Guide* are the intermediate level texts for sport psychology in the American Coaching Effectiveness Program. If you have not done so, I recommend that you read the introductory level text *Coaching Young Athletes* (Martens, Christina, Harvey, & Sharkey, 1981).

Coaches Guide to Sport Psychology is organized into three parts. Part I provides a perspective for the study of the other two parts by asking you to examine your philosophy of coaching and presenting a framework for understanding motivation, a phenomenon that is related to every chapter in the book. Part II focuses on the two major psychological skills you need to be a successful coach— leadership and communication skills—and part III focuses on the psychological skills your athletes need to be successful. The psychological skills that I will emphasize for coaches are also skills that athletes should develop, and the skills discussed for athletes are skills coaches should possess.

This book is no "pop psych" book that tells you how to make yourself a better person in just thirty minutes a day, or in six weeks. The easy answers you might like to find in this book are not here because the answers are not easy. If they were that easy, I would not need to write this book; somebody would have done it long ago. (Some have already done so, but their books have not been widely accepted because their approaches do not work.)

The psychology of sport is a complex subject, and although the solutions to the problems are not simple, they can be understood and mastered by you and your athletes. I have made every effort in this book to present these psychological skills in an understandable and practical way.

You and your athletes will not, however, develop these psychological skills overnight, nor will you fully understand them by quickly reading this book. To develop these psychological skills, you must practice the techniques outlined. You will need to practice them just as you have your athletes practice and train to master the physical skills of your sport.

Accompanying this book is a *Study Guide*, which provides you with more information about these psychological skills, and outlines methods and exercises for practicing these skills. Thus I highly recommend that you enroll in the ACEP Master Level course that utilizes this book and the *Study Guide*.

Coaches of high school, college, or adult athletes will find this book useful, whether they are coaching male or female athletes. The psychological skills you will learn are useful not only for professional and Olympic athletes, but for athletes at any level who wish to remove psychological barriers in order to enhance performance.

Read the book once to absorb as much as you can of its total content. Then begin to reread each chapter, and if you are taking the course, work through the exercises in the *Study Guide*. It is a cliché to say that "you get out of it what you put into it." An orginal idea, no—but true, yes. Give this book your best and you will be a better coach.

PART I
Psychological Perspectives

It is my objective in part I to help you develop a perspective for considering all the subject matter in this book. Two topics especially pervade every other topic to be considered here—philosophy and motivation.

Philosophy is the foundation from which you will develop your entire approach to sport psychology. Your philosophy may be based on the premise that athletes need to be directed and driven to excel. Or you may espouse the view that direction and motivation come from within, and that athletes need only be provided an environment that nurtures them to pursue excellence. Or your philosophy may be one that totally discounts the significance of psychological factors in sports. (I assume you picked up this book by accident, if you hold this viewpoint.)

Many coaches do not have well-developed philosophies, nor have they had the opportunity to examine their philosophies in a structured way. Chapter 1 is intended to help you take a critical and constructive look at your philosophy—at your beliefs and values. It will ask you to come to know yourself, to bare your soul, in order that you can become more conscious of your philosophy of life and of coaching. It will ask you to examine your objectives as a coach in considering the place of psychology in your coaching and the psychological methods you will use to achieve your objectives. Chapter 1 contains fewer answers than it does questions, but these thought-provoking questions are intended to lead you to answers. These answers are the principles and values that will constitute your coaching philosophy.

Your philosophy very much prescribes how you view motivation. In chapter 2 you will learn about the different approaches to motivation and what research has taught us about this complex phenomenon. Every chapter in this book pertains directly to motivation. The effectiveness with which you communicate and your style of leadership will affect the motivation of your athletes. And athletes' motivation is directly influenced by their psychological skills in managing stress, controlling attention, and setting realistic goals, the subject matter of part III.

Chapter 2 is designed to help you formulate a perspective of motivation that will be consistent with your philosophy, and to provide a framework for considering the factors that influence motivation. In this way you will better understand the implications, provided in other chapters, for motivating your athletes.

Chapter 1
Philosophy of Coaching

The word *philosophy* used to turn me off. Nothing seemed more impractical than philosophy, and I see myself as a practical person. But I have learned that nothing is as practical as a well-developed philosophy about life and about coaching. My philosophy guides me everyday; it helps me interpret the events in my life and it gives my life direction.

The word *philosophy* to me means the pursuit of wisdom; it helps me answer fundamental questions about what, why, and how. My philosophy is the way I view objects and experiences in my life; it's the way I view people and my relationships with them. And it is the values that I hold about all these. The philosopher Epictetus said, ''The beginning of philosophy is to know the condition of one's own mind.''

Do you know the condition of your own mind? Is your philosophy of life well formulated? Is your philosophy of coaching well defined? Or are you uncertain about your beliefs on important issues in life and in coaching sports? Such uncertainty leads to inconsistency in behavior, which often destroys personal relationships and creates chaotic conditions within a team.

The key to developing a philosophy of coaching, then—and of life—is coming to know yourself. In this chapter I'll ask you to consider some facets of yourself and issues pertinent to coaching sports in order to help you further develop your coaching philosophy.

WHY PHILOSOPHY?

You might wonder why I begin a book on sport psychology with a chapter on philosophy. It is because philosophy is the foundation of psychology. Philosophy is derived from self-awareness, and self-awareness is an objective of psychology. The information about psychology that I present in this book will be understood and reacted to in substantially different ways, depending on your coaching philosophy. Thus I did not want to write a book about sport psychology unless I first built a foundation for it.

Your philosophy will give you direction in using the psychology I present. As one philosopher said, ''If you don't know where you are going—any road will get you there.'' To be successful you need to know where you're going, and throughout this book I'll provide a road map. But it's up to you to select the right roads. Coaches without well-developed philosophies lack direction and readily succumb to external pressures, as exemplified in the following story told by Ralph Sabock:

There was an old man, a boy, and a donkey. They were going to town and it was decided that the boy should ride. As they went along they passed some people who exclaimed that it was a shame for the boy to ride and the old man to walk. The man and boy decided that maybe the critics were right so they changed positions. Later they passed some more people who then exclaimed that it was a real shame for the man to make such a small boy walk. The two decided that maybe they both should walk. Soon they passed some more people who exclaimed that it was stupidity to walk when they had a donkey to ride. The man and the boy decided maybe the critics were right so they decided that they both should ride. They soon passed other people who exclaimed that it was a shame to put such a load on a poor little animal. The old man and the boy decided that maybe the critics were right so they decided to carry the donkey. As they crossed a bridge they lost their grip on the animal and the donkey fell into the river and drowned. The moral of the story is that if you try to please everyone you will finally lose your ass. (1985, pp. 49-50)

When you are coaching, it will be your philosophy much more than knowledge of the sport that will keep you from losing your ass. Having a philosophy will remove uncertainty about formulating training rules, style of play, discipline, codes of conduct, competitive outlook, short- and long-term objectives, and many other facets of coaching. If you will give the same amount of time to the development of your philosophy as you do to the development of your technical knowledge of the sport, you will be a better coach.

DEVELOPING YOUR PHILOSOPHY

You already have a philosophy about life and probably a philosophy about coaching. The philosophy may or may not be well developed in your mind. You may be conscious of your perspective of life or it may reside more at an unconscious level, depending largely on how much you have reflected on it. Even though you may have a well-developed philosophy, remember that philosophies are ongoing—lifelong in their development.

Many famous coaches are well-known for their coaching philosophies. The names of John Wooden, Joe Paterno, Bobby Knight, and "Bear" Bryant come to mind as coaches with whom we associate specific philosophies. These coaches discovered early in their careers that the art of coaching was using broad philosophical concepts in a skillful way to enhance the pursuit of their goals, regardless of whether others agreed with their particular coaching philosophies.

A philosophy consists of beliefs or principles that serve as guides to action. These principles help you cope with the myriad of life's situations. Often some of your beliefs or principles are formative. Events test these developing principles by placing you in situations where you are uncertain about the best way to respond. When you do respond, the consequences are evaluated against your principles. If the evaluation is favorable, it strengthens your principles. If it is unfavorable, and repeatedly so, you may search for a different principle.

Some coaches, however, give little consideration to this evaluative process. These coaches, consequently, have philosophies that are insufficiently developed to meet the demands of coaching. Other coaches form philosophies that are inflexible and less productive in achieving their objectives. And still others adopt philosophies that are incongruous with the values of society.

I am especially impressed with John Wooden's philosophy, with his emphasis on teaching and performance rather than winning. But recognize that Wooden's philosophy represents his cumulative wisdom over a lifetime of coaching. He did not begin coaching with the philosophy he espoused at the end of his career. So don't expect to have all the answers immediately. Keep an open mind, examine your beliefs and values from time to time, and benefit from the experience of wise coaches such as John Wooden.

Of course you must develop your own philosophy of coaching, but it also must be acceptable to the society in which you live. You cannot acquire a philosophy by reading this book or by adopting the philosophy of a famous coach. A philosophy is not acquired from any one source, but from all your experiences. A philosophy is useless unless you own it and nurture it. This chapter is intended to help you think about some of the components that I hope will hasten the development of a useful philosophy for you. The poet Elbert Hubbard (cited in Sabock, 1985) wrote:

If I can supply you with a thought
you may remember it or not.
But if I can make you think a thought for
  yourself,
I have indeed added to your stature. (p. xi)

It may be useful to think of your philosophy as comprising three different levels: a philosophy of life, a philosophy of coaching, and a philosophy of the particular sport you coach (e.g., the techniques and strategies you use).

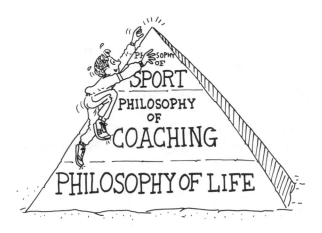

Usually your philosophy of life will shape your philosophy of coaching, and your philosophy of coaching will influence your philosophy of sport. Sometimes, however, coaches adopt principles in sports that are inconsistent with their larger principles of life.

I recall coaching with a math teacher who was one of the kindest persons I knew. He clearly followed the principle of the Golden Rule in his interactions with others until he stepped onto the football field. For some reason, when he coached he became a tyrant. He abused the players physically and psychologically, only to return to the classroom the next day as a warm, sensitive, highly effective math teacher. I never did learn why he abandoned the Golden Rule when coaching. I suspect somewhere he developed the mistaken notion that a good coach must be highly authoritarian, unkind, and abusive to athletes.

Coaching athletes should be approached in exactly the same way you approach interacting with other people in all other spheres of your life. Of course, that does not mean that if you are abusive to athletes, you should also be abusive to others! My meaning here should be clear.

Developing a useful philosophy involves two major tasks. The first is to develop greater self-awareness, to come to know yourself better. The second is to decide what your objectives are in coaching, which in turn will shape the way you see your role as a coach and consequently many of your behaviors as a coach. In the next section of this chapter you will learn more about knowing yourself. Then, in the following section, you will be asked to consider your coaching objectives, that is, what you value in coaching.

SELF-AWARENESS

If you don't know who you are, how can you help your athletes come to know who they are? If you are not at peace with yourself, it's improbable you can help your athletes to be at peace with themselves. If you don't have direction or commitment, it's unlikely you can impart these to your athletes. If you find it difficult to behave with reasonable consistency, it's unlikely that your athletes will respond with appropriate consistency. If you lack character in guiding your athletes through the competitive experience, it's unlikely that you will build character in those you guide.

Remember this when you assume the tremendous responsibility of being a coach: Your athletes are much more likely to become what you are than what you would like them to be. Consequently, you cannot provide consistently positive direction for your athletes unless you know who you are. A coach who has his or her own values clarified is better able to help athletes work through conflict and confusion.

Only through self-awareness can you arrive at the conclusion that you want or need to become more competent in some facet of your life. This requires being honest with yourself about who you are—sometimes a painful experience. When taking the first look at themselves, some people do not like what they see so they run from themselves. You can increase your self-awareness in two ways:

- By listening to yourself in order to understand your feelings and reactions to the events in your life and the causes of these feelings and reactions.
- By requesting feedback from other people on how they see you and how they react to you.

Who Am I?

Now is the time for some thought and reflection. Read each question; then turn the book over and reflect for a few moments on your answer. Don't merely read through the list and move on. Take some time to acquaint yourself with your self. Ask the following questions:

- Who am I?
- What do I want in life?
- Where am I going?
- What is my goal in life?
- Is my behavior appropriate to my life's goals?
- Am I proud or ashamed of who I am?
- Am I happy or unhappy?

These are tough questions. We should all periodically take a break in our busy lives and answer these questions for ourselves. Now consider five questions specific to coaching:

- Why do I coach?
- Am I coaching for the right reasons?
- What are my goals as a coach?
- Am I a good coach?
- What would make me a better coach?

Answers to all these questions, and countless others, form your self-concept—the beliefs you have about yourself. Most of the beliefs you have about yourself are acquired from how you perceive other people responding to you. These beliefs are unconsciously assumed, and often you have little awareness of their source.

The Three Selves

Your self-concept can be thought of as three selves. The *ideal self* refers to the person you would like to be. It represents your values, your sense of right and wrong. It is what you expect and demand of yourself, and is typically based on moral principles acquired from your family and from other important people in your life.

The *public self* is the image you believe others have of you. You want others to believe certain things about you so that they respect you, love you, help you meet your goals. If others believe the wrong things about you, they may ignore you, reject you, or punish you.

The *real self* is the sum of those subjective thoughts, feelings, and needs that you see as being the authentic you. The real self is continually changing, and the healthy person strives to honestly know him- or herself and to relate this inner self to the realities of the outside world. Through interactions with others, through the communication process, you come to understand, accept, and experience the real self.

Sometimes there is a conflict between the real and the other selves, resulting in anxiety, guilt, and perhaps even self-hatred. When a feeling, thought, or experience conflicts with your beliefs about yourself you may feel threatened and distort, deny, or ignore the experience. In this way you protect your self-concept, but when you are overly protective, you deny yourself an opportunity to grow from these experiences. To maintain good mental health, you should strive to keep your public and ideal selves compatible with your real self.

Seeing yourself accurately requires insight, or the ability to view yourself objectively. None of us are able to do so with complete objectivity, but some are able to see themselves more accurately than others. To help you look at your ideal, public, and real selves, Table 1.1 contains a list of some roles and characteristics that are significant to the job of coaching. Complete the table by following these procedures:

1. For the first role listed, rate yourself first as you would like to be (your ideal self).
2. Then rate yourself as you believe you are seen by others (your public self).
3. Next rate yourself as you perceive yourself really to be (your real self).
4. Then proceed to the next role or characteristic and again rate your three selves.
5. Finally, to help you look at your three selves, rate these selves on this continuum.

−3,	−2,	−1,	0,	+1,	+2,	+3
Negative self			Neutral			Positive self

If the role or characteristic is a positive one, give yourself a +1 to +3. If you are entirely neutral about the item, give it a 0. If the role or characteristic is a negative one, give yourself a −1 to −3. Remember, learning to know yourself requires you to be honest with yourself.

Now look at your ratings. Do you see any substantial discrepancies between your three selves? If so, why do you think they exist? What can you do about the discrepancies? If you are feeling courageous, ask someone who knows you very well to review your ratings. Discuss with this person any discrepancies they see. Remember, others really only know your public self.

Self-Esteem

Self-esteem pertains to an inner conviction about our competency and worth as human beings. Too often those of us in the sport world

base our self-esteem on our wins and losses in competition. We esteem ourselves by diminishing someone else's esteem, by displaying that we are more competent in a contest. Genuine self-esteem, however, is not competitive or comparative. *Positive self-esteem is viewing yourself as a competent and worthy person, and feeling good about that.* Self-esteem is not achieved by defeating others, but by living up to your own standards.

Your success as a coach is strongly related to your self-esteem, to how you value yourself. If you have confidence, you will help develop confidence in those around you. If you feel worthy as a person, you will recognize worth in others.

How do you judge yourself? Do you feel you are a competent person? Do you feel you are a worthy person? Nathaniel Branden in *Honoring the Self* (1983) begins his book by stating: "Of all the judgments that we pass in life, none is as important as the one we pass on ourselves, for that judgment touches the very center of our existence" (p. xi). How we relate

Table 1.1
Knowing Your Three Selves

Item	Ideal Self (As you would like to be)	Public Self (As you believe you are seen by others)	Real Self (As you perceive yourself)
Rating Scale: −3, Negative Self	−2, −1,	0, +1, Neutral Self	+2, +3 Positive Self
Knowing yourself as . . .			
an athlete			
a coach			
a mother or father			
successful			
honest			
anxious			
empathic			
domineering			
loyal			
humble			
needing recognition			
respected			
stubborn			
powerful			

to our selves affects how we relate to others, to the world around us.

Branden continues by observing,

> A commitment to awareness—the will to understand—is the central pillar of positive self-esteem. . . . It entails the behavior of seeking to integrate to the best of our ability and knowledge, that which enters our mental field—as well as the effort to keep expanding that field. A commitment to awareness, then—a commitment to thinking as a way of life—is both a source and an expression of positive self-esteem. (p. 45)

Your success as a coach, then, is strongly related to your perception of yourself as a competent person. Your judgment of your self-competence is vital because we make ourselves worthy of living by making ourselves competent to live. Thus self-awareness is the first step toward knowing yourself and your competence, and toward making a choice as to whether or not you wish to change current, ineffective patterns of behavior to effective ones.

Some years ago *I'm OK—You're OK* (1967) was the "hit" self-help book. In it, Thomas Harris described four basic positions or attitudes that we each can take toward ourselves and others. Read the characteristics of each of these positions and consider which one best describes you.

I'm Not OK, You're OK

- You feel at the mercy of others.
- You need much support, acceptance, and recognition from others.
- You worry about getting others to give you the reassurance and support you need.
- You doubt yourself.
- You place little value on yourself.
- You frequently have alibis for not doing things.

I'm Not OK, You're Not OK

- You give up hope of being happy.
- You prefer not to be around others.
- You feel little acceptance or support from others.

- Even when others try to give support, you cannot accept it because those providing it are bad, weak, and "not OK."
- You reject yourself.

I'm OK, You're Not OK

- You reject support from others.
- You feel you are fine as long as others leave you alone.
- You are independent.
- You don't want to get involved with others.
- You reject the support and acceptance of others because they are "not OK."
- You let others know you're fine, but they're not.

I'm OK, You're OK

- You feel you are worthwhile and valuable.
- You feel others are also worthwhile and valuable.
- You like yourself and others.
- You like to get involved in meaningful relationships.
- You are happy.
- You see life as a meaningful, worthwhile experience.

Look at Figure 1.1, which portrays these four positions as falling on two continuums and complete the following steps:

1. You are to determine each of four famous people's positions on the two continuums and place them in the appropriate quadrant. To do this, first determine how far up or down you would rate the person on the "I'm OK, I'm not OK" dimension.
2. Then determine how far to the right or left that person belongs on the "You're not OK, You're OK" continuum. Put the person's initials in the location and quadrant you judge appropriate.
3. Rate these people: Adolf Hitler, John Kennedy, Margaret Thatcher, and Peanuts' Charlie Brown.
4. Now place yourself on the figure.

After completing the exercise, reflect for a few moments on where you placed yourself.

Are you satisfied with this position? Would you like to change? What will it take to make a change?

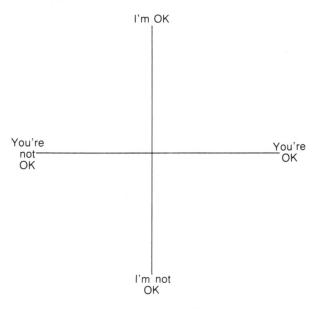

Figure 1.1 Evaluate yourself with regard to how you perceive yourself and others.

Self-Disclosure

The significance of self-disclosure in developing self-awareness is expressed well by David Johnson in *Reaching Out* (1981).

> By disclosing myself to you, I create the potential for trust, caring, commitment, growth, and self understanding. How can you care for me if you do not know me? How can you trust me if I do not demonstrate my trust in you by disclosing myself to you? How can you be committed to me if you know little or nothing about me? How can I know and understand myself if I do not disclose myself to friends? (p. 15)

Some coaches believe it is inappropriate to disclose themselves to their athletes. They feel that they must stay detached in order to be good taskmasters. I disagree with this view, for when it is analyzed, the reason for the detachment is either to extract more from the athletes in order that the individual or team will win, or to conceal the fact that the coach lacks a positive self-concept and fears what the athletes will see. John Powell understood this when he wrote:

> I am afraid to tell you who I am,
> because, if I tell you who I am,
> you may not like who I am,
> and it's all that I have. (1969, p. 15)

It's true; our self-worth is our most important possession. I will come back to this theme often in this book.

So how revealing should you be about yourself? To be self-disclosing does not mean to reveal intimate details about your past life. It means sharing with your athletes how you feel about what they say and do, or about events that you have shared. Self-disclosure must be relevant to your relationship and appropriate to the situation you are in. You can be too self-disclosing. If a person is untrustworthy, misinterprets or overreacts, you would be foolish to be self-disclosing.

Some coaches believe being silent is being strong, but it is not. Strength is the willingness to take risks in your relationship with your athletes, to disclose yourself with the intent of building a better relationship. Being self-disclosing in this way means you are being "real," being honest and genuine, first to yourself and then to your athletes.

You need to recognize that if you are not appropriately self-disclosing, your athletes will not share their thoughts and feelings with you. Without this intimate knowledge of your athletes, you cannot hope to help them develop the psychological skills discussed in part III.

You can't disclose your feelings and reactions if you don't know what they are. Self-awareness, therefore, is the first step to self-disclosure. And in turn, through self-disclosure you receive feedback from others and this feedback helps you further your own self-awareness.

Study Figure 1.2 for a moment. How much of the total self that you know is known by others? How much of you do you purposely choose not to reveal to others? How much of you is known to others, but not known to yourself? You can't answer this question of course! Do you dare ask others to find out this information? Of course, you want to know what others know about you that you don't know. Or do you? It's also interesting to wonder how much of you is unknown to yourself and others. What can you do to learn more about this hidden side of you? Provocative questions, are they not?

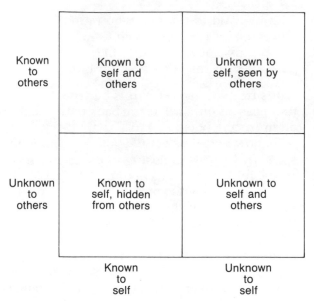

	Known to self	Unknown to self
Known to others	Known to self and others	Unknown to self, seen by others
Unknown to others	Known to self, hidden from others	Unknown to self and others

Figure 1.2 Evaluate how much you know about yourself and how much others know about you.

YOUR COACHING OBJECTIVES

In *Coaching Young Athletes*, the American Coaching Effectiveness Program (ACEP) Level 1 text, I reviewed the major objectives for coaching. If you have not read chapters 1 and 2 of this book, I suggest you do so before proceeding.

Two Major Objectives

In *Coaching Young Athletes* three broad objectives are identified that are widely accepted: (a) to win, (b) to have fun, and (c) to help athletes develop physically, psychologically, and socially. In a sense, fun is helping athletes develop, so really there are two major objectives and these will be the focus of this section— winning and athletes' development. No other decision you make about your role as coach will be as important as the one you make about the emphasis you give to each of these objectives. It will be the heart of your coaching philosophy.

Winning

Winning is an important objective to pursue. Athletes and coaches should try their best when they agree to compete in sport. But at

what costs are you willing to pursue the goal of winning? Are you willing to risk your own health or the health of your athletes? Do you put winning ahead of your athletes' personal development, ahead of your family? What is a proper perspective on winning? These are important and difficult questions to answer, but you will have to answer them every day that you coach, so let's look at some of the issues involved.

A former university swim coach, Frank Iverson, observed that when he first started his career he coached to enhance his own ego. He relished the power the position gave him, and when his authority was questioned, he took it as a personal affront. Coaching permitted him to continue to compete vicariously through his swimmers. A meet was not a meet to see who were the best swimmers; the purpose of a meet was to see who was the best coach. When his swimmers won, Frank owned the success, and when they lost, Frank *sometimes* owned the failure. You see, Frank had this ingenious tendency to get the swimmers to own their failures by discrediting their performance in some way.

Development

That was Frank in the early years of his career; but Frank changed. Some said he lost his competitiveness, and others said he mellowed. It was not any single event that led to the changes. Just gradually over the years Frank's coaching philosophy shifted from being a *win-centered* coach to an *athlete-centered* coach. No longer did his swimmers have to win races to be successful in Frank's eyes, or for Frank to feel successful himself.

The development of the athletes as swimmers and as people became Frank's new measurement of success. The swim team had a 3.2 grade point average, Frank would proudly tell you. Although it took more than ten years of coaching for Frank to see it, helping his athletes develop self-discipline and autonomy, to be responsible for themselves, was more important than winning races.

The Challenge

Why do coaches become win-centered? (You will learn more about what motivates people in the next chapter.) Perhaps it is because they succumb to pressure from the public through the media, or from administrators, parents, or even the athletes themselves. Perhaps, as in Frank's case, it is a way to continue to compete vicariously. When this occurs, coaches coach not to help athletes achieve their goals of winning and self-development, but to achieve the coaches' personal goals.

More than likely, however, coaches become win-centered because they associate their self-worth with the wins and losses of their team. As you will see throughout this book, our self-worth is the most important possession we have and we will go to great lengths to protect it and nurture it. Consequently, when coaches link their self-worth with their team's wins and losses, winning becomes all important—losing is a direct affront to their self-worth. Now the adage, "Winning isn't everything, it's the only thing," is entirely applicable to these coaches. When coaches link their self-worth with winning and losing, their goals are totally self-centered: They no longer care about what they can do for their athletes, but what their athletes can do for them.

Do you coach to win for any of these reasons? Is coaching your ego trip? Do you link your worth as a person with the wins and losses of your athletes? Or do you understand what Frank Iverson learned after ten years of coaching?

The ACEP Philosophy

In *Coaching Young Athletes*, I expressed the ACEP philosophy about these objectives as being "Athletes first, winning second," which has become ACEP's motto. This athlete-centered philosophy places the highest regard on the people being coached, whereas a win-centered philosophy places the highest regard on the outcome of competition. As you read this section, evaluate your current philosophy as you evaluate the ACEP philosophy. Then decide if you want to make any changes in your philosophy.

The "Athletes first, winning second" philosophy means that every decision a coach makes is, first, in the best interest of the athlete, and second, in the interest of winning. It does not mean that winning is unimportant, but that it is not as important as the development of the athletes.

Although "Athletes first, winning second"

is the phrase used to convey the ACEP philosophy, this concept goes beyond the athletes. It means you do what's best for all those with whom you interact in your role as coach, be they your players, the other team's players, other coaches, officials, parents, and so on.

These two objectives, although they may appear as dichotomies, actually fall on a continuum. The extreme athlete-centered coach would always consider what's best for the athletes first; winning is never given preference. On the other extreme of the continuum, winning is the ultimate objective; it's the reason for sport, and the win-centered coach will do what's best for the athletes only as long as it does not jeopardize winning. Athlete-centered coaches see the sport as existing for the athletes; win-centered coaches see the athletes as resources to achieve their objective of winning.

Look at the continuum in Figure 1.3. Where do you place Bobby Knight on the continuum? Put a BK where you think Knight belongs. Where do you place John Wooden? Put his initials on the appropriate point of the continuum. Now, where do you place yourself on this continuum? Insert your initials. Then put an S where you think your supervisor would put you and put an A where your athletes would likely put you. Think about your position for a few moments. Would you like to see it change?

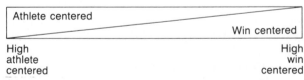

Figure 1.3 Determine your position on the athlete-centered versus win-centered continuum.

From Principle to Practice

"Athletes first, winning second" is a simple, straightforward philosophy and I have met few coaches who disagree with it when asked. On the other hand, I have met few who consistently put this philosophy into practice—and a philosophy really is not the principles you preach; it's the principles by which you live.

When confronted with the question of prioritizing winning and development, many coaches contend that they want both and that they coach to achieve both. And they rightfully point out that winning can help athletes develop by giving them self-confidence and earning them scholarships. On the other hand, at times you will have to choose one over the other. Furthermore, it is not always easy to discern which action places the athlete before winning or vice versa. Consider the following three examples, which illustrate the problem.

Margie, your star athlete, is injured. It's the most important game of her life, and even though she can function only at 75 percent of her normal level, she will help you win the state championship if she plays. Margie desperately wants to play; it will be the culmination of three hard years of training for her. The doctor advises you that there is a 10 to 15 percent chance she could reinjure herself seriously if she plays. Do you let Margie play?

Fred is a problem athlete on the team whose potential is great but whose attitude is awful. You've tried several times to counsel Fred, but so far nothing has changed. Fred disrupts practice and you see signs that his negative attitude is adversely affecting some of the other members of the team. Fred's mother, however, told you recently that Fred looked up to you and really wanted to be a part of the team. If the truth be known, though, you don't especially like the youngster. Do you keep Fred on the team?

Kevin, one of your starters on the team, has been in constant academic trouble. You happen to overhear in the locker room that two other members of the team sat next to Kevin in class and gave him the answers on a mid-semester geometry examination. Without this help, Kevin would have flunked the course and been ineligible to play on the team. You confront the two with what you overheard, and they admit they did it because it would help the team. Now what do you do?

How you would respond to each of these situations is likely to depend on many other specific things that you would need to consider for each of the examples. But in the end these problems would test your values concerning winning and the athletes. These would be difficult decisions, but coaching is a difficult profession—that's what makes it challenging!

Here are a few more situations that will challenge your philosophy of coaching:

You know that you can intimidate an official into a position where your team is likely to receive a favorable ruling on a close judgment call. You also believe that this kind of intimi-dation is not what coaches should demonstrate to athletes. Do you intimidate the official?

The opposing coach has not been playing within the spirit of the rules, although technically within the letter of the rules. You have an opportunity to retaliate, and although you would not technically be cheating, all your players will know you are not playing within the spirit of the rules. Do you retaliate?

You want to help your athletes become responsible individuals, and you know that to learn responsibility athletes need to be given opportunities to exercise responsibility. But some athletes are likely to act irresponsibly, and the consequences of this irresponsibility would dim your chances of winning. How do you reconcile this dilemma?

Athletes do not become better competitors by sitting on the bench all season. Yet it seems only right that the better athletes should play; they earned the right. Furthermore, playing less than your best team is not providing the opponent with the best competition possible. How do you resolve this problem?

It's often said that good teams have the "killer instinct"; they know how to put their opponent away. Yet coaches are not regarded well when they humiliate an opponent by running up the score. How do you resolve this dilemma?

Most coaches genuinely subscribe to the "Athletes first, winning second" philosophy. From research and hundreds of coaching clinics where coaches ranked their priorities for these two objectives, fewer than 2 percent acknowledged that winning is their first priority. The problem, as illustrated in the above examples, is implementing the "Athletes first, winning second" philosophy. A major obstacle to its implementation is the powerful nature of competition. Let me explain.

Evidence indicates that humankind has an innate (although not instinctive) tendency to compete, because competition is one means of meeting our needs. The goal of the competitive process, of course, is to win, which demonstrates our competence and strokes our ego. This goal is immediate and clearly defined. Success or failure is quickly discerned when the contest ends. The outcome is often public and the rewards of winning are often extrinsic and significant.

On the other hand, the goal of helping athletes develop into better humans—physically, psychologically, and socially—is neither immediate nor clear-cut. Success in achieving the goal is difficult to discern, and only rarely are the rewards public or extrinsic.

Consequently, the power of the competitive process may easily engross coaches in the pursuit of victory, even at the expense of athletes' development—unless their philosophy of "Athletes first, winning second" is well established. It requires coaches with well-developed philosophies to maintain this perspective when they are in the heat of battle, when their team is treated unjustly, when they have suffered an agonizing defeat.

Some may see the "Athletes first, winning second" philosophy as placing too much emphasis on the individual and not enough on the team. Many coaches contend that what is really important is for athletes to learn to place the team ahead of themselves. I concur with this view if it means that one or two individuals must forego their personal goals in order for the team to achieve its goals. When coaches are faced with the choice of helping one athlete at the expense of the team or doing what's best for the majority, I vote strongly for the majority.

However, some coaches may use the plea— "in the best interest of the team"—as a means of goading players to do whatever is necessary to win. Thus the team becomes a powerful excuse to abandon the "Athletes first, winning second" philosophy.

Consider the example of Fred presented on page 12. If you decide to have Fred leave the team, is it really because he will hurt the development of the other athletes, or is it because his bad attitude may affect the other players' motivation and jeopardize the team's chances of winning? The "Athletes first, winning second" philosophy cannot tell you whether or not to cut Fred from the team. It only guides you toward the right and wrong *reasons* for deciding what you decide.

Next time you find yourself deciding something for the good of the team over one of the individuals, ask yourself: Are you putting winning ahead of the individuals? Is that what you want to do?

The ACEP Philosophy Summarized

Coaching is a *people's* business, and thus the most important facet of your philosophy will concern your perception of human relationships, not only with your athletes, but with fellow coaches, administrators, parents, officials, and others. Will you choose to have close, personal relationships, which are essential to helping individuals, or will you choose to remain cool and removed, focusing more on winning and athletes as objects to help you win?

Coaching, to me, is helping athletes develop their physical, psychological, and social abilities to their greatest potential. This helping process is dependent upon the coach's skill in enabling athletes to develop these abilities. It's assisting, not demanding, change. Coaching is, and should be regarded as, a *helping profession*, and as such, coaches become counselors and advisors, not dictators. Coaching is giving of yourself, your energies, knowledge, skills, and most of all your wisdom. In short, it's sharing your philosophy with your athletes.

To me, the "Athletes first, winning second" philosophy means all of the following:

- Every player plays when the coach judges it is in the best interest of the youngster to play, not when it is in the best interest of winning.
- Injured athletes don't play until they have completed the rehabilitation program appropriate for their injury.
- The coach leaves his or her ego at home during contests; self-worth is not judged on the basis of the team winning or losing. This means being proud when the team plays well, regardless of the outcome, and being disappointed when the team's members fail to give a good effort, regardless of the outcome.
- Society's pressures and enticements to pursue winning at any cost are resisted, and the coach stays committed to his or her philosophy.
- The coach's role is to allow the athletes to develop to their fullest by providing them with decision-making opportunities that help them assume greater responsibility for themselves.
- Coaches influence the lives of athletes in many ways—the most profound way is by shaping athletes' values. A coach can bring his or her own philosophy of coaching—of life—to the athletes by living it and communicating it. Doing so shows you care.

Harry Levinson writes in *The Exceptional Executive*,

Has the leader a right to mold and shape? Of what use is aging, experience, and wisdom if not to be the leaven for those who are younger? Of what use is pain if not to teach others to avoid it? The leader not only has the right; if he is a leader, he has the obligation. (1968, p. 128)

A well-developed philosophy of life and coaching will be among your best friends as you pursue your career in coaching. The development of your philosophy is based substantially on coming to know yourself, and thinking through important issues in response to which you establish principles for guiding your actions. Appropriate disclosure of your self to your athletes helps you to know yourself better, and thus develop your philosophy further, and helps to develop a trusting relationship with your athletes. Sharing your philosophy with your athletes by word and deed will help them develop their own philosophies.

This chapter's purpose is not to provide answers as much as it is to stimulate your thinking about critical issues pertaining to your philosophy of coaching. You are especially encouraged to examine the significance you give to winning and to helping athletes develop physically, psychologically, and socially. I expressed what the ACEP philosophy means to me and hope you will examine this viewpoint carefully. But the most important ingredient of a philosophy is that you own it. Espousing the tenets of someone else's philosophy without acting in a way that is consistent with these tenets is deceiving yourself and others. Remember a philosophy is not really expressed by what you say, but by what you do!

SUMMARY

1. A philosophy consists of beliefs or principles that serve as guides to action.
2. The development of your coaching philosophy involves developing greater self-awareness and deciding what your coaching objectives are.
3. You can become more aware of yourself by analyzing your views on many issues and by paying more attention to how others respond to you.
4. It is helpful to distinguish between your ideal, public, and real self.
5. Your success as a coach is strongly related to your self-esteem, to how you value yourself.
6. Self-disclosure is important because it helps others get to know you. Those others, in turn, help you to know yourself. Being appropriately self-disclosing is also important in that it builds a trusting relationship between you and your athletes.
7. Every coach must decide how important winning and helping athletes develop physically, psychologically, and socially are as objectives.
8. Win-centered coaches often are motivated to pursue winning at almost any cost because they evaluate their self-worth on the outcome of the game and season results.
9. The ACEP philosophy of "Athletes first, winning second" places the highest priority on coaches making decisions that are first in the best interest of athletes, and second, in the interest of winning.
10. On many occasions coaches are forced to make critical choices between these two objectives. The direction of these choices more accurately reflects a coach's true philosophy than his or her words.

Chapter 2
Motivation

Coaches need not be told the importance of motivation, nor is it a revelation that motivation is a complex topic. Some coaches believe motivation is too complex to be understood, or if it can be understood, it remains impossible to motivate people. "I just can't understand why he does that," exclaims a coach in frustration after his best runner drops out of a race feigning an injury. Or from a more positive perspective, "I've never known a more persistent competitor. I wish I knew what drives her to excel; I'd package it and give it to every member of my team—and myself," comments another coach.

OVERSIMPLIFYING MOTIVATION

Because motivation is complex, the tendency is to simplify it by latching on to one particular approach. In this section, several oversimplified approaches are reviewed, revealing some common myths held by coaches about motivation.

The Donkey Approach

Some coaches who are bewildered by the complexity of motivation take the "donkey" approach to motivating their players. They conclude from superficial observation that people and donkeys are much the same—stubborn and stupid. The only way to drive players is the carrot (reward) and stick (punishment) approach, with emphasis on the stick in the form of swearing, chastising, hitting, and other forms of physical and psychological abuse.

The Stork Approach

Other coaches see motivation as something they give to players, much like a fairy tale stork delivering a baby to its mother. Coaches have motivation and deliver it to their players when they choose, often dispensing it in the form of words with which they wax eloquently in oratorical pep talks. Coaches who follow the "stork" approach subscribe to the single motive fallacy, the assumption that players have one goal and that whatever little bundle of joy the coach chooses to deliver will satisfy this goal.

Other Simple Approaches

Donkey and stork coaches oversimplify motivation because of their frustration with its complexity. Other coaches also deal with motivation in a simplified way by using one of the following approaches:

1. Coaches may leap on a few principles and advocate these as the keys to motivation. You will hear these simple

recipes frequently in talks by successful coaches or read them in coaching magazines. "The key to motivation is to be organized, develop trust with your athletes, and be knowledgeable about the game," states one coach. He's not wrong, but it's only a small part of the motivation story.

2. Coaches may use gimmicks to motivate athletes through elaborate reward schemes, use of slogans or posters, or even bizarre pep talks such as the one given by an Eau Gallie, Florida coach who bit off the head of a live frog to "fire up" the team. Gimmicks may be helpful (although I do not recommend frog decapitation), but they too are only a small part of the total motivation picture.

3. Some coaches purchase motivational packages that come in the form of written materials, audiovisual aids, and consultants who may call themselves sport psychologists. Most motivational packages are superficial and not worth the money spent on them. Moreover, they are short-term approaches to what is a long-term challenge. Coaches cannot transfer to others their responsibility for directing the motivation of their players; the coach is too vital a part of the team to abdicate this responsibility. The use of consultants who truly know sport psychology can be beneficial; but once again, this is only part of developing a comprehensive approach to motivation.

4. William Warren, in his book *Coaching and Motivation* (1983), concludes that the best way to motivate is to select motivated players. He writes:

> Surround yourself with players who think as you do, and who care about you, your program and teammates. If this entails weeding out the players who are not dedicated to you, your program or the team—well, it's not an enjoyable task to consider, but it may be necessary for your own mental health as well as for your team's well-being. (p. 45)

Selecting motivated players may or may not be an option available to you. Furthermore, your philosophy of coaching will help you decide how much you subscribe to Warren's approach. For those coaches who are interested in helping athletes develop, then helping them develop motivation may be the most significant achievement for a particular player.

In his book, Warren proclaims a new definition of motivation: "Finding ways to get players to do things they might not want to do on their own" (1983, p. 22). Initially this definition seems innocuous enough, but think about it a moment. It assumes that athletes do not *want* to do something (the donkey approach) and the coach will deliver the motivation to make them do it (the stork approach). This is not only an oversimplified view of motivation, it is a very negative one.

A Motivational Misunderstanding

Some coaches incorrectly assume that athletes are not motivated when they balk at doing everything the coaches' way. But often athletes who balk at the directives of coaches are highly motivated to play sports—they're just not motivated to play according to the structure and methods dictated by the coach. Some athletes want to do it their own way, and when they do, coaches may view these athletes as discipline problems, especially those coaches who relish the power of their position.

The source of this conflict between coach and athlete often emanates from coaches seeking to meet their own needs through the team rather than considering the athletes' needs. I recall observing a man coaching sixth-grade boys in football for a period of about six weeks. Practices were hard work and highly structured. The kids often appeared bored and antagonistic to the coach who constantly threatened and administered discipline. The coach frequently expressed frustration to his assistant with the lack of motivation his team showed, usually expressing it in front of the team.

What the coach failed to realize was that

most of these young players wanted to play football for *fun*, not to do drills and calisthenics all day. Nor did they want to be yelled at. When the coach left at the end of practice, many of the players would stay behind and play a pickup game of football. The entire atmosphere changed: Everyone hustled and there was a lot of laughing and very intense playing. Because the coach had deprived the players of attaining one of their major goals in joining the football team—to have fun—they met their need when he departed.

There are two useful lessons about motivation in this example. One is that often a coach's greatest challenge in motivation is not to help athletes acquire it, but to avoid destroying their intrinsic motivation to play the sport. The second is that coaches ought to keep practices fun, organizing them for variety and maximum involvement of all the players. Do you see any relationship between these two points?

Some Limits

On the other hand, some players may have needs that are outside the scope of a team and your ability to meet. Some players may pass your way who lack adequate self-restraint or who have extraordinary needs for attention, causing them to be constantly disruptive. For you to devote inordinate amounts of time helping such individuals deprives the other players of your coaching. Coaches, of course, cannot solve every player's problems; some will be beyond your skills to help, anyway. All in all, you will have some tough value judgments to make regarding whom you help and whom you refer to others for help.

A Pep Talk

Some coaches respond to the study of motivation by saying, "I don't want to know all the theories of motivation. Just give me the principles, the secrets." If it were that easy, you would have learned these "secrets" long ago. Some coaches want to know only where the stork gets those little bundles so that they can deliver them as needed. Coaches must go be-

yond just asking *how* to motivate and learn more about *why* people are motivated.

If you asked me to give you five principles of motivation that apply to all people at all times in all situations, I could not do it. We do not have absolutes about motivation, we have relativisms. Knowing how to motivate athletes involves knowing what the athletes' goals (needs) are and how they perceive the situation, including how they perceive you as their coach. The failure of coaches to use motivation effectively stems mostly from their failure to fully understand what motivation is. So motivate yourself now to get "inside" motivation and understand how it really works.

DEFINING MOTIVATION

The basic issue, from a coach's perspective, is a simple one: "How do I get my players to change their behavior, be it their performance in games or other behaviors?" Your objective may be to help athletes increase the *quantity* of their behavior (e.g., run more miles), the *quality* of their behavior (e.g., shoot free throws more accurately), or the *direction* of their behavior (e.g., come to practices regularly, quit swearing, emphasize defense).

Psychologists consider motivation to consist of two dimensions: intensity and direction. *Intensity* is concerned with how activated or energized the person is, that is, how much effort is being given to reach a certain goal. You will learn in chapter 5, "Energy Management," how athletes are able to manage their intensity, and how performance is affected by not having enough or having too much intensity.

Direction is concerned with choosing a goal. Psychologists talk about people approaching or avoiding a task, and understanding why they do so. In sports, coaches are frequently interested in knowing why a talented youngster will not play a particular sport, or why someone quits the team. Coaches also want to know why some players are so doggedly persistent in playing a sport when they apparently would be better playing a violin. The answer to these questions lies in the goals of the person. Understanding the person's needs, which are the bases of the person's goals, is among the most important aspects of motivation. You'll learn more about this shortly.

MOTIVATION BASICS

Motivation is influenced by so many factors that we would need several encyclopedic volumes to consider them all in depth. However, the more vital components of motivation are small in number and quite understandable.

In this section you will learn essential information about four key topics:

- Intrinsic and extrinsic motivation
- Direct and indirect methods of motivation
- Locus of control
- Athletes' needs and motivation

As you read about each of these, keep in mind constantly what the information suggests for your approach to dealing with motivation.

Intrinsic and Extrinsic Motivation

Motivation has two sources, from inside the person (intrinsic) and from outside the person (extrinsic). People who are *intrinsically* motivated have an inner striving to be competent and self-determining, to master the task, to be successful. These qualities of competence, self-determination, mastery, and success are goals pursued by those who are intrinsically motivated, and when achieved are their own rewards. In sport, athletes who play the game because they love the game are intrinsically motivated. They play for inner pride, which is what compels them to do their best even when no one is watching.

Extrinsic motivation comes from other people through positive and negative reinforcements. (Reinforcements are those things that increase or decrease the likelihood of certain behaviors recurring.) These reinforcements may be tangible items, such as trophies or money, or intangible items, such as praise and public recognition. When these reinforcements are received, they are known as extrinsic rewards.

It is entirely possible, and most often likely, that athletes play sports for both intrinsic and extrinsic rewards. However, the importance that each athlete assigns to these two types of rewards can vary substantially. These individual differences are important for coaches to understand.

Extrinsic Rewards

The most basic principle of human behavior and motivation is the *law of effect*, which says this:

> Rewarding a behavior increases the probability that the behavior will be repeated, and punishing a behavior decreases the probability that the behavior will be repeated.

Applying the law of effect by using extrinsic rewards, and to a much lesser extent punishments, can be very effective in motivating athletes when the rewards and punishments are properly used. Often, though, they are not; problems occur when (a) appropriate reinforcers are not used, (b) they are not made contingent on the appropriate behaviors, and (c) they are not given at the right time.

B.F. Skinner is preeminent in the development of the field known as *behavior modification*, or the principles of using reinforcements. Coaches have been either wildly enthusiastic about behavior modification, seeing it as a panacea to motivation, or they have been adamantly opposed, viewing it as a corrupt means of manipulating people and denying them freedom. I hope you will see behavior modification a bit more neutrally; it's not all a coach needs to motivate athletes effectively, but it is a useful set of tools for certain types of motivation problems.

Space does not permit an adequate summary of the principles of behavior modification in this book. Most of the basics are presented in *Coaching Young Athletes* and I highly recommend you read Karen Pryor's *Don't Shoot the Dog!* (1984), which provides an excellent discussion of behavior modification—for people too. Also, in the *Study Guide* you will have an opportunity to learn more about, and to practice, behavior modification techniques.

Two final comments about extrinsic rewards. First, coaches tend to think of themselves as the only source of rewards (the stork). However, through instruction and creation of a warm, supportive environment, coaches can encourage athletes to reward each other. When fellow athletes give the rewards, the coach appears to be less in control of the athletes, or less manipulative, and as a result more rewards can be given out. Furthermore, research has demonstrated that athlete-administered rewards are more effective than coach-administered rewards in motivating swimmers to practice. Finally, coaches can use extrinsic rewards to help athletes learn to reward themselves, which in essence develops intrinsic motivation. We now consider these intrinsic rewards.

Intrinsic Rewards

Why not use behavior modification exclusively if it is so effective? Because extrinsic rewards typically lose their reinforcement power more quickly than intrinsic rewards. In Maslow's hierarchy of needs, the deficiency-based needs are more easily satisfied; once a need is satisfied, it no longer is a goal and loses its power to reward. Thus trophies, medals, money, and other forms of extrinsic rewards tend to lose their reward power more quickly than the intrinsic rewards of feeling competent and satisfied, which are self-fueling rewards. In other words, when a person plays soccer for the sheer joy of playing soccer, and then experiences that joy, the motive to play again is reinforced.

One of the problems with extrinsic rewards is that the more rewards a person gets, the less need he or she has for the same type of reward in the future. Thus as extrinsic rewards are earned they become less valued. Especially in professional sports, the exorbitant salaries soon exceed any reasonable need to purchase materials and services. Money is not the reward sought, but becomes an indication only of how much the person is valued by the team.

What coaches should strive to accomplish, therefore, is to transform extrinsic motivation into intrinsic motivation. Extrinsic rewards can be especially helpful in getting a person to be initially interested in a sport. I recall how this happened to me in high school wrestling. I was on the *C* team in basketball as a sophomore, and I suspect the coach recognized my wrestling talent in the way I played basketball! He politely discouraged me from pursuing basketball while arranging with the wrestling coach to invite me out for that sport.

I knew nothing about wrestling; it had no intrinsic value to me at all. But I gave the sport a try because initially I wanted to show the basketball coach I was a good athlete and because the wrestling coach was very encouraging (extrinsic rewards). By my senior year I no longer needed those two sources of extrinsic rewards. I had developed a real love for wrestling because my efforts had been successful and I felt competent as a wrestler (intrinsic rewards).

For this transformation from extrinsic motivation to intrinsic motivation to occur, three important elements were involved:

1. There were powerful extrinsic rewards to which I responded.
2. I experienced initial success (i.e., the extrinsic rewards made me feel more competent).
3. The wrestling coach nurtured the development of intrinsic motivation by letting me know in many little ways that winning trophies and medals was not the ultimate reward, but feeling satisfied with my own accomplishments was.

There is an art to the use of extrinsic rewards to develop intrinsic motivation. It's important that the rewards are not excessive or presented in such a way that the athletes perceive the coach is trying to control their behavior. Athletes will react negatively to what they perceive to be sly manipulation. The rewards also should be contingent on accomplishment. Giving everyone a reward for participation has no real power to build intrinsic motivation. It is also very important for athletes to understand that extrinsic rewards are nice momentos of a successful experience, but that the primary purpose for playing is the enjoyment and satisfaction of accomplishment.

Undermining Intrinsic Motivation

Just as it is possible for extrinsic rewards to enhance intrinsic motivation, extrinsic rewards can undermine intrinsic motivation. An example of the way this can occur is revealed in the now classic story of how an old man solved his problem of children making too much noise outside his house. One day the old man called the kids up to the house, telling them he really liked hearing them play and wanted them to make even more noise because he was hard of hearing. He offered to pay each twenty-five cents for doing so. The children played, made terrific noise, and later collected their money. The next day after playing and making much noise, they went to be paid and the old man apologetically explained he could pay only fifteen cents. The next day the children played, made noise, and when they went to be paid the old man explained he was running low of money and could pay them only five cents. Then he told them that tomorrow he would not be able to pay anything, but certainly hoped they would continue to play. The indignant children declared they were not going to play for the old man for nothing!

When extrinsic rewards are offered in such a way that athletes perceive the rewards are being used to control them, or even to bribe them, intrinsic motivation is likely to be undermined. When asked about what he was offered when recruited by various colleges, Earvin "Magic" Johnson, the outstanding Los Angeles Lakers basketball player, said, "I received my share of offers for cars and money. It immediately turned me off. It was like they were trying to buy me, and I didn't like anyone trying to buy me." Dean Ryan (1979) found that football players who received scholarships had less intrinsic motivation than those players who did not receive scholarships.

How extrinsic rewards may undermine intrinsic motivation has been a popular topic about which much has been learned. Evidence reveals, especially with children, that when an activity such as sports is already intrinsically motivating, offering extrinsic rewards can decrease intrinsic motivation under certain circumstances.

For example, a young girl develops an enjoyment of soccer by playing with her brothers and sisters and the neighborhood kids. Later she plays on the school team where she receives much more recognition from her peers and teachers for her excellent play. She makes the league all-star team, receives trophies and medals, and her name appears frequently in the newspaper. She loves the recognition and the awards, which are prominently displayed in her room at home.

After several years of such recognition, will she continue to be motivated to play primarily for the intrinsic rewards or will she want to play only for extrinsic rewards? If her need for these extrinsic rewards is satisfied, will her interest in soccer die?

The answer is, "It depends." Those conditions likely to lead to the undermining of intrinsic motivation are the following:

- The activity is intrinsically motivating to the person at the outset.
- The extrinsic rewards are also important to the person in that they have reinforcement power.
- The extrinsic rewards are perceived as *controlling* the athlete's behavior rather than *providing information* about how well the athlete played.
- The extrinsic rewards are given regardless of the person's performance; that is, they are not contingent on performance. In other words, the extrinsic reward tells them they are being rewarded for playing the sport, not particularly for playing it well.

Remember, though, extrinsic rewards have the *potential* to enhance intrinsic motivation when the rewards are perceived as providing information about the athlete's competence and are given on the quality of the performance. Extrinsic rewards are also useful to help develop interest in a sport when a person does not have initial intrinsic motivation to participate. Gradually, coaches who are skilled motivators will slowly withdraw or deemphasize the extrinsic rewards and place emphasis on the intrinsic rewards of the sport. Furthermore, because sport tends to provide many extrinsic rewards for winning (the outcome), coaches can use extrinsic rewards to acknowledge how well the person played (the performance) regardless of winning and losing. The importance of using extrinsic rewards to emphasize the achievement of performance goals is discussed in chapter 10.

Direct and Indirect Motivation

You may select to use direct or indirect methods to motivate your athletes, or as many coaches do, use both. When you call players into your office and appeal to their pride in themselves in hopes they will practice harder, you are using the *direct* method. When you assign players who are on one squad to a second squad because they are being influenced adversely by members of the first squad, you are using the *indirect* method. This method means changing the situation in hopes of influencing the athletes' motivation.

Direct Methods

One of three direct methods may be used to influence the athlete—compliance, identification, and internalization. The *compliance* process relies on the use of extrinsic rewards and punishments. "If you win today, we won't have practice on Monday," or "If you don't shape up and listen, you'll run twenty laps," are examples of compliance.

The compliance process can be an effective means of motivating, especially among athletes who do not have well-developed standards of behavior and who have weak self-concepts. Overreliance on the compliance process, however, may be a problem because often it is desirable to motivate players with goals other than to receive extrinsic rewards. Coaches who seek a deeper commitment—internalization of the goal—will find compliance inadequate.

In *identification*, the second direct method, the basis of motivation is the coach's relationship with his or her athletes. A coach using the identification method might say, "If you care about the team, you'll do this for me." Identification is actually a disguised form of compliance. Implicit in the statement, "If you care about the team . . .," is the understanding that if you behave as I request, you will be re-

warded. And if you do not, you will be punished.

To successfully use the identification process to motivate, coaches must have a positive relationship with their players so that the players feel compelled to meet the request. Coaches who rely heavily on punishment and negative reinforcements alienate athletes who then couldn't care less about doing whatever is requested by the coach. Instead, they obey the coach because they fear punishment.

The third method of direct influence is *internalization*, which seeks to motivate by appealing to players' own beliefs and values, not by administering rewards or punishments. "Bob, you've worked hard to prepare for this game. You should have confidence in that preparation, and I'm confident you'll play the best you can. I want you to know that I'll be proud of you however the game comes out," is an example of what a coach may say to motivate a player through the internalization process.

Which of these direct methods of influence you may use most likely will be determined by (a) what works with a given athlete, and (b) your coaching philosophy. The pragmatic coach will not only discover which of these techniques works best with certain players, but which of the methods he or she is more effective in using. Research indicates that athletes between the ages of five and ten are often not sufficiently mature to respond well to the internalization approach. So initially, compliance and identification are more effective; but by the time players are in junior or senior high school, internalization should be effective and preferred. On the other hand, some players have been so conditioned through the compliance process that internalization is less effective.

Then, you will need to consider what your coaching objectives are. A wise person once said, "There is no greater treason than to do the right thing for the wrong reasons." If winning is your first objective, you'll rely on compliance and identification extensively. These techniques are easier and less time-consuming, and when used correctly are effective.

If your primary objective is helping athletes develop, especially psychologically so that they acquire positive self-concepts and an integrated value system, you will first use compliance and identification to help your players respond to internalization methods. That is, you will help your players shape their values and beliefs, and then you will be able to appeal to these using the internalization process. Internalization moves athletes toward being intrinsically motivated and becoming more responsible for themselves.

Indirect Methods

The indirect method alters the situation or the environment—either the physical or psychological environment—in order to enhance motivation. For example, some coaches will change the location of practice just to increase motivation. The psychological environment can be changed by adding or removing the presence of certain people or by changing their behavior. Perhaps one of the most effective changes that can be made is the attitude of the coach—a positive one rather than a negative one. Another powerful way to change the psychological environment is to give athletes more control over the situation. I will discuss this important topic more in the final section of this chapter.

Locus of Control

People differ in the responsibility they perceive for the rewards and punishments they receive, which is called *locus of control*. People who are inclined to explain the events in their lives as resulting from external forces, such as luck, chance, and powerful other people, are called *external controls*.

People who are *internal controls* are more likely to perceive the events in their lives as being dependent upon their own behavior. They believe that in most cases, if they perform well or poorly, appropriate consequences will follow. They do not consider what happens to them to be purely a matter of luck or chance, and do not see their fate as always being in the hands of other people.

Most people have some qualities of both internal and external control, but tend to view the world predominantly more from one perspective or the other. Therefore you can subjectively identify people on a single continuum as shown in Figure 2.1.

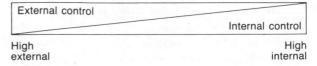

Figure 2.1   Evaluate yourself on this external-internal control dimension.

How do you rate yourself on this important personality quality? Where would you put Horatio Alger, Cinderella, and Vince Lombardi? (In the *Study Guide* you will find a means for measuring internality/externality.)

Lower socioeconomic groups and minorities tend to be more external controls because they tend to perceive that the rewards they receive or fail to receive are not the consequence of their own actions. Athletes, especially good athletes, tend to be more internal because they have learned that their abilities and efforts bring them the rewards of athletic success.

Whether players are internal or external controls may influence both their performance and the methods you use to motivate them. Internal control athletes are skill oriented and more motivated to achieve, while external control athletes are chance oriented and fear failure more. Internals tend to achieve more than externals because their reactions to failure are less negative, they are more persistent, and they can delay gratification of rewards longer. Internals are more likely to raise their goals after success and lower their goals slightly after failure—both healthy, adaptive responses.

On the other hand, success tends not to reinforce externals to attempt higher goals; because they attribute their success to outside forces, they do not derive personal satisfaction from success. Externals, consequently, are more inclined to set unrealistically high or low goals, and take unnecessary risks.

Internal control athletes are more influenced by the internalization process of motivation, and externals are influenced more by identification methods. Internals are especially motivated when they are given the opportunity to exert greater control over their own lives.

Being predominantly internal is obviously desirable and coaches should strive to help athletes develop this characteristic. To do so, you should (a) help athletes experience situations in which their personal actions produce desired consequences, and (b) teach athletes to set realistic goals and to take personal responsibility for their actions (see chapter 10 for specific steps to accomplish this). The psychological skills introduced in part III are also effective means for teaching internality. Sport provides an especially good format for teaching responsibility if coaches will make the effort to do so.

One warning: While externals deny responsibility they should accept, high internal control coaches and athletes may perceive greater control over the outcome of a contest than actually exists. The outcome of a contest is only *partially* controlled by a player or team; the opposing team, officials, luck, and other environmental events also determine the outcome. The danger in assuming greater control about the outcome is that coaches and athletes can blame themselves for losing when they should attribute the loss to other reasons. This problem is one of the primary reasons why the self-confidence levels of many athletes are so fickle. I'll elaborate on this problem more in chapter 10.

Athletes' Needs and Motivation

If there is such a thing as a secret to motivation, understanding what athletes need would be it. A need unmet becomes a goal, and helping your athletes meet their goals provides you with a passkey to their motivation. So let's see what we know about athletes' needs.

Among the better known theories of motivation and personality is Abraham Maslow's hierarchy of needs. Maslow (1962) asserts that people attempt to satisfy their needs according to a system of priorities (see Figure 2.2). These priorities can be divided into two general categories—deficiency needs, such as hunger, thirst, sex, safety, and security, which have highest priority; and growth needs, such as love, self-esteem, and self-actualization. According to Maslow, once a need is satisfied and remains so, it no longer is a need, and the person moves up the hierarchy to the next higher need.

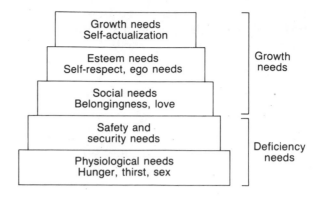

Figure 2.2 Maslow's hierarchy of needs.

While Maslow's theory makes intuitive sense, there is little support, if any, for the hierarchy he proposes. However, the needs he identifies are useful in helping you think about the goals athletes may have for competing.

From numerous sources, the evidence indicates three prominent needs that athletes seek to fulfill by participating in sports.

- To play for fun, which meets the need for stimulation and excitement.
- To be with other people, which meets the need to affiliate with others and belong to a group.
- To demonstrate competence in order to meet the need to feel worthy.

Before looking at these three needs more closely, another caution. Some coaches have used personality tests to help understand the needs of their athletes. It is my opinion that general or sport-specific personality tests tell you less about the needs of your athletes and how to motivate them than effective communication with them can tell you about their interests and needs. (In the *Study Guide*, you'll find some useful tools for determining these needs.)

Glenn Patton, the swimming coach at the University of Iowa, uses a novel approach to learn about his swimmers' interests and needs. He has every member of the team interview another member, and then the interviewer reports the findings of the interview in a team meeting. This technique is enjoyable and lets not only the coach know the athletes' needs, but also the other team members so that they, too, can help meet these needs. At the same time, this kind of an approach builds team unity.

Need for Stimulation

Each of us has wired into our genetic makeup the need for a certain amount of stimulation and excitement, or arousal as psychologists call it. I say "certain amount" because if people get too little stimulation they will seek more (watch children who become bored), and if people get too much stimulation they will seek a quieter environment. Positions such as those held by air traffic controllers—and coaches—can offer too much stimulation, leading to stress and eventual burnout. (The problem of burnout among coaches is discussed in chapter 8.) Some individuals prefer an optimal arousal level that is quite high and others prefer an optimal arousal level that is much lower.

When we experience optimal arousal—fun —we are neither bored nor anxious, and this state is known as being in *flow*. Flow is the feeling that everything is going just right and you are totally absorbed in the activity, feeling very much in control. (You will learn more about the flow phenomenon in chapter 7.)

Sport itself possesses qualities that increase the possibility of experiencing flow and having fun, largely because it's challenging, creative, and so absorbing of mind and body. But sport can be turned from fun to work, and some coaches have a knack for doing this. When coaches overstructure practices, create a negative environment, remove the athletes' freedom, or make excessive demands, then sport may become drudgery for athletes.

Wise coaches have known for a long time that they must meet athletes' need for fun. Yet they also know that athletes must practice— and practice can be monotonous and thus little fun. The creative coach finds a way to do both. Here are a few examples:

- Fit the difficulty of the skill to the ability of the athlete. No one finds it fun to lose or fail constantly. Build in some success.
- Keep practices stimulating by varying the activities.
- Keep everyone active. Don't give players time to get bored by having them stand in long lines.
- Give different athletes the opportunity to

perform the more enjoyable tasks in practices.
- Help athletes set realistic performance goals.
- Allocate some time in each practice when the athletes can just play the game without receiving evaluation or feedback from the coach.
- Permit athletes to play a greater part in determining what will be done in practice.

Recognize this about athletes who are motivated primarily to have fun: They may not be as committed to achieving excellence as athletes motivated to enhance their self-worth. Some coaches expect every member of the team to be as committed as they themselves are. Athletes who are motivated primarily to meet their need for fun may become problems for coaches who have taken much of the fun out of practices, and perhaps even out of games. They may engage in creative activities to make the sport fun, but these activities often annoy coaches because they disrupt the highly structured practice regimen. These athletes are seen as "goof-offs" and may therefore be considered discipline problems.

Some coaches cannot tolerate these athletes and may dismiss them from the team. They want athletes who are committed to winning only. This is another philosophical issue you need to consider. Do you have room on your team for athletes who have a high need for fun? Just how much tolerance do you have on your team for athletes who do not conform entirely to your structure?

Need for Affiliation

Some individuals choose to participate in sports because they want to be a part of a team; they want to belong to a group that adds significance to their lives. These people are motivated foremost to affiliate with other people and to be accepted by them. They are motivated largely to meet this need, not to achieve fame or recognition. They often are willing to accept sitting on the bench and getting to play only occasionally. Coaches can motivate athletes with a high need for affiliation especially through the identification process because they want to be accepted by the coach and team.

Players who are primarily motivated to

meet their affiliation need may be similar to athletes motivated to have fun. Performing well and winning at all costs are not as significant to them, although they will inculcate this goal, if it is a team goal, because they want to be a part of the team. Coaches who recognize this can still motivate these athletes to pursue excellence by using the affiliation motive as a powerful reward.

Need to Feel Worthy

I believe the need to feel worthy—competent and successful—is the most powerful and most prevalent need in sports. The need to feel worthy can be met in sport by demonstrating competence that other people recognize, or it can be met by athletes recognizing their own competence without being esteemed by others. When skills are less well developed, and when a person does not have a mature, positive self-concept, being judged competent and successful by others is very important. It helps athletes move toward being able to judge their own self-worth in the absence of others, which is an important ability to be developed.

In *Coaching Young Athletes* the significance of self-worth in enhancing motivation is explained in depth, but I will briefly summarize the important points here. Children quickly learn that their self-worth depends largely on their ability to achieve, and our society teaches them that winning means being successful, and losing means being a failure. Consequently, participation in sports is potentially threatening because players feel their achievement in sport is a reflection of their self-worth. Success-oriented athletes—those who are predominantly successful and therefore perceive that their ability is high in sport—see winning as a consequence of their ability and blame failure on insufficient effort. This is a healthy view.

Failure-oriented athletes—those who have predominantly unsuccessful experiences in sport and perceive their ability as low—attribute losing to a lack of ability and their rare wins to luck or an easy opponent. Thus they blame themselves for losing and do not take credit for winning, which obviously is unhealthy. Failure-oriented athletes have very poor self-esteem.

Failure-oriented athletes attempt to protect their self-worth by putting forth only token effort so that others will not discover their feared lack of ability. Their reasoning is that if they try hard and still lose, then everyone will know they lack ability. If they give only token effort, others won't know whether it's the lack of effort or their ability that caused the failure. This behavior is a desperate attempt on the part of athletes who dread failure to protect their self-worth, but the token effort strategy almost guarantees that they will fail.

Failure-oriented players prefer not to play sports because it so unequivocally identifies winners and losers, but sometimes extrinsic motives or other factors keep them involved. Then they use either the token effort strategy or many excuses to blame factors other than their own ability for their failures.

Coaches often mistake the token effort strategy as a lack of motivation on the part of failure-oriented athletes, but actually they are highly motivated—motivated to avoid the threat to their self-worth. So what can you do to help this type of athlete? Positive reinforcement and identification procedures may be helpful if the failure orientation is not too strong, but often these athletes reject positive reinforcement because they have such low self-regard. They tend to respond best to internalization procedures, but only after you help them redefine their goal. That goal is not to focus on winning, an outcome, but on their own performance, something they control. I will elaborate in chapter 10 on the significance of this type of goal in helping all athletes perform better.

Now let's look at two coaches who approach motivation in different ways.

TWO STYLES OF COACHING AND MOTIVATION

In *Coaching Young Athletes* you were introduced to the command style of coaching, characterized by coaches making all the decisions, and the cooperative style of coaching wherein coaches share the decision making with their athletes. Now let's look at these two styles of coaching to see how they approach motivation.

Command Style Coaches

The commander, much in the image of General Patton or Woody Hayes, takes the following view:

- I am responsible for organizing the elements of an effective team—money, equipment, facilities, people, and so on.
- I am responsible for directing the players' efforts, motivating them, controlling their actions, and modifying their behavior to fit the team's needs.
- Without my direction, the players would be passive, even resistant, to the team's goals. Athletes must, therefore, be persuaded and controlled by rewards and punishments—their activities must be directed.

Cooperative Style Coaches

The cooperative style coach takes a quite different view:

- I am responsible for organizing the elements of a competitive team—money, equipment, facilities, people, and so on.
- Athletes are not by nature passive or resistant to team goals. If they are, they have become so because of previous experiences that restricted their opportunity to be responsible and in control.
- Motivation, potential for development, capacity for assuming responsibility, and the ability to work toward individual and team goals are all present in my athletes or can be developed. I do not supply these qualities for team success, but am respon-

sible for making it possible for players to develop and exhibit these qualities through sport.

Some Other Differences

Examine Table 2.1 to see other differences in the way command style and cooperative style coaches see their role.

Table 2.1
Differences Between
Command and Cooperative Style Coaches

Command Style	Cooperative Style
Tends to subscribe to the "win first" philosophy	Tends to subscribe to the "athletes first" philosophy
Sees players as predominantly external controls	Sees players as predominantly internal controls
Relies heavily on compliance and identification processes	Uses all the methods of motivation, generally striving to use internalization
Favors extrinsic motivation	Favors intrinsic motivation

Cooperative style methods are used mostly by coaches who (a) have high self-esteem, (b) once played for coaches who subscribed to this style, and (c) are high in empathy. Command style methods are used more by coaches who (a) have low self-esteem, (b) once played for coaches who used the command style, and (c) are low in empathy. The methods of the command style are easier to implement but generally less successful, whereas cooperative style methods are much more difficult to implement but are substantially more successful in motivating athletes.

More and more today, coaches are using the cooperative style and enjoying greater success —both in winning and in helping athletes develop. If you are still relying on command style techniques, thorough study of this book and the companion *Study Guide* will help you move toward cooperative style methods.

CONTROL AND RESPONSIBILITY

All roads for enhancing motivation lead to one place from my perspective—helping athletes become responsible for themselves by permitting them to control their lives. From numerous sources, the tide of scientific evidence rises to the same conclusion: Deny individuals the right to control their own lives and you destroy motivation, achievement, self-responsibility, and self-worth. Provide individuals the right to control their own lives, nurture their development, and you enhance all these qualities.

This final section of chapter 2 is my sermonette. I believe deeply in the importance of nurturing self-responsibility by allowing people to assume control of their own lives, not only to enhance motivation but to enhance total development. First, I will make the case for the importance of having control, and then I'll describe how coaches may unwittingly deny such control. The chapter concludes with specific recommendations on how you can develop responsibility in your athletes by sharing some of the control.

Significance of Control

Edwin Moses, the world's greatest 400-meter hurdler, has not lost a race since 1977. How does he stay motivated to sustain this high level of performance when no one provides him with a serious challenge? If the source of Moses' motivation was totally extrinsic, his needs would have been fully met sometime ago. But Moses runs predominantly for intrinsic rewards—being the best he can be—and there is none better!

This source of intrinsic motivation, I suspect, comes from Moses' being very much in control of his own life; he's responsible for every aspect of his training and preparation for competition. Moses is not unlike many other great athletes. Achieving at the upper end of a person's capabilities demands the motivation that comes with being responsible for yourself.

The significance of control, of course, is not at all unique to the world of sport. Carl Rogers

in *Freedom to Learn for the 80's* (1983) describes the failure of our education system to teach young people to assume responsibility and control for their own learning. The traditional educational approach follows the command style, with teachers so totally controlling the learning process that they stifle motivation to learn. Rogers marshals compelling evidence to show that in nontraditional schools where students are given responsibility and control, both motivation and achievement are greatly enhanced.

Richard de Charms (1976) conducted an extensive research project in the East St. Louis school system. The study first showed how teachers denied children responsibility and control for their own learning, and how this resulted in teachers spending most of their time maintaining order and disciplining the children. The consequence was a dismal amount of learning with the children tending to be more external than internal. They saw themselves as "pawns," pushed around by others rather than being responsible for their own fate.

de Charms' next step was to retrain the teachers to return some of the control to the students. Initially it was hard for the teachers to do this; the classrooms became chaotic because the students did not know how to handle this new responsibility. But after several weeks, with teachers providing general structure and guidance but not assuming total control, the students discovered they could enjoy learning by exerting some control over what and how they learned. As they demonstrated greater responsibility, more control was given to them. By the end of the year, far more learning had taken place, discipline problems had significantly decreased, and attendance had greatly improved—all signs of motivated behavior.

Here are some additional examples of how lack of control suppresses motivation:

- Several psychological theories postulate an innate drive in humankind to be competent and self-determining. Research has shown that when individuals are denied control during their developmental years, they assume such undesirable personal qualities as being high external controls, highly anxious, and low in achievement motivation.

- When older people who have been placed in nursing homes feel they have lost control, they have significantly more physical and psychological health problems.
- Hospitals have discovered that not assuming total control over the lives of their patients during convalescence increases the rate at which they get well, mostly because the patients are happier.
- Children who are raised in environments where they perceive they have no control develop feelings of *learned helplessness*. These children suffer substantial motivational losses, are sad and depressed, and are very resistant to future responsibility training.

Control in Sport

Most coaches subscribe to the objective that athletes should become more responsible for themselves. Yet many do not ensure that responsibility is developed by giving athletes the opportunity to exercise responsibility.

The problem is simply this: When athletes are given certain responsibilities, sometimes they do not use them wisely. They do not always make the best decisions and these errors can cost the team the chance to win. Coaches who feel society's pressure to win, or who coach first for their own ego enhancement, will be quick to withdraw such responsibilities.

The coach of a women's track team desired to control every aspect of the members' lives. They often resisted, but he justified it by saying he had learned from past experience: In his early coaching years, six of his runners became pregnant. So his 9:00 p.m. curfew the nights before races and his automatic expulsion if members of the team entertained male visitors in their rooms may appear understandable—but it's not.

Coaches who subscribe to the "Winning first, athletes second" philosophy often contend that, "If I show them how to win, then they'll become responsible for themselves." That simply isn't true, and many athletes who are winners in sport have been losers in life because they never learned how to take control of their lives. It's not the outcome of winning that develops responsibility, it's the process used in pursuing winning.

Coaches deny athletes the possibility to exercise decision-making skills and assume responsibility in several ways. They may, for instance, make all the decisions for their athletes with regard to the training program. The athletes have no input into the training regimen—they simply follow it. Certainly the coach should know best how to train young athletes, but coaches could teach athletes how to develop their own training program, giving them more and more responsibility as they learn more. Athletes are more likely to design better training programs once they know how, because they also know their own bodies better than the coach, and, as you'll learn in chapter 10, they are more likely to be committed to a training program they themselves have designed.

Coaches can also deny athletes the opportunity to make decisions about learning sports skills by prescribing exactly how a particular technique must be done. The Fosbury Flop would never have been developed if Fosbury practiced high jumping only the way his coach told him to. Stan Musial, with his highly unorthodox stance, would probably never have been the great hitter he was if he had not done it his way. Coaches must give athletes room to learn what is the best way for them to perform a skill. Seldom is there only one *right way* to perform complex sport skills.

Coaches may also overcoach during the learning process because they are impatient with the rate at which athletes learn. Thus they constantly give athletes information about what they are doing wrong. Often this information is inconsistent and is more than the athlete can handle, which only hurts learning. When coaches overcoach, they deprive athletes of the opportunity to learn how to make adjustments and how to perform a skill correctly. For more information on teaching sport skills and providing feedback, consult the *Coaches Guide To Teaching Sport Skills* in this series.

Among the most enjoyable aspects of sports is making decisions about what strategy will be used. Commonly coaches make this decision, especially in sports like basketball and football, denying athletes yet another opportunity to learn to make decisions for themselves. Few would argue that coaches can make decisions better—that is, better for winning but not necessarily better for the athletes' development.

Denying athletes the opportunity to learn to control their own lives extends well beyond practices and games. Some coaches are guilty even of taking total control of the lives of their athletes—particularly those athletes who hold promise for stardom. They tell them what courses to study, when and where to study, whom to see socially, how to use their money, and on and on. Athletes who endure such coddling often have exceptional difficulty reentering society when their playing days are over, for they lack the decision-making skills to function effectively.

Not for a moment do I believe coaches deliberately deny athletes the opportunity to make decisions, learn responsibility, and acquire control over their lives. Instead, coaches are so steadfast in their pursuit of victory that they do not see some of the long-term consequences.

Enhancing Responsibility Development

Some coaches mistakenly assume that giving athletes more responsibility for themselves is a mandate for complete abdication of control. It's not. It's encouraging athletes to take as much responsibility as a coach judges they can manage. It's giving a little more responsibility as the athlete demonstrates the wise use of responsibility. It's taking constructive action to help athletes who have erred in using their responsibility.

The athlete should not expect, nor be given free rein, to do anything he or she chooses, but should be given choices within a structured situation. The athlete needs to learn to concentrate on striving for goals within certain constraints, those being primarily that a person's own goal seeking cannot interfere with the goal seeking of others.

The coach who facilitates this type of development in assuming responsibility is not necessarily a democratic coach. All the judgments implied above are not voted upon—they are the responsible decisions of the coach. The athletes are given structure and rules by which they must live, just as we all must. But this structure and these rules are so arranged that it is possible for athletes to develop their capacity to set their own goals and learn to strive for them. To resign from the task of structuring the situation is to give up the major responsibility of being a coach. To accept the responsibility is to meet the difficult

challenge of deciding how much structure will provide an optimum climate for the development of an athlete's own responsibility.

What can coaches do to help athletes become responsible, autonomous human beings? The most important thing is believing deeply that athletes are more important than winning. Helping an athlete to develop into a responsible person is very much a long-term objective. It's achieved by countless little events that cumulatively permit the athlete to experience life and to grow from these experiences. It requires the coach to communicate that he or she cares for the athlete as a human being, accepting and trusting the person.

Coaches must also have empathy—the ability to understand the emotions and attitudes of the athletes, to see the world as they see it. Empathy creates trust between coach and athlete, which is essential for both if decision making is to be shared.

Coaches need to coach less on techniques and strategies and more on the development of psychological skills, such as those discussed in parts II and III of this book.

Coaches can help athletes to set short- and long-term goals that are realistic without imposing their own goals on the athlete. In turn, athletes should be counseled to examine the causes for their successes and failures in sport, and to assign them to the correct sources. If the outcome is in fact their personal responsibility, then that should be accepted. If the outcome is the result of some external factor, then that needs to be acknowledged as well.

In the past coaches approached motivation with the attitude, "We'll make them do it." Then they learned, "We'll make them want to do it." And at last we've discovered, "We'll make them responsible to do it."

SUMMARY

1. Motivation is a complex topic that does not lend itself to simplistic approaches such as the donkey and stork approaches.
2. A coach's challenge is not only to find a means to motivate, but to avoid destroying the intrinsic motivation of his or her athletes.

3. Motivation is concerned with the intensity and the direction of behavior.

4. Athletes may be intrinsically motivated —an internal striving to be competent— or extrinsically motivated—a need to obtain rewards or recognition from others—or both.

5. Extrinsic rewards can be a powerful source of motivation for athletes. Coaches should be skillful in applying the principles of behavior modification that rely on the use of extrinsic rewards.

6. Intrinsic rewards tend to be more enduring sources of motivation because they are self-fueling. Extrinsic rewards, when used correctly, can help develop intrinsic motivation.

7. On the other hand, extrinsic rewards can undermine intrinsic motivation when the athlete is already intrinsically motivated, when the rewards are perceived as controlling the athletes' behavior, or when the rewards are given noncontingently.

8. Coaches can motivate athletes through such direct methods as compliance, identification, and internalization, and through indirect methods that alter the situation.

9. Athletes differ in the responsibility they perceive for the rewards and punishments they receive. Some athletes are high external controls and others are high internal controls. Internal controls are more easily motivated by the internalization process, and externals by identification methods.

10. A key to motivation is knowing the needs of your athletes. The major needs relevant to sport are (a) the need for stimulation or fun, (b) the need to affiliate with other people, and (c) the need to feel worthy.

11. Coaches can easily create discipline problems for themselves when they fail to meet the players' need to have fun.

12. The need to feel worthy is the most important need to be met in order for athletes to develop a strong motivation to achieve rather than a fear of failure.

13. Command style coaches assume all responsibility for directing athletes, including being the source of their motivation. Cooperative style coaches share the responsibility for team activities with athletes and seek to provide an environment that stimulates the athletes' intrinsic motivation to play.

14. Athletes are more motivated and become more responsible for themselves when coaches provide them with opportunities to control and manage their own lives.

PART II

Psychological Skills for Coaches

Coaching is a demanding, difficult profession that requires exceptional skills. Society expects coaches to be super-human beings. Bill Libby writes in *The Coaches*, "Theirs may be the worst profession—unreasonably demanding and insecure and full of unrelenting pressures. Why do they put up with it? Why do they do it?" (1982, p. 4).

More and more coaches are succumbing to the pressures of their profession. Newspapers report a growing number of men and women who are burning out or finding other alternatives more attractive because coaching demands are so great.

Coaching is only now emerging as a profession. Many who enter coaching have not formally prepared to be coaches. Our society, and especially administrators who employ coaches, believe that having played the sport is the major qualification for being able to coach. Furthermore, some people believe that the better an athlete has played, the better coach he or she will be. The assumption apparently is that the skills and knowledge of outstanding athletes make for better teachers and tacticians of the game.

These beliefs are without substance. Just because individuals were proficient at playing a sport does not mean they will necessarily be effective coaches. Coaches need to know not only the techniques and tactics of their particular sport, but also how to teach these things to their athletes. They must possess not only the psychological skills essential to being good athletes—energy management, stress management, attentional skills, and goal-setting skills—they must possess leadership and communication skills as well.

Coaches sometimes see leadership as being an intangible quality that is mysteriously bestowed on people, but leadership is a set of complex skills. "Leaders are made, they are not born; and they are made just like anything else has ever been made in this country—by hard effort. And that's the price that we will have to pay to achieve that goal, or any goal," said Vince Lombardi (Dowling, 1970, p. 79).

With hard work, you can develop your leadership skills. Chapter 3 assists you by providing a contemporary and progressive look at leadership, discussing the four components you must consider in exerting leadership skills. You will learn how leaders provide direction by acquiring vision and developing insight. This chapter will tell you how coaches lead teams to pursue their goals through the development and management of team culture.

The most important leadership skill is the ability to communicate effectively. Communication skills are what separate highly successful coaches from less successful coaches. The very essence of coaching *is* communication.

In chapter 4 you will have the opportunity to assess and improve your verbal skills—those skills that are necessary for sending and receiving messages effectively. You will also learn about nonverbal communication skills, a vital part of the communication process. And finally, we will look at conflicts and how to develop effective confrontation skills.

First through awareness of the components of leadership and communication skills, and then through greater self-awareness, particularly in regard to those same skills, you can begin a concerted effort to improve as a leader and as a communicator. The activities in the *Study Guide* will be of help, but the most important steps are recognizing the need to improve your skills and committing yourself to the hard work.

Chapter 3
Leadership Skills

If you are like most coaches, you played sports for many years before you began coaching. Once you assume the role of coach, you must make the difficult transition of getting things done through others. You can no longer play the game yourself, even though you may yearn to do so; you have to help your players play the game. The skills needed to do that are not at all the same skills you needed when you were playing. Consequently, many coaches are ill prepared to assume the leadership role of coach.

In this chapter you will learn more about what leadership is. We will examine the four components of effective leadership, see how leaders provide direction, and how coaches build team culture.

UNDERSTANDING LEADERSHIP

While reading through the massive literature on leadership, I gained two impressions. First, the leadership literature in psychology, including sport psychology, contains pounds of pulp and ounces of information. Never have so many said so much to tell us so little. And second, the essence of leadership, what sets it apart from other human processes, is ill conceived in psychology.

Hence I decided to look at the leadership literature in management, which led me into the plethora of new business books on excellence. These books frequently cite examples of outstanding leadership not only from business, but from sports. What I discovered was that American business has learned a great deal about leadership by observing and analyzing how great coaches lead. Thus this chapter is based on what outstanding coaches and business executives do as leaders, as observed by behavioral scientists and manage-ment analysts, combined with what psychologists and sport psychologists have learned.

Leadership Defined

Leadership is simply this: First it's knowing how to chart a course, to give others direction by having a vision of what can be. A team without a leader is like a ship without a rudder. Second, leadership is developing the social and psychological environment—what business calls the *corporate culture* and I'll call *team culture*—to achieve the goals the leader has charted. This culture consists of selecting, motivating, rewarding, retaining, and unifying members of your team—players, assistants, everyone who helps your organization.

Excellent coaches—leaders—give the team vision, and know how to translate this vision into reality. Coaches, in their leadership roles, seek to develop an environment whereby each and every athlete has the maximum opportunity to achieve success, and in so doing achieve team success. The coach is concerned not only with the physical environment, but the psychological and social environments as well.

Leadership, formally defined, is the action of an individual to influence others toward set goals. It is often confused with management. Management consists of planning, organizing, staffing and recruiting, scheduling, budgeting, and public relations. Leaders perform these functions, or delegate them to others, but they also do more. Leaders determine the direction for the future, and then marshal the resources within the organization to pursue that vision. Managers simply handle the routine, never questioning whether the routine should be done. This distinction is significant in sport, for too many teams are overmanaged and underled.

Leadership emphasizes interpersonal relationships and has direct impact on motivation, whereas management necessarily does not. Tom Peters and Nancy Austin write in *A Passion for Excellence*:

> Coaching is face-to-face leadership that pulls together people with diverse backgrounds, talents, experiences and interests, encourages them to step up to responsibility and continued achievement, and treats them as full-scale partners and contributors. Coaching is not about memorizing techniques or devising the perfect game plan. It is about really paying attention to people—really believing them, really caring about them, really involving them. (1985, p. 326)

I recommend you read that quote again. Coaching is a *people* business, and excellent coaches become students of people. To be an excellent leader—an excellent coach—you must develop the psychological skills, especially the interpersonal skills, to move people to action. Communication skills are essential —talking, listening, pleading, arguing, negotiating, encouraging, consoling. Coaching is as demanding of communication skills as marathoning is of conditioning skills.

I subscribe to the "great man" theory of history. Individuals who exert leadership make a difference. Excellence in teams is a product of superior leadership by individuals who have acquired specific skills that give them both vision of a future that can be obtained and the ability to commit people to pursue that future. Excellence doesn't just happen. It comes from preparing yourself to lead and working hard when leading. It's been said that people can be divided into three classes:

- The few who make things happen,
- the many who watch things happen,
- and the vast majority who have no idea what happened.

There is a ring of truth in that statement.

Transformation Leadership

In *Leaders: The Strategies for Taking Charge* (1985), Warren Bennis and Burt Nanus describe a leader as "one who commits people to action, who converts followers into leaders, and who may convert leaders into agents of change" (p. 3). Leadership viewed from this perspective is congruent with the philosophy espoused in the first two chapters of this book. It's a collective process—you and your players working together to meet each other's individual needs and common goals. This type of leadership, known as transformative leadership, involves a *dynamic relationship* in which you not only influence the team, but the team influences you. It is a psychological contract between you and your athletes, the contract containing a variety of expectations and actions on both sides. Your demands on the athletes may be reciprocated by the athletes' demands on you.

Leadership from this perspective is not unilateral—it is an impressive yet subtle sweeping back and forth of energy between you and your team. This approach to leadership can move your athletes to become more responsible, more in control of their lives. It can help them acquire the skills that will permit them to lead now and tomorrow.

Power

Power is the basic energy to initiate and sustain action, which permits you to translate intentions into reality. Power is essential for you to move the team to achieve its objectives, yet it is greatly distrusted because it is so often misused. Leadership is the wise use of power, and power is gained by effective leadership.

Because you are the appointed coach, you have the authority to direct, but that doesn't make you the leader. A coach does not become a leader until the team members acknowledge or legitimate his or her authority. Power is this authority—the power becomes usable when those being led acknowledge the leader's authority. In short, you must earn the respect of the team to have the power needed to achieve excellence. This respect is earned by demonstrating ability through superior skills and knowledge, and by attaining credibility through a clear commitment to the team.

In transformative leadership, you empower the staff and players to help achieve team goals. Empowerment is another way of granting athletes responsibility. When you empower members of your team they

- are more likely to feel they are making a difference, a contribution to the team goal;
- learn new skills that enhance their physical and psychological performance;
- feel more committed to the team, thus increasing their motivation;
- experience more enjoyment from participation, which meets their need for fun.

FOUR COMPONENTS OF EFFECTIVE LEADERSHIP

Leadership was once thought to be an innate quality—people were either born to be leaders or they were not. The "great man" theory of leadership (not to be confused with the great man theory of history) did not survive long, because it became apparent that excellent leaders for some tasks were poor leaders for other tasks.

Astute observers noticed that all leaders did not act alike—they had different styles. Although there were many variations, the styles generally fell into two categories, widely referred to as the autocratic style and the democratic style. Much enthusiasm accompanied this discovery, along with substantial research exploring which style worked best for which kinds of tasks.

Recognizing that one style was more effective than another for certain tasks, researchers began looking at other situational variables. Thus the notion developed that it was really the situation that gave ordinary people the opportunity to become leaders. This was called the "big bang" theory, as if something spectacular happened to cast an ordinary person into a leadership position.

While investigating how leadership styles interact with the task to be undertaken, researchers also observed that not all those who were being led responded in the same way. In other words, followers differed in their personalities and needs, and thus responded to leadership in different ways.

This brief history of leadership research, then, identifies four components of leadership that have received scrutiny:

- The leader's qualities
- The style of leadership
- The nature of the situation
- The follower's characteristics

As you proably have already concluded, a complete understanding of leadership requires consideration of all these factors and how they interact to influence the leadership process (see Figure 3.1). A review of what we know about each of these components will prepare you to look at what leaders actually do.

Figure 3.1   The four components of effective leadership.

Qualities of Effective Leaders

While there are no qualities that are absolutely essential for all leaders to possess, there are some qualities that many successful leaders have in common. It does not require years of research to know what these are. As a little experiment, look over the list of leadership qualities in Table 3.1, comparing the two dimensions. Underline those you think leaders are more likely to possess. The answers are listed on page 45 at the end of this chapter.

It's quite easy to identify the basic qualities of leaders. But many people have all these qualities and still are not leaders, suggesting that these tend to be *necessary* but not *sufficient* qualities to be a leader. Leaders tend to have some other qualities as well.

Table 3.1
Qualities of Leaders Test

Unintelligent	Intelligent
Assertive	Passive
Self-confident	Diffident
Persuasive	Unpersuasive
Rigid	Flexible
Intrinsically motivated	Extrinsically motivated
Motivated to achieve success	Motivated to avoid failure
External control	Internal control
High self-awareness	Low self-awareness
Optimistic	Pessimistic

Empathy

Great leaders have the ability to adopt the perspective of the other person, understanding how that person perceives events and experiences emotions. This quality is called empathy, and should not be confused with sympathy. The empathic person *understands* how the other person feels; the sympathetic person *feels* emotions of regret for a person experiencing troubles.

Researchers in the helping professions have learned that empathy is *the* most vital quality for success as a helper. In my view, it is the most important quality that distinguishes outstanding coaches and leaders from less effective ones. To help athletes develop the psychological skills discussed in this book, empathy is essential. Empathy lets you know the interests and needs of your athletes, which you recall is not only a prerequisite for leading them, but for motivating them. The seed of empathy is genuine caring; its soil is communication skills, especially listening skills, and its sunshine is helping. Empathy then involves three steps:

1. Recognizing the need to be empathic.
2. Taking the time to understand the members of your team.
3. Taking action, based upon this understanding, to help the team members obtain their goals.

Empathy is not likely to occur when coaches assume they know the needs and expectations of their athletes without communicating with them, or when they treat everyone the same despite individual differences, or when they fail to recognize that a person may have changed. But the good news is that all of us have the capacity to be empathic. We simply need to decide to make the effort, to take the time, to attend to the feelings of others.

Other Qualities

Here are some additional qualities that effective leaders are likely to possess:

- They tend to act like leaders; they're not one of the boys or girls.
- They not only are problem solvers, they are problem finders. They look to identify problems in the early stages of development and then take corrective action.
- They develop trust in others by being reliable and tirelessly persistent.
- They have self-control.
- They constantly strive to develop and improve their own skills.
- They esteem others, helping others to develop self-worth.
- They are concerned with and responsive to time.
- They are flexible and pragmatic, not rigid and esoteric.

Leadership Style

A leader's style refers to the way that a leader typically approaches helping the group accomplish the task at hand and helping to satisfy the group's needs. It is a tendency on the part of a coach to lead the team in a particular way. When you think of John Robinson, Tom Landry, Casey Stengel, and Red Auerbach, you quickly can identify differences in their styles of leadership. Coaches approach sport with the qualities discussed above, and these influence how they lead. Qualities such as optimism/pessimism, assertiveness/passiveness, cautiousness/boldness, and rigidity/flexibility are particularly strong dispositions that are likely to influence a coach's style in most situations.

The two styles widely recognized to be of significance—the autocratic style and the democratic style—are shown in Table 3.2.

These two styles are often considered dichotomous; you are either one or the other. As we learned in the previous chapters, though, most human qualities fall on a continuum, and this is true for leadership styles

Table 3.2
Comparison of the Autocratic and Democratic Styles of Leadership

Autocratic Style	Democratic Style
Win-centered	Athlete-centered
Command style	Cooperative style
Task-oriented	People-oriented

as well. Moreover, even if you are autocratic, you are not necessarily also task-oriented. Thus what really constitutes these styles are broad, general orientations.

Can a leader adopt both styles? Yes, and the best leaders do—and this is *the* important point about these styles. Figure 3.2 is an adaptation of Robert Blake and Jane Mouton's (1969) managerial grid, showing how coaches can integrate both styles. Study this figure for a moment, and then rate yourself.

The "9,9" coach is the ideal coach—a person who is flexible and adaptable with his or

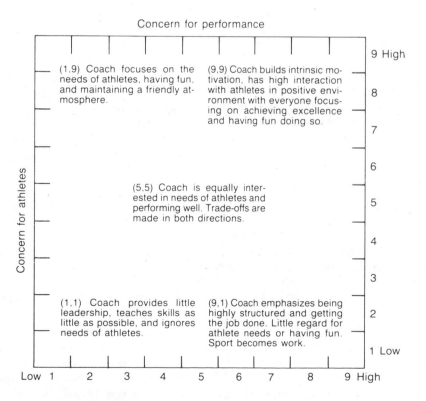

Figure 3.2 The coaches' leadership style grid (adapted from Robert Blake and Jane Mouton, 1969).

her leadership style. This style is neither autocratic nor democratic, but a blend of the two; the method appropriate for the situation is used. This style calls for directing, even forcefully, when the situation demands it, and empowering staff and team members with responsibilities for achieving team goals. Because the position of coach in our society typically involves so much power, and because the task of coaching must be performed effectively under demanding time constraints, the autocratic, highly directive style is necessary—at times. Unfortunately, the directiveness needed on the field may carry over into all other phases of the coach's behavior as leader, and this is unnecessary and undesirable. Thus a challenge for coaches is to learn when to use each of these styles, and the many variations of them.

Situational Factors

The basic premise of the situational approach to the study of leadership is that different situations require different leadership functions to be performed. The most important situational variable is the task at hand. As was just mentioned, "on-field" leadership requires quick action in sports, and thus it is not effective to use a democratic style in such a situation. Decisions must be made quickly, and the responsibility for those decisions rests with the coach. Nevertheless, coaches are frequently seen consulting with assistant coaches and players when making these decisions.

Another important aspect of the task at hand in sports is whether the sport is a team or individual sport. Team sports require more coordination and structure of group effort during the contest than do individual sports, thus requiring greater directiveness by the coach. A less directive approach, therefore, may be preferable for individual sports, and a more directive approach for team sports.

Research has found that athletes in team sports prefer task-oriented leaders more so than athletes in individual sports. Athletes in sports that are more variable and dynamic, such as basketball, prefer more task orientation than athletes in nonvariable, closed sports, such as swimming. It also appears that athletes who are less skillful prefer coaches who are more task-oriented, who can teach

skills well. Conversely, highly successful athletes prefer coaches who are more athlete-oriented, who will provide emotional support and work *with* the athlete rather than direct the athlete.

In addition to the task, four other situational factors have been found to be related to leadership effectiveness: tradition, available time, assistants, and the number of individuals in the group.

1. *Tradition*. A group that has a history of one type of leadership style is not likely to respond well to a change in that style regardless of who the leader is.
2. *Available time*. As noted above, when little time is available, the task-oriented, autocratic style is more functional than the democratic style.
3. *Assistants*. The more assistants a leader has, the more important it becomes to prepare them to lead in the same direction as the leader.
4. *Number in group*. It is difficult to use the participative, democratic style with large teams, although assistants, if they are available, can help to achieve greater participation.

Remember that situational factors determine in part who will be a successful leader. However, different sports possess many common situational factors. Thus the style of leadership and the qualities of the leaders probably have more similarity in sport than in general.

The situational approach alone, however, gives insufficient attention to the characteristics of those being led—the followers—and to the processes of leader-follower relations over time. Therefore, we now consider some of the followers' characteristics that have been found to be important.

Followers' Characteristics

Obviously, good leaders must consider the athletes' personalities and values, just as they need to do when they consider motivation. As in all relationships, the leader not only influences the followers, the followers influence the leader in that the leader must respond to the followers. When followers are not warm and receptive to direction, leaders are more likely to use an autocratic style.

Research shows that athletes differ in their desire and need for structure. Some are ready to accept considerable responsibility without a great deal of direction, and others are not. Athletes who handle uncertainty well, who identify closely with the team goals, and who possess high levels of skill and knowledge about the sport need less direction than their counterparts. At present, we still have much to learn about how followers influence leadership.

Becoming a Leader

What becomes evident about these four components of leadership is that leaders must be flexible, or adaptable. There is no one way to lead all people in all situations. The four components all help you consider how you will lead, and how you will select leaders among your team members. In selecting a team captain, for example, you would most likely look for athletes who are intelligent, self-assured, and assertive.

From the information presented, you also may realize that you are not sufficiently assertive or weak in some other quality, and thus you can take action to develop these qualities further. You may recognize that your communication skills are not as effective as you believe necessary to be the best coach possible. Thus you will want to study chapter 4 carefully.

Remember that the major styles of leading are not dichotomous, but are forms of leadership each of which are appropriate for certain tasks to be performed effectively. Your coaching philosophy will greatly influence which style you can use for different situations. If you perceive that the objective in a certain situation is to help an athlete develop, you will likely be more athlete-centered. If you see that the objective is to win the game, you may be more task-centered. When you are faced with competing objectives, you will have to make a choice based on what you value most.

Knowing that followers influence leadership helps you understand why what worked so well one year may work miserably the next. It explains, too, why it has become common practice in professional sports to replace the coach when things are not going well—it's the easiest change to make.

There is no one recipe for success as a coach, but here are some hints about leadership that may be useful:

- Know and train yourself to acquire the skills possessed by leaders.
- Develop both styles of leadership and use them appropriately.
- Know and support your team members.
- Adapt to the changing demands of your role as a coach.
- Act like a leader.
- Delegate but don't abdicate. Empower members of your team with responsibilities, but be selective with how much responsibility is delegated.
- Build an effective team by developing the psychological environment—the team culture (more on this point later).

WHAT LEADERS DO

The most significant thing to know about leadership is what leaders do and how they go about doing it. You will learn what they do in this section, and throughout this book you will learn how they do it. The following six actions set leaders apart from followers; the quality of these actions distinguish the effective leader from the ineffective leader.

- Leaders provide direction; they set goals by having a vision of the future. The next section of this chapter elaborates on this vital function.

- Leaders build a psychological and social environment that is conducive to achieving the team's goals—what business calls the "corporate culture." The last section of this chapter deals with this topic.
- Leaders instill values, in part by sharing their philosophy of life. The significance of having values, and of coaches imparting those values to their athletes, was addressed in chapter 1.
- Leaders motivate members of their group to pursue the goals of the group. This action was the focus of chapter 2.
- Leaders confront members of the organization when problems arise, and they resolve conflicts. This vital but often neglected action is considered in chapter 4.
- Leaders communicate. This is the critical skill needed for leaders to engage in the five actions just mentioned. It is the topic of the next chapter.

Providing Direction

You may say that the direction—the goal—in sports is obvious. The goal is to win each game, the league championship, the state title, the national championship, a world record, and so on. Throughout this book, however, I will argue that this is not the goal that excellent coaches pursue when leading their teams. Of course, every team wants to win all that it can, and so the aforementioned goal should be the one pursued. But as John Brodie (1974), the former quarterback for the San Francisco 49ers, noted: "You play to win. There's no doubt about that. But if winning is your first and only aim, you stand a good chance of losing" (p. 78). Leaders provide direction not by focusing on the outcome of winning or losing, but on the steps that lead to winning, and on the other goals they consider to be important for the team.

How do leaders know what the right direction is? Leaders acquire the ability to have vision—to set realistic goals that beckon the group to action. Hickman and Silva (1984) say, "Vision is a mental journey from the known to the unknown, creating the future from a montage of current facts, hopes, dreams, dangers, and opportunities" (p. 151).

Once coaches have direction, have charted a course, they focus not only their own attention, but the attention of the team, on this course. First they must communicate the direction successfully, striving to obtain commitment to it. Such commitment cannot be achieved by edict or coercion, although many coaches have sought to establish direction in this way. True commitment comes through persuasion; it comes from creating enthusiasm by helping the team to see that it is possible to achieve a certain goal. Effective coaches appeal to the emotions and to the spirit of the team members, addressing their values and aspirations. Excellent coaches do not state their goal just once, but repeat it again and again and arrange the physical and psychological environment to reinforce that goal.

Vision

Vision comes mostly through preparation. Leaders acquire vision by seeking information from any appropriate source—from history, books, reports, observation, and especially from other people. Because leaders rely so heavily on other people for their information, they must possess good listening skills and must be able to ask good questions. Once the available information is obtained, they sift through it, analyze it, and interpret it. The quality of this interpretation determines whether or not true insight is gained.

Vision also comes from intelligence, a quality noted earlier that leaders possess. And intelligence comes from preparation—from educating oneself to be able to outthink, outplan, outteach others. Those who can select the right strategy for the right situation, under the pressure that sport often imposes, earn the right to be called leaders. To implement superior strategy does not come from raw intelligence, although that helps; it comes mostly from educated intelligence—and that involves becoming a student of the game. To provide direction, to have a vision, to implement strategy, all require that you know your sport, your athletes, and your competition well. Knowledge is the edge, but it's not the only factor—coaches need insight.

Insight

Insight refers to the phenomenon of gaining an understanding of something in a way not readily apparent. It first requires obtaining a full understanding by gathering all the available information. Then some creative thinking is required through intense concentration. Insight comes by developing as many ways to solve a problem as possible, weighing each, and then selecting the best. For insight to occur, you must be cautious not to get trapped by old, habitual, comfortable ways of seeing the world. (You will find several useful exercises in the *Study Guide* for improving your insight.)

Leaders gain insight by asking the right questions, which helps them penetrate to the core of the problem. Leaders gain insight by encouraging disagreement and discussion from group members at the right time. Leaders gain insight by taking the time to step back from their organization to engage in introspection—an in-depth look at what's happening within the group. Some additional qualities of insight (adapted from Hickman and Silva, 1984) are listed below.

- After gathering information, leaders synthesize it by first breaking it into its parts, then restructuring it to expose the problem and reveal solutions.
- When an approach to a problem fails to work, leaders drop it and pursue the problem from another angle.
- Leaders tenaciously pursue difficult problems over a long period of time.
- Leaders do not worry about asking dumb questions in order to get to the heart of a problem.
- Leaders entertain unusual ideas without immediately labeling them "crackpot."
- Leaders know how to set up procedures for acquiring information and then immerse themselves in all the information they can get about a problem.
- Leaders picture situations and possible solutions with vivid imagery.
- Leaders set aside time regularly to engage in thinking.

Coaches can develop the ability to set direction through vision and insight mostly by preparing themselves. Become a student of the sport, become a student of the sport sciences, practice thinking, and discipline yourself to solve problems in the manner just described. As Thomas Edison said, "Genius is 10 percent inspiration and 90 percent perspiration."

Nurturing Team Culture

Having direction—a vision—for your team is the first vital act of leadership. But it's the ability to put this vision into action, to make it become reality, that enables a coach to advance to the throne of leadership. Putting a vision into action requires the coach to develop and maintain an effective *team culture*.

What some coaches do not understand, what keeps them from becoming successful, is their failure to nurture a team culture. Instead, their energies are expended developing physical skills and conditioning, and planning a masterful strategy for the next game.

Team Culture Defined

Team culture is the way things are done on a team—it's the social architecture that nurtures the team psyche. Team culture is concerned with building a climate for success. When coaches talk about developing a winning attitude, instilling commitment, inculcating pride, building team spirit, they are talking about team culture.

Team culture is concerned with how rewards are given, who communicates with whom about what, practice procedures, game protocols, acceptable reactions toward winning and losing, dress codes, and so on. Team culture is about the style of leadership used by the coach, which determines how power is distributed and decisions are made.

Team culture, then, is comprised of the formal organizational systems that the coach establishes for moving the team toward its goal, and the many informal factors that operate in any dynamic organization. These formal and informal processes have great influence on the soul and spirit of the team—the team psyche.

When team culture is not adequately developed, or is incompatible with the team direction, then the team will function substantially below its performance capabilities, and widespread dissatisfaction is likely. Poor team culture results when athletes are constantly subject to criticism, when conflicts develop between athletes and coaches or among athletes themselves, when athletes feel alienated, when coaches exert too much control, when feelings of futility and frustration reach a threshold.

Far more coaches fail to achieve their objectives because they lack awareness or the ability to develop team culture than because they lack good direction or knowledge of the game. John Wooden's last national championship team was considered by many to be weaker in talent and ability than other prominent teams in the country that year. From all accounts of that team, UCLA won a national title more because of a very powerful and effective team culture than because of superb talent.

Emphasizing the importance of the coach nurturing team culture does not mean that every member of the team must conform rigidly to the dictates of the coach. Building team culture is a *team* process, and thus must involve the team. To dictate every standard of appropriate behavior is not leading the development of team culture; it is imposing the coach's power on the team and is highly likely to have an adverse effect on the building of a positive team culture. A positive culture must have room for individualism and the sharing of responsibility.

Components of Team Culture

John Robinson, former coach at the University of Southern California and now coach of the Los Angeles Rams, is considered one of the most successful football coaches in the nation. When coaching at USC, a school rich with football tradition, Robinson fostered the "USC Mystique"—the winning tradition, the championship ideal, the destiny to be successful. This mystique was reinforced by coaches frequently mentioning the USC tradition, by photos of Heisman trophy winners, and by other memorabilia conspicuously displayed where the athletes could see them daily.

Robinson places ultimate importance on the dignity of each player, which he feels is essential for a cohesive team. He emphasizes positive reinforcement in practice sessions while giving constructive feedback. Players know precisely what is expected of them, and in turn what to expect from the coaching staff. There are no surprises.

The team comes first in Robinson's philosophy—athletes are expected to sacrifice personal goals for team goals. The young players are constantly reminded how "paying their dues" on the second, third, and fourth teams will be rewarded later when they make the first team.

Coach Robinson, known as the "Ice Man,"

approaches the game with a very businesslike attitude, and the team reflects that point of view. There are no pep talks, and little emotion is wasted prior to the game; but inspired play during the game is quickly rewarded.

The use of slogans is not favored by Robinson. He says, "We sell tradition, not slogans." He also does not use the helmet award system so popular in football—giving stickers to players to put on their helmets when they perform exceptionally well. He feels such stickers have little significance.

Robinson avoids denigrating the opposition or commenting about personalities when meeting the press. He permits his players to meet with the press, but controls these meetings so that they do not interfere with practice or games. He believes learning to handle the press is one way athletes can learn to handle stress.

Players are given honest feedback about how they play in practices and games, with emphasis on how to improve. When the team loses, the coaching staff analyzes what went wrong and presents this information to the players without placing blame. Failure is viewed as a means to learn and a means to become a better football team.

Robinson follows a highly consistent, evenhanded approach in leading the team. Thus he knows it is important to inculcate his assistant coaches with these views, and he especially emphasizes treating players with respect. (This description of John Robinson is adapted from Mechikoff and Kozar, 1983.)

John Robinson knows what team culture is. He recognizes its many aspects, and not only has a firm position about them, but actively takes steps to develop them. The more important components of team culture, some which Robinson has identified, are as follows:

- *Team tradition*. Obviously coaches want to build a winning tradition and replace a losing one, but other traditions are also important to develop—such as a team that never quits, good sportsmanship, a smart team, and so on.
- *Basic operating procedures*. These concern how players are selected, rewarded, trained, practiced, and prepared for competition. The procedures deal with how equipment and facilities are managed, assistants employed, and public relations handled. They are all the systems a coach

puts into place to accomplish the many things that need to be done to operate the team.

- *Management of information.* Who is privy to what information? How does certain information get passed on to assistant coaches and to the players? How is information directed to the coach? How is information managed during the games, when traveling, during the off-season? The answers to these questions determine how information is managed.
- *The nature of the sport.* Individual sports commonly have a different team culture from team sports because team sports require precise coordination of efforts under strict time constraints. Combative sports tend to have different team cultures from noncontact sports, and single-sex sports differ from mixed-sex sports. The team culture, of course, needs to be suited to the type of sport you coach.
- *The power, influence, and status structure within the team.* Does the coach retain most of the power or is it shared with assistants and players? Are team members encouraged to help other players or do the coaches want to provide all the instruction? Is there a strong pecking order in the team based on players' skills? The answers to these questions reveal how the team culture functions.
- *The leadership style of the coach.* This is probably the most significant factor influencing the team culture, and it has been discussed throughout this chapter.

Developing Team Culture

A group of Harvard professors in the late 1920s and early '30s conducted a series of studies at the Western Electric Company in Hawthorne, Illinois that have taught us much about team culture. These studies initially tested the hypothesis that workers would be more efficient if their lighting was increased. The results were positive. Then the lighting was decreased. Again the workers increased their productivity, much to the astonishment of the professors.

This led to a series of other studies in which researchers lengthened the rest periods, shortened them, offered refreshments and took them away, shortened the work week, and changed the method by which workers were

paid. In every case production increased, which initially baffled the professors. After much analysis, however, they realized that the significant factor in the studies was not the change in the work environment, but the attention being paid to the workers because they were part of a special group. This attention fostered a sense of group cohesiveness and motivation. They also observed that the boss in the experimental group behaved differently from the boss in the control group in the following ways:

- He showed interest in each employee's achievement.
- He demonstrated pride in the accomplishments of the group.
- He helped the group work together.
- He regularly posted feedback about their performance.
- He consulted the workers before changes were made.

The workers in the experimental group, as compared to the control groups, exhibited other changes:

- They took pride in their own achievement.
- They felt satisfaction from the interest shown by outsiders in their work.
- They did not feel they were being pressured to change.
- They developed a sense of confidence and candor.

These conditions, discovered nearly sixty years ago in the now classic Hawthorne studies, are still highly important in developing team culture. Implement the first five behaviors well, and you are likely to obtain the last four.

In chapter 2, I mentioned how you can engineer the environment to enhance motivation. Developing or modifying the team culture to produce desired behaviors is an excellent example of social or behavioral engineering. Developing team culture, however, is not something successful coaches delegate to anyone else. They recognize that it is the most difficult task facing coaches. When coaches talk about "turning a team around," or when they recognize that their team needs some psychological training, they are recognizing the need to change the team culture.

How do you recognize the need to change the team culture? You should always be working on the team culture—every time you meet with an athlete, every practice, every contest, every action you take has some influence on the team culture. Nevertheless, some definite signs indicate when your team culture is in trouble:

- The team is not playing as well as it used to, or it appears to be playing below its capability.
- Your assistant coaches are complaining.
- There are conflicts among members of your team.
- You feel uncomfortable communicating with assistants and players, and they with you.
- There is confusion about assignments, signals are missed, and relationships are unclear.
- Signs of apathy and disinterest are evident.
- There is little response at team meetings.

When seeking to change the team culture, some coaches err by taking a very short-term orientation. Changing the team culture is not accomplished overnight or even in a week; it is a gradual process. On the other hand, when teams are constructed quickly, such as all-star teams that represent a region, or national teams that represent us internationally, there is little time to develop team culture. This is probably one reason that these hastily created teams with enormous individual talent do not play as well as might be expected. Sport administrators increasingly are recognizing this

problem and are now having national teams play together longer before engaging in international competition.

Some coaches also err by not fully grasping the scope of team culture and the complexity with which it operates. A coach cannot simply announce, "We'll have no more bickering on the team," and expect this to be any type of permanent solution to internal friction. Nor is giving a pep talk about how everyone needs to be more committed likely to result in any lasting change. When the team culture is in trouble, you must look hard to discover what is interfering with maximum effort. Then you must devise a strategy to remove the obstacle or to build the right system. Tinkering with the team culture thoughtlessly can cause devastating problems. Thus it is vital that you involve the other members of the organization in determining what the obstacles are. Remember—they are part of the culture.

Lee Iacocca is a contemporary American hero for his success in pulling Chrysler out of bankruptcy. Iacocca had a vision first—build a better car for less money—and then he sought to implement that vision by taking three culture-building steps. He worked to instill commitment. He rewarded competence. And he maintained consistency in his direction and management.

Coaches can build commitment by

- involving players in defining team goals;
- recognizing that team goals must be compatible with individual goals;
- giving players responsibilities that they can accommodate;
- demonstrating superior skill and knowledge of the sport;
- treating each player with respect.

Coaches can reward competency by

- taking time to notice it;
- rewarding it promptly;
- rewarding excellent performance and effort, not outcomes that are beyond the control of the athletes;
- teaching the players to reward each other.

Coaches can maintain consistency by

- developing a sound coaching philosophy;
- taking a long-term rather than a short-term perspective;
- sticking with a well-thought-out plan when adversity occurs.

Conclusion

No one book can tell you how to build your team culture. This book, I hope, first has created an awareness of the need for you to attend to your team culture, and second offers some assistance in building your team culture. But you should also rely on your past experiences. Think about teams you have coached before and how their cultures differed from one another. Study other coaches; learn not only how they play the game, but how they develop their team cultures. Finally, look inwardly for greater self-awareness. Are you having a positive or negative impact on the team culture?

When coaches chart out a meaningful course for the team and build an effective team culture, they become excellent leaders. Neither objective can be ignored. The process through which these directions are imparted and team culture built is *communication*, which is the topic of the next chapter.

SUMMARY

1. Leadership, not to be confused with management, is the sum of the actions coaches take to influence their teams toward achieving team goals.
2. Transformative leadership is a dynamic process in which you not only influence the team, but the team influences you.
3. A coach does not become a leader until the team members acknowledge or legitimate his or her authority. This authority is power, which becomes usable only when the team members acknowledge that authority.
4. The four components of effective leadership include (a) the leader's qualities, (b) the style of leadership, (c) the nature of the situation, and (d) the followers' characteristics.
5. There are a number of qualities that leaders tend to possess; these qualities tend to be necessary, although not sufficient unto themselves, for one to be a leader.
6. The most effective leadership style is a combination of both autocratic and democratic orientations, with a skillful understanding of which style to use when.
7. Those situational factors known to influence a coach's leadership style are the nature of the task, tradition, available time, assistants, and the number of individuals on the team.
8. The characteristics of those being led also influence the leadership process, but as of yet we do not understand these influences well.
9. Two of the most important functions of leaders are that they provide direction toward goals and they develop team culture.
10. Coaches determine the direction for achieving goals by acquiring vision through extensive preparation and by gaining insight through in-depth analysis.
11. Developing and nurturing team culture is a vital task of the coach in being a successful leader.

Answers to Table 3.1. intelligent, assertive, self-confident, persuasive, flexible, intrinsically motivated, motivated to achieve success, internal control, high self-awareness, optimistic

Chapter 4
Communication Skills

7:06 a.m.—My wife reminds me that we have dinner tonight with her mother and I'm to invite her to join us at the cottage this summer. I'm overwhelmed with excitement.

8:14 a.m.—Mrs. Waterman calls expressing concern about the bruised thigh Neil received in practice last night. I suggest it isn't serious.

9:32 a.m.—I meet with Principal Jones. He's upset that our travel expenses are over budget. I try to explain the circumstances, but he isn't in a mood for listening.

10:55 a.m.—I finish teaching gymnastics to the ten o'clock class. It's my favorite class. I enjoy teaching when the students show interest.

12:14 p.m.—See Hank in the hallway. He looks right through me. I wonder if he's upset about what I told him yesterday?

12:45 p.m.—The usual faculty group have lunch in the "home ec" kitchen. There is some intense discussion about how our union should renegotiate the contract with the school board for next year. Mary Ellen really jumps on Gwen about her apathy on the whole issue.

2:20 p.m.—See Hank at the water fountain and ask him if anything is bothering him. He just gives me a piercing look and walks off. The turkey.

3:48 p.m.—The trainer asks if we have any more tape. I look and we're out. I chew him out for not having it on hand, but know I should have reordered last week.

4:30 p.m.—I show the team a new zone defense. Everybody seems confused. Maybe it's because this is the first time I have taught it.

6:15 p.m.—I leave the locker room and say good night to Charlie, the janitor. He wishes me luck in the upcoming game.

6:30 p.m.—We have dinner with my mother-in-law. After saying hello, I'm not able to get in another word, but I do a lot of head-nodding while thinking about why I was so miserable at teaching the new zone defense.

9:38 p.m.—Hank calls and says he wants to talk to me first thing in the morning. I agree, but wonder what's up.

10:57 p.m.—My wife rolls over on my pillow and whispers . . .

Our lives are filled with a flow of communication—we talk, read, write, gesture, listen, teach, console, persuade, demonstrate, observe, and so on. In the coaching profession it usually is a steady stream—sometimes a roaring river—of communication. We communicate verbally and nonverbally; we communicate by words and by actions. It is hard to imagine a world without communication—without ever knowing what other people think or without sharing our thoughts. Without communication, life would hardly be worth living. And thus, by improving your communication skills, you improve your own life in a very direct way.

Even before humankind invented language, communication flourished in nonverbal forms, just as it continues to do today. Each time I visit a non-English speaking country I'm amazed at how readily I can communicate my basic needs nonverbally—and how I miss being able to communicate beyond these basic needs.

Language is among the greatest inventions of humankind, yet at times it can be the bane of our existence. In *Three Roads to Awareness* (1970), Don Fabun writes, "Man is the only creature on earth who can talk himself into trouble. After a couple of million years of practice, we've become pretty good at it" (p. 15).

To be successful in influencing others and in permitting others to influence you—to be a leader, a coach—you must master communication skills, both verbal and nonverbal. Thus the objective of this chapter is to provide you with information that will help you (a) identify your strengths and weaknesses as a communicator, and (b) improve your communication skills. In this chapter you will learn more about

- expressing yourself,
- improving your listening skills,
- understanding nonverbal communication, and
- developing conflict and confrontation skills.

But reading this chapter is far from being enough; you must practice these skills. No one wants to ride in an airplane with a pilot who has done nothing more than read a book on how to fly; and you won't earn your communication wings simply by reading about communication. You will need to take the following steps to improve your communication skills:

1. Become aware of the need to improve a certain skill.
2. Identify the behaviors involved in improving your communication skills.
3. Practice the behaviors.
4. Receive feedback concerning how well you are performing the behaviors.
5. Integrate the new or improved communication skill into your day-to-day communication patterns.

This chapter will help you with the first two steps. The exercises in the *Study Guide* are useful for Steps 3 and 4, although you will need to do even more on your own to learn some skills well. Step 5, of course, is in your hands entirely.

Communication skills are much like sports skills, and you should recognize the five steps above as those you use in teaching sports skills. You might view this chapter as a chalk talk; it sets the stage for you to acquire these skills.

Part of the problem in learning communication skills is that less skillful communication patterns are so well ingrained, it's difficult to let them go. To do so requires first recognizing them and then having the motivation to

root out these stubborn patterns—not unlike what you try to accomplish when coaching your athletes. Also, many of us have a tendency to feel we are fairly good communicators—it's just that everyone else seems to do such a lousy job of it!

COMMUNICATION BASICS

A simple communication act of one person sending a message to another person involves six elements, as shown in Figure 4.1. An example will illustrate: You want to tell Wally he will not be starting today's game.

Figure 4.1 The six elements of the communication process.

1. The communication process begins when you decide that you want someone else to know what you know, value what you value, feel what you feel, or decide what you decide. In this case, you decide Wally should know he will not be starting today's game.
2. You must translate the thought to be communicated into a message, called *encoding* the message. You decide simply to tell Wally he will not be starting the game, without additional explanation.
3. Now you send the message to Wally. In this case, you articulate the words, "You will not be starting today's game, Wally."
4. The message you send goes through some channel. Most likely you speak the words, which produce sound waves and are heard by Wally. But you also can deliver the message through sign language, for instance, if Wally were deaf, which would involve his interpreting light waves from your symbolized language. The message can also be delivered over the phone, or by an audio

or video recording, and so on. These are simply examples of different channels.

5. Wally receives your message and now must interpret it, what is called *decoding* the message. Wally hears your words and understands their meaning.
6. Wally now thinks about this message and has some type of internal response. He could be angry, upset, relieved, uninterested, and so on.

Were you successful in this communication? It depends on what your intention was and how Wally responded to your message. When the message you intended to communicate is not what Wally heard, then the problem is called *noise* in the communication process. Noise can occur anywhere between the six steps. The common sources of noise are these:

- The sender's past experience provides a frame of reference for sending the message, such as beliefs, attitudes, and personality. These things may distort the message.
- The sender lacks sufficient skill in encoding the message. For example, you can't put your thoughts into words, or you don't know how to reveal certain feelings.
- The communication channel can have noise, such as other players making a lot of noise in the locker room, a bad telephone connection, and so on. Also, speech problems, such as stammering and annoying or distracting mannerisms of the sender or receiver, can create noise in the channel.
- Within the receiver, noise commonly occurs in the decoding process because of the receiver's past experiences, which also form a frame of reference for receiving and interpreting the message.

Let's consider some possibilities. If your intention was merely to let Wally know he would not be starting, regardless of how he felt about it, then you were successful. He received the message and understood the meaning—he would not be starting the game today.

Perhaps your intention, though, was to let Wally know he would not be starting today but also that this was not any type of negative judgment on your part about his ability. You intended to tell him that he is not starting today because you want to let Phil have a chance to play against a weaker team. You are very happy with Wally's play, and this decision is not a negative reflection on him in any way. You merely wanted to give Phil, who has patiently sat on the bench most of the season, an opportunity to start, especially because Phil's parents are here today.

While you intended to communicate the full reason for Wally not starting, perhaps you decided he would understand without additional explanation. You reason, "He knows how I feel about him." Or perhaps you were very busy when you saw Wally and delivered the message without the reason because you were in a rush. Or possibly you simply forgot to deliver the full message, even though it was your intention to do so. These are all examples of noise that interfered at the sender's end of the communication process.

Another source of miscommunication could have occurred as you told Wally, "You will not be starting today." Wally immediately became angry so you decided not to explain the reason for your decision if he was going to act so childishly. In this case, Wally's initial response created noise in your head, which interfered with delivering the full message. How often has this happened to you?

Let's say you delivered the entire message to Wally, but when he heard, "You won't be starting today," he immediately became wrapped up in his own thoughts about why you were doing this to him. Consequently, he never heard the reason why. Or Wally heard the reason why, but you expressed it in a very insincere way and your facial expressions and body gestures were interpreted by Wally to mean you were insincere. Perhaps your relationship was such that Wally didn't trust you, so he simply didn't believe the words you spoke.

Here is another example that illustrates how noise pollutes the communication process. You're in the office busily preparing the afternoon practice schedule when Shirley walks in to talk with you.

"Hi coach," Shirley says meekly.

"What is it, Shirley?" you grudgingly inquire without looking up from your desk.

"Coach, have you ever had any members of the team who had a drinking problem?" she inquires.

With a brief glance, you say, "Only one," in such a tone that it implies you have little patience with such matters.

Shirley asks reticently, "What did you do about it?"

"I had to let her go," you say. "We don't have room on this team for alcoholics. Look Shirley, I'm busy now. Anything else I can help you with?"

"No. See you later coach."

You can see all types of communication problems in this example as it's presented, but would you see them if you were living it?

The first source of noise in this example is that you were so preoccupied with your work you didn't listen to what Shirley was really asking. You understood the words, but perhaps you failed to hear the underlying meaning, which might have been, "Coach I have a drinking problem, and I need help." Only with empathy, some well-targeted questions, and full focus on the communication process would you be likely to determine if that was what Shirley really wanted to communicate.

With the blunt response she received, if Shirley had a drinking problem, you would be among the last to know about it. Because of the relationship you had with Shirley, she did not feel comfortable presenting the problem to you straightforwardly, so she tested you—and you flunked.

Here is another possible way you might respond to Shirley: Almost before she gets the question out, you jump on your soapbox about the evils of drugs and alcohol. You're so interested in what you have to say that Shirley never gets to tell you what she wants—that she has an alcohol problem and needs help. You think you have really set her straight, but Shirley leaves feeling very frustrated.

When you consider all the possible noise that can cause us to misunderstand each other, it's amazing how we ever communicate successfully. Look at our language. There are over 600,000 words in the English language, plus or minus a few thousand, but the typical, educated adult relies on only about 2,000 words in daily communication. That makes it easier, but of these 2,000 words, the 500 most frequently used have 14,000 dictionary definitions. And words, of course, are not the only means by which we communicate.

Successful communication is enormously difficult and depends on eliminating or controlling the noise. To communicate success-fully you must recognize that each person with whom you communicate has had different experiences from yours. If you are to be understood by the other person, and if you are to understand the other person, you must come to know that person's frame of reference. Can you see why empathy is so important?

SENDING MESSAGES

The very word *coach* suggests that persons in this profession send many messages. Coaches instruct, encourage, discipline, organize events, and evaluate players' performances, all of which require sending messages. Coaches have been credited with being much better at sending messages than receiving them, but judge that about yourself after learning more about sending messages. In this section you will learn how to send effective messages, and you will acquire some useful information about a special type of message—feedback.

Understandable Messages

The most important judgment you need to make is when a message needs to be sent. Some coaches talk too much, rambling on about things that bore others or distract athletes from practice. Some coaches talk too little, assuming others know what they think or want.

In Table 4.1 are 14 guidelines for sending effective messages. Read the guideline and the explanation for the guideline. Then rate whether this is a strength or weakness in your communication skills by circling the appropriate number.

Guidelines such as these have the inherent flaw of being read and quickly forgotten. They can be useful in improving your ability to send effective messages only if you will take action to improve any deficiencies. You will find some helpful exercises in the *Study Guide* to practice sending better messages.

Table 4.1
Guidelines for Sending Effective Messages

1. Your messages should be direct.

Coaches weak on this quality assume others know what they want or feel, or how the coach feels about them. Rather than expressing their message directly, they hint at what they have in mind or they tell someone else, hoping the message will get to the right person indirectly.

How strong are you in sending direct messages?

1	2	3	4	5
Weak				Strong

2. You should own your messages.

Use "I" and "my," not "we" or "the team," when referencing your messages. You disown your messages when you say, "The team feels . . .," or "Most people think you are . . .," when it is really what *you* believe. Using others to bolster what you have to say implies cowardice in expressing your own messages.

How strong are you in owning your messages?

1	2	3	4	5
Weak				Strong

3. Your messages should be complete and specific.

Provide the person with whom you are speaking all the information he or she needs in order to fully understand your message. Watch for leaps in logic, unknown assumptions, and unstated intentions.

How strong are you in making your messages complete and specific?

1	2	3	4	5
Weak				Strong

4. Your message should be clear and consistent. Avoid double messages.

"I really want to play you Mary, but I don't think this is a good game for you. I think you're a fine athlete, but you'll just have to be patient." This example of a double message—acceptance and rejection—leaves Mary confused and probably hurt. Double messages have contradictory meanings, and usually are sent when you are afraid to tell the person directly something that may offend him or her.

How strong are you in sending clear and consistent messages?

1	2	3	4	5
Weak				Strong

5. You should clearly state your needs and feelings.

Our society frowns on those who wear their emotions on their sleeves. So we tend *not* to reveal our feelings and needs to others. Yet if you want to develop close relationships, you need to share your feelings, for this opens the door for the other person to do the same. And this is the only way to come to know, and thus be able to help, the other person. It's also important to state your needs, for no one else knows them as well as you. Others can help you meet your needs if you will trust them with this information.

How strong are you in clearly stating your needs and feelings?

1	2	3	4	5
Weak				Strong

6. Your messages should separate fact from opinion.

State what you see, hear, and know, and then clearly identify any opinions or conclusions you have about these facts. You say to your son when he returns home late one night, "I see you've been out with the Williamson kid again." In the context in which it is spoken, the message is received by your son, but he is not certain exactly what your concern is about the Williamson boy. A better way to send this message would be (a) "That was the Williamson kid, was it not?" (verifying a fact); and then (b) "I'm concerned that you spend time with him. I fear he will get you into trouble" (stating your opinion). Although your son may not be pleased with your opinion, this message is far less ambiguous than the first one.

How strong are you in separating fact from opinion in your messages?

1	2	3	4	5
Weak				Strong

(Cont.)

Table 4.1 (Cont.)

---

7. You should focus your message on one thing at a time.

You begin discussing how to execute a particular skill, and in the middle you jump to complaining about how the team hasn't been practicing well. Are your messages frequently disjointed thoughts because you don't take the time to organize your thinking?

How strong are you in focusing your messages on one thing at a time?

1	2	3	4	5
Weak				Strong

8. You should deliver your messages immediately.

When you observe something that upsets you or that needs to be changed, don't delay sending a message. Sometimes holding back can result in your exploding later about a little thing. Responding immediately also is a sound principle for giving effective feedback.

How strong are you in delivering messages immediately when you see the need to do so?

1	2	3	4	5
Weak				Strong

9. Your messages should not contain hidden agendas.

This means that the stated purpose of the message is identical with the real purpose. Hidden agendas and disguised intentions destroy relationships. Ask yourself these two questions to determine if your message contains hidden agendas:

- Why am I saying this to this person?
- Is it because I want him or her to hear it or is there something else involved?

How strong are you in avoiding messages that contain hidden agendas?

1	2	3	4	5
Weak				Strong

10. Your messages should be supportive.

If you want the other person to listen to your messages over time, you cannot deliver them with threats, sarcasm, negative comparisons, or all types of judgments. Eventually the person will avoid communicating with you or will simply tune you out whenever you speak. Your cumulative messages need to demonstrate support for the person.

How strong are you in sending supportive messages?

1	2	3	4	5
Weak				Strong

11. Your verbal and nonverbal messages should be congruent.

You tell your player it was OK to make the error, but your body gestures and facial expressions belie your words. The two conflicting messages confuse your player and hurt your credibility in future communication.

How strong are you in making your verbal and nonverbal messages congruent?

1	2	3	4	5
Weak				Strong

12. Your messages should be redundant.
(That is, you should repeat the message. Get the point?)

That's correct. Repeat the key points in a message to reinforce what you are saying. However, too much repetition results in the other person not listening, so you must be discriminating in your redundancy. Also, you can be redundant by using additional channels of communication to bolster your message—show a picture or video along with explaining the skill, for example.

How strong are you in making your messages optimally redundant?

1	2	3	4	5
Weak				Strong

(Cont.)

Table 4.1 (Cont.)

13. You should make the messages appropriate to the receiver's frame of reference.

This point was discussed in the last section. Your messages can be much better understood if you tailor them to the experiences of the person with whom you are communicating. For example, it is inappropriate to speak in complex language to young athletes who do not have the vocabulary to understand what is being said.

How strong are you in sending messages that are appropriate for the receiver's frame of reference?

1	2	3	4	5
Weak				Strong

14. You should obtain feedback that your message was accurately interpreted.

Look for verbal and nonverbal evidence that the person with whom you are speaking is receiving the message as you intended. If none is given, ask questions to solicit the feedback: "Do you understand what I am telling you, Susan?" or "Are you clear about what you are to do?" are examples.

How strong are you in obtaining feedback to make certain the person understands your message?

1	2	3	4	5
Weak				Strong

Now sum up your ratings. The following subjective scale will help you assess your skill in sending messages effectively:

61 - 70	Excellent
51 - 60	Good
41 - 50	Average
31 - 40	Weak
30 or less	Help!

Feedback

Feedback is a special form of sending messages, and the guidelines presented certainly apply. However, because coaches particularly spend much of their time giving feedback, some additional observations are noted here. Feedback comes in various forms and it is useful to recognize the differences (Dyer, 1976).

Objective Descriptive

This type of feedback describes as clearly and objectively as possible the behaviors observed. "Your knees were bent when you were leaning out over your skis," is an example. This type of feedback does not evaluate; it seeks to help the other person look more clearly at his or her behavior. The quality of this type of feedback is very important in facilitating your athletes' learning of skills.

Direct Descriptive

When giving this type of feedback, you first describe a person's behavior, and then describe how you reacted to it. "When you walked away from me, it made me feel very angry." This type of feedback is powerful because it gives the person receiving it a clear picture of his or her behavior and what impact it had on you. Direct feedback of this type, however, must be given in a relationship of trust and concern, with a desire to improve the relationship.

Direct Evaluative

A less desirable form of feedback occurs when you directly evaluate another person's behavior without describing what led to the evaluation. "You are an obnoxious young man," or "I think you're neat," are examples.

When giving feedback, you need to consider what your motivation is for doing so. It should be (a) to reward and support the person receiving the feedback, (b) to help someone improve his or her performance, or (c) to improve your relationship with that person. Unfortunately, at times we give people feedback to punish, hurt, or put them down. That almost always hurts or destroys a relationship. (See *Coaches Guide To Teaching Sport Skills*, Christina & Corcos, 1988, for more information on how to give feedback effectively.)

Receiving Feedback

Just as it is important to give feedback effectively, it's essential to obtain feedback about your own behavior, about your performance as a coach. You can obtain such feedback by observing how others respond to your coaching, by requesting feedback directly from other individuals—perhaps from your players, their parents, and other coaches—and by soliciting written evaluations.

Recognize that when your players and assistants share feedback with you, it is a high-risk activity for them. How you respond to the feedback will determine if they will give you truthful feedback in the future. Here are a few suggestions for receiving feedback.

- Listen and don't explain or justify. You're likely to explain or justify your actions when they are criticized, believing the person giving the feedback has misunderstood your action. He or she may have, but this type of response is seen as defensive behavior and stifles the flow of feedback communication. Listen and try to understand the other person's point of view; remember, you are under no obligation to accept it.
- Ask for more feedback. When receiving feedback directly from another person, follow up with questions such as, "Can you tell me more about that?" or "What do you think the cause is?" This will en-

courage more feedback by showing you are interested and open to the feedback.

John Wooden obtained written feedback from his players regularly about such issues as who were the best shooters, rebounders, defensive players, and passers. He asked the team to tell him who worked the hardest, who were the most talented players, who were the most unselfish, and who played best together. This feedback, gathered systematically by Wooden, gave his players a chance for input into the decision-making process and provided Wooden with an opportunity to check his own perceptions.
- React honestly. When people want to know what your reaction is to their feedback, which they often do, tell them your honest feelings.
- Express appreciation for the feedback. Let people know you appreciate the trust they have in you that is reflected in their willingness to share the feedback.

LISTENING SKILLS

You're at a noisy party, and the hostess is telling you how your swimming team has such nice boys, and on and on. You are trying to be polite, nodding approval to her nonstop patter, but actually you are tuning in to a conversation next to you about politics. Suddenly, you notice silence from your hostess. You realize she has asked you a question, but you have no earthly idea what it was. You apologize and ask her to repeat the question.

Some variation of this scenario has happened to just about everyone. Sometimes we listen with only half an ear, or we may hear, but we don't really listen. Listening well is a skill and hard work. When others listen closely to you it's flattering, because it tells you that they think what you have to say is important and they care about you.

When you are a good listener, people enjoy talking with you. When you are a good listener, people feel satisfied that they have been heard and understood. When you are a good listener you don't miss out on information that may be important to you.

People who don't listen are bores, and they frequently misunderstand what others tell them. Listening well may be the weakest of all our communication skills. A speaker once said:

"We hear half of what is said, (50%)
We listen to half of that, (25%)
We understand half of that, (12.5%)
We believe half of that, (6.25%)
And we remember half of that."(3.125%)

I was listening when he said that and remembered it—because there is a ring of truth in that statement. Seventy percent of our day is spent in verbal communication—reading, writing, speaking, and listening. Of this 70 percent, listening occupies approximately 45 percent (Sathre, Olson, & Whitney, 1973). Unquestionably, listening is a common communication activity, and yet we have so little training in doing it well.

Evaluating Your Listening Skills

In Table 4.2 (p. 56) are fourteen common causes of not listening. Think about your general patterns of listening and indicate the frequency with which you encounter each of these blocks by marking the appropriate column.

Improving Your Listening Skills

The prerequisite for improving your listening skills is wanting to, of course. Good listening is hard work; it requires intense concentration and mental activation.

Active Listening

By far the most useful tool for improving listening is what Dr. Thomas Gordon (1974) has labeled *active listening*. Rather than just passively hearing what is being said, you participate actively in the communication process as a listener. Active listening involves paraphrasing what you think the speaker said. It is especially useful when you are having an important, and perhaps complex or abstract, conversation. Use such lead-ins as, "What you're telling me is . . ."; "I understand, you mean . . ."; "Let me see if I've got this right, you said . . ." Paraphrasing keeps you involved in the conversation, reduces misunderstandings, and helps you remember what was said.

In addition to paraphrasing what the speaker said, you may need to ask questions for clarification. You may need more background or other facts to understand, or you simply may have missed a point in a rapid-fire conversation. Active listening also involves the use of nonverbal communication to ask questions with looks of the eyes, tilts of the head, an inquiring lift of the shoulder, gestures, and shifts in body positions.

When you understand the message, active listening involves feedback to the speaker about what you have understood from the message. Then, without being judgmental (unless the speaker requests you to evaluate), tell the speaker how his or her message affected you. This gives the speaker a chance to correct any misconceptions that may have inadvertently been conveyed. The feedback to the speaker should follow four rules: It should be clear, it should be honest, it should be immediate, and it should be brief. (You will find an active listening exercise in the *Study Guide*.)

More Tips

In addition to active listening, you can do several other things to improve your listening skills.

- Listen with empathy. Try to understand where the speaker is coming from.
- Listen with openness. You can't hear a message if you are evaluating or judging the message while it's being delivered.
- Be mentally prepared to listen. Delay im-

Table 4.2
Listening Skills Test

Rating Scale:	Never 1	Seldom 2	Sometimes 3	Often 4
1. You find listening to others uninteresting.	1	2	3	4
2. You tend to focus attention on the speaker's delivery or appearance instead of the message.	1	2	3	4
3. You listen more for facts and details, often missing the main points that give the facts meaning.	1	2	3	4
4. You are easily distracted by other people talking, chewing gum, rattling paper, and so on.	1	2	3	4
5. You fake attention, looking at the speaker but thinking of other things.	1	2	3	4
6. You listen only to what is easy to understand.	1	2	3	4
7. Certain emotional-laden words—such as homosexual— interfere with your listening.	1	2	3	4
8. You hear a few sentences of another person's problems and you immediately start thinking about all the advice you can give.	1	2	3	4
9. Your attention span is very short, so it is hard for you to listen for more than a few minutes.	1	2	3	4
10. You are quick to find things to disagree with, so you stop listening as you prepare your argument.	1	2	3	4
11. You try to placate the speaker by being supportive through head-nodding and uttering agreement, but you're really not involved.	1	2	3	4
12. You will change the subject when you get bored or uncomfortable with it.	1	2	3	4
13. As soon as someone says anything that you think reflects negatively on you, you jump in to defend yourself.	1	2	3	4
14. You second-guess the speaker, trying to figure out what he or she *really* means.	1	2	3	4

Now add up your score. The following subjective scale will give you some help in determining how well you listen.

15 - 24	Excellent
25 - 34	Good
35 - 44	Fair
45 - 54	Weak
55 +	Can you hear me in there?

portant conversations that will require especially good listening skills until you are mentally fresh. Also, for certain types of listening, you may need to do some preparation so you know more about the subject or the speaker.

• Practice improving your concentration. (See chapter 9 for more information on this.)

• Remind yourself not to judge a speaker by his or her appearance or reputation, but by the content of the message.

• Listen with your eyes by observing the body language of the speaker to determine if what is said verbally is congruent with what is said nonverbally.

• Listen for the main ideas without getting caught up in minor points or facts.

- Build your vocabulary and listen to difficult expository material to improve your comprehension.
- When possible, remove distractions in the environment. When this is not possible, exert greater attentional control by narrowing your focus on the speaker.
- Be committed to becoming a better listener—and practice.

NONVERBAL COMMUNICATION SKILLS

Nonverbal communication—the messages we send to each other without uttering a word—is a fascinating topic. So much has been learned in recent years it would take a separate book, such as Mark Knapp's *Nonverbal Communication in Human Interaction* (1978), for you to fully understand the complex nature of this form of communication. In this section the objective is simply to create an awareness of the different facets of nonverbal communication. The *Study Guide* contains more information about this topic, and several useful and enjoyable exercises for improving your nonverbal communication skills.

The field of nonverbal communication is commonly organized into three parts:

1. Body language, or what is called *kinesics*
2. Spatial relations, or *proxemics*
3. Paralanguage, or the way in which words are spoken.

Kinesics

Body language refers to how we communicate through our physical appearance, our posture, gestures, touching behavior, and especially the changes in our facial and eye movements. Let's briefly look at each of these aspects of kinesics.

Physical Appearance

In each culture, stereotypes develop that are based on physical appearances. In our society, we tend to believe fat people are more talkative, good-natured, and trusting while thin people are more ambitious, stubborn, and pessimistic. Skin color has been a cause of prejudice in our society for a long time, and even hair length was a means of judging people—especially athletes—in the 1960s and '70s. Many coaches were especially negative toward athletes who had long hair during that time. Here is an example.

"Long hair on boys and men is the sign of a sissy and should be banned from American athletic fields," according to the lead article in an issue of the Texas High School Coaches Association's magazine.

Tony Simpson, head football coach at Northshore Junior High School in the Houston suburb of Galena Park, said, "God made man to dominate woman and, therefore, meant for man to wear short hair.

"If common sense dictates that long hair on a man is a disgrace, let's stop compromising our common sense by allowing it," Simpson told his fellow coaches. "A good hair code will get the abnormals out of athletics before they become coaches and bring their 'loser' standards into the coaching profession." (*Chicago Tribune*, May 22, 1973, Section 3, p. 3)

It's rather amazing how athletes at one time were judged on physical appearance, and how time can change our views about what is important in athletics. Today we're much more concerned about truly significant problems, such as chemical abuse in sports.

Posture

We also communicate with our posture. A slumped posture is a sign of feeling low, fatigued, and inferior whereas an erect posture connotes feelings of confidence, openness, and energy. The way people walk also communicates how they feel. When people are sad, they shuffle along, head down, hands in their pockets, moving along ever so slowly. Happy, achieving people show enthusiasm in their walk by a rapid, purposeful pace with free-swinging arms and upright posture. Even our breathing reveals something about how we feel. Rapid breathing is associated with excitement, fear, anxiety, or extreme joy.

Officials in sports such as basketball are especially good examples of the importance of nonverbal communication. Some officials by their posture, walk or strut, and other gestures communicate arrogance, while others communicate self-confidence, and still others meekness.

Gestures

We especially communicate with gestures and various body movements. Are you aware of how others talk with their hands or how you talk with your hands? Table 4.3 contains a short test to see how well you can match the gesture with its common meaning in our society.

Table 4.3
Test for Recognizing Common Gestures

Gestures	Meaning
1. Tugging on ear	A. Puzzlement
2. Rubbing hands together	B. Grief
	C. Superiority
3. Folding arms across chest	D. Desire to interrupt
4. Scratching head	E. Anger or frustration
5. Locking hands behind head	F. Reference to self
	G. Anticipation
6. Extending arms out in front with palms up	H. Openness
	I. Closed or competitive attitude
7. Rubbing neck	
8. Uncrossing legs and holding slightly apart	J. Sincerity
9. Pointing index finger to self	
10. Wringing hands	

You can check your answers by referring to the answer key on page 65. How many did you get correct? If you got eight or more correct, you are very observant of other's body language. If you had difficulty with this test, either you need to become more attentive to what others are communicating to you by their body language or you simply have difficulty recognizing these gestures when they are taken out of context. Regardless, as you interact with people or watch television during the next few months, give greater attention to these gestures to see how readily you recognize what they say within the context of

the total communication interaction. Also, look at the messages you send nonverbally. Are they what you want to say?

Touching

Touching others is another common form of body language used to express affection, to calm, or to interrupt, depending on the context. How would you touch another person to communicate these three messages? A hug works well for expressing affection; holding the other person's hands in yours just in front of your chest is used to calm and reassure; and a slight touch on the speaker's arm may be used to interrupt.

The handshake is a common way we communicate by touch, and some people put a great deal of stock into what a handshake tells them about a person. A weak, clammy handshake compared to a firm, positive grip are commonly thought to be windows to a person's personality.

Facial Expression

Another means of communicating by kinesics is through the face, our most expressive body part. The eyes and mouth especially communicate a great deal, and we tend to study these when listening to others to determine the meaning of their messages. Below is a short list of some messages we commonly communicate with facial expressions. First try to visualize how you would express each message, and then look in the mirror while expressing it to see if the face you create matches the image you had visualized.

- Interest in what's been said
- A come-hither look
- A disinterested glance
- A surprised look
- A look that could kill
- A suspicious look
- A sexy look

We better stop here before someone sees you and you get yourself in trouble!

The amount of time we spend in eye contact with another person is another way we communicate. When *both* people are looking directly into each other's eyes, this is called the *line of regard.* Long looks into another person's eyes convey either romantic notions or conflict and anger, and you are not likely to confuse the two. When people are uneasy about communicating a potentially negative message to another person, the line of regard tends to be very short in time.

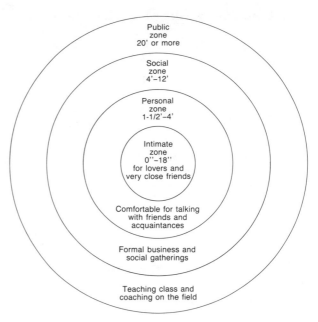

Figure 4.2 The four zones that define the space we use in various social interactions.

Proxemics

Proxemics is the study of how you communicate by the way you use space—the distance between you and others, how you arrange furniture and other objects for social interaction, and how you respond when others invade your territory. "If you can read this, you're too close" is a bumper sticker that attempts to regulate space between cars. People don't put up such signs to regulate space between them, but they do use other signals.

Animals have an instinct called territoriality —an automatic response to protect their territories. Territoriality is not an instinct in humans, but we do have a tendency to demonstrate similar behaviors. Your territory may be the personal space around you, your home, office, or the playing field or gymnasium. This territory is where you feel safe and comfortable. When others invade it, you are usually quick to respond to protect it.

Edward T. Hall (1966), the father of proxemics, has described four distinct zones, shown in Figure 4.2, that we use when interacting with others. Notice how a person will back off when someone imposes into their intimate space. Also people tend to feel embarrassed or threatened if circumstances force them to

share this space. In a crowded elevator, for example, people avoid eye contact and draw away or tense up if touch is unavoidable.

We tend to encourage intrusions into our personal space by people we like, and resent intrusions by strangers or people we dislike. Yet many cultural differences determine acceptable distances for personal space. Latins, for example, have a much closer personal zone than North Americans, which sometimes creates uncomfortable situations. Many other cultural differences exist with regard to proxemics, and the context of the relationship between the communicators greatly influences how we perceive what is being communicated by spatial relationships.

Paralanguage

Paralanguage refers to all the vocal components of speech, considered separately from the actual meaning of the words, and is a relatively neglected facet of communication. The components of paralanguage are as follows (McKay, Davis, & Fanning, 1983):

- Pitch—the highness or lowness of the sound of your voice.
- Resonance—the richness or thinness of your voice.

- Articulation—the way you enunciate the words.
- Tempo—the speed at which words are spoken.
- Volume—the loudness or softness with which you speak.
- Rhythm—the emphasis placed on different words and the cadence of the speech.

"It's not what you say, but how you say it" expresses well what paralanguage is all about. How you say it can betray your true feelings, moods, and attitudes by revealing what you would never reveal verbally. So let's see what you know about the basics of paralanguage. In Table 4.4 answer each question *true* or *false* without looking at the answers and explanations that follow.

Now for the answers.

1. *True*. The pitch goes up when you experience intense feelings of joy, fear, or anger.
2. *False*. Thin voices indicate these qualities. Rich resonance is associated with firmness, self-assurance, and strength.
3. *True*. But this type of speech would be inappropriate for a formal meeting where decisive speech is expected.
4. *True—sometimes*. Speaking too fast can make the listener nervous, and may indicate the speaker is insecure. A slower tempo may sound more sincere and thoughtful.
5. *False*. A loud voice tends to connote these qualities. Loudness may also suggest aggressiveness, an overinflated ego, or exaggerated belief about the importance of the message. A soft voice is associated more with trustworthiness, caring, and understanding. It can also reveal a lack of confidence or that the message is considered unimportant.
6. *False*. Rhythm of speech is learned early, but you can readily learn to place emphasis on certain words to convey different meanings.

The monotoned speaker who fails to vary pitch, tempo, rhythm, and so on, is quickly perceived as a bore. The person who skillfully uses paralanguage engrosses us in what he or she has to say. Tape a conversation of yours and listen to how you use these elements of paralanguage. In the *Study Guide* you will find further help on how to develop this communication skill.

Importance of Nonverbal Communication

We all recognize that nonverbal communication is very important in fully understanding a message when two or more people are communicating. Why else will we fly from one side of the country to the other, or halfway around the world to meet personally with someone? Because we know the significance of a face-to-face discussion!

Albert Mehrabian (1968) analyzed typical communications between two people and concluded that the total impact of the message was divided in this way:

7%	Verbal (words)
38%	Paralanguage
55%	Body language

Clearly what we do, and how we do it, speaks more loudly than what we say!

Body language and paralanguage also reveal considerable information about our unconscious feelings and attitudes and our hidden selves, as we discussed in chapter 1. Because we know nonverbal messages are less

---

Table 4.4
A Test of Your Paralanguage Knowledge

T F 1. The pitch of your voice is lowered when you are tired, calm, or depressed.

T F 2. Rich resonance suggests insecurity, weakness, and indecisiveness.

T F 3. A slight slur or drawl may add to an atmosphere of comfort or intimacy.

T F 4. Fast talkers convey excitement and often are persuasive.

T F 5. A soft voice is usually associated with confidence and enthusiasm.

T F 6. The rhythm of your speech is learned early in life and is very difficult to change.

likely to be under our conscious control, and therefore harder to hide, we tend to believe the nonverbal messages more than the verbal messages. For example, you ask a player what's wrong. She shrugs her shoulders, looks down and away, frowns, and mutters, "Oh ... nothing, I guess. I'm just fine." You know from the nonverbal messages that her words do not reveal her real feelings, so you probe further to find out what is wrong.

Our nonverbal messages, while being more powerful than verbal messages when communicating our feelings and emotions, often are more difficult to interpret accurately. We all tend to have stereotypes about what various nonverbal messages mean, and the likelihood of misinterpreting certain messages is considerable. Caution is needed to avoid placing much trust in these messages, especially when looking at them outside of the total communication context.

Begin today to become more observant of nonverbal communications. See how well you can read the nonverbal messages of others by using your active listening skills to feed back what you think you understood. Also, practice your own nonverbal messages, and strive for congruence among the various forms of verbal and nonverbal communication. Although at times it is difficult, the effective communicator masters the ability to have both verbal and nonverbal messages agree with or complement each other.

CONFLICTS AND CONFRONTATIONS

Many people believe a good relationship has no conflicts. That idea is totally false. Every relationship of any substance has conflicts and disagreements. It is the failure to handle these conflicts in a constructive way that can destroy relationships, not the conflicts themselves. In this final section of chapter 4, you will learn how to manage conflicts better by learning what conflict style to use for different situations, and you will learn how to confront others successfully to resolve a conflict.

Conflicts

Whenever the action of another person prevents, obstructs, or interferes in some way with your goal or actions, a conflict is likely. The very nature of coaching—a competitive environment involving many relationships with others—means conflicts are frequent and inevitable. Thus it is vital that you learn the skills to resolve conflicts constructively. It is when you avoid conflicts and confrontations, or stifle discussion of differences between you and other people, that you will have serious problems in your relationships.

The first step toward resolving conflicts is to look at how you presently manage them. To make this assessment, you need to consider how important it is

- to achieve your personal goals that are being threatened by the person with whom you are having the conflict, and
- to maintain a good relationship with that person.

David Johnson (1981) has described five conflict styles that are based on how important your personal goals are and how important the relationship is. Read each description carefully and consider which style you typically adopt.

Turtles

When a conflict is eminent, turtles pull into their shells. They are quick to sacrifice both their personal goals and the relationship by avoiding the person with whom they are having a conflict. Turtles fear confrontation or believe that confrontation will be useless in solving the problem.

Sharks

Sharks try to force on their opponents their own solutions to the conflict. They are concerned primarily with achieving their own goals and have little interest in maintaining the relationship. Sharks consider a conflict a game—one person wins and one loses—and they plan to win by attacking, overpowering, and intimidating if necessary. How the other person feels is of little consequence.

Teddy Bears

The relationship is most important to teddy bears. Thus they are willing to give up their personal goals when a conflict occurs. They believe conflicts always harm relationships, and because of their great need to be accepted and liked, they avoid jeopardizing the relationship by sacrificing personal goals.

Foxes

Foxes are concerned with achieving both goals, at least to a moderate extent. They prefer a compromise if possible, one where both sides gain something. "You give up part of your goal and I'll give up part of mine," is the attitude of the fox.

Owls

Owls also want to achieve both goals, but more than to a moderate extent. They value both their goals and the relationship highly. Owls are satisfied only when they fully achieve both their own goals and the other person's goals, and when they have strengthened the relationship.

Selecting a Conflict Style

People tend to have a dominant style, but they also will use other styles for certain types of conflicts. Which of the five conflict styles do you tend to use in the following relationships?

- With your spouse or closest friend
- With your boss or supervisor
- With your players
- With officials
- With other coaches

It will be useful for you to keep in mind that no one conflict style is appropriate for every relationship or encounter. Instead you should select the best strategy for resolving the conflict based on how much you value your personal goals and the relationship. Here, then, is Johnson's (1981) recommendation as to when each conflict style is appropriate to use.

When the goal is unimportant and you care nothing about the relationship, use the *turtle* style. For example, a fan comes out of the stands and is verbally abusive to you after the game. Being a turtle is usually wise.

When your goal is important, but the relationship is not, you may wish to be a *shark*. When buying a used car, if you are dealing with an offensive salesman, a shark may be best.

When the goal is of little importance to you, but the relationship is of great importance, being a *teddy bear* is best. When a group of the players' parents want to set up an advisory group to consult with you regularly about team activities, you may find it more important to retain a positive relationship than to resist this movement, which you view as relatively inconsequential.

When both the relationship and your goal are of moderate importance, and you are in a situation where you both cannot get everthing you want, then compromise is appropriate. For example, you have two players competing for the same position and both want to be playing all the time. Being a *fox* to resolve this conflict is the clever thing to do. Recognize that compromise in conflict situations is often necessary to maintain a relationship, and the compromise may well be positive for you as long as it does not require you to compromise your values.

When both the goal and the relationship are highly important you will want to be an *owl*. Typically, to resolve this type of conflict, a confrontation is necessary.

Confrontations

A confrontation is a face-to-face discussion with the individual with whom you are having a conflict. Confrontations are useful not only for major conflicts, as suggested in the owl style, but for minor conflicts as well.

Confrontations are a part of sport—a big part—and you will have your fair share of them if you strive to be an effective coach. Yet confrontations need not be heated arguments that elicit hostility. When they are, it is more likely a consequence of coaches lacking the skills to confront the other person effectively.

Why Confront?

Consider these situations:

- You have good reason to suspect that one of your players is responsible for vandalizing the locker room, so you decide to confront her about it.
- You no longer can remain silent after repeated poor calls by the official, so you confront him about it.
- One of your player's parents continues to interfere with your coaching by attempting to assist you, even though you haven't requested his help. While you welcome

the intent of the parent, his actual coaching often is incorrect and results in confusion among the players. Thus you decide to confront the parent about the problem.

- A coach from another team fails to obey the league rules by not playing all the girls on the team in each half of the game. You decide to confront her about this.

These are but a few of the situations likely to occur when you coach and are justifiable reasons for you to initiate a confrontation. You see, the purpose of a confrontation is not to put others "in their place," but to get them to examine their behavior and its consequences. But some coaches are so unskilled at initiating confrontations that they inevitably create arguments and escalate feelings of hostility. Other coaches avoid confrontations if at all possible because they are terribly stressed by the anticipated negative encounter. Avoiding confrontations or initiating confrontations unskillfully aggravates the relationship. With some effort, however, you can acquire better confrontation skills. These skills will help you not only in your coaching, but in all of your social interactions.

How to Confront

Here are five important steps for initiating successful confrontations.

1. *THINK.* Before you charge after the umpire, blurt out a put-down, or scream commands at a player—*think*. Think if what you are about to say will result in a successful confrontation—one in which you get the other person to examine his or her actions, one in which you achieve your goal without damaging the relationship—or will it be another event that escalates the conflict? Don't let your emotions speak for your thoughts.

2. *UNDERSTAND.* Ask yourself if you are accurately *understanding* the other person. This requires you to have empathy, which is a quality emphasized throughout this book. When you confront others, let them know that you are trying to understand their position. Without understanding, confrontations almost inevitably are ineffective or destructive.

Understanding is easier said than done. Because conflicts and resulting confrontations tend to be emotion-laden, it is very likely that you will unknowingly have perceptual distortions of your own and the other person's behavior, motivation, and position. These misunderstandings make it difficult to resolve the conflict unless they can be openly discussed.

3. *CARE.* Show that you *care* about the people you confront, that you are for them, that you value your relationship with them. Being aloof, antagonistic, domineering, or competitive does not convey that you care; it only causes others to dislike or resent you. Your motivation should be to achieve your goal to help the other person achieve his or her goal, rather than to show you are right, or to punish, or to be vindictive.

Remember, too, that in a conflict both you and the other person are likely to have mixed feelings about each other. You may feel hostile toward the other person because of the source of the conflict, but try not to forget the positive qualities of the other person. It is also important that you determine whether or not the other person is ready to accept the confrontation. If a person is already emotionally upset or confused, it is a poor time for a confrontation.

4. *BE TENTATIVE.* Confront the other person *tentatively*, expressing that you wish to explore together his or her actions to see if your perceptions are correct. Being somewhat tentative helps the other person consider what you are saying more easily. If you come on like a shark, those you confront are more likely to feel you are attacking them and will quickly raise their defenses. On the other hand, you don't want to be so tentative that the message loses its impact. You must find a balance; you don't want to give the impression you are accusing, but rather that you are inviting the person to examine the problem as you see it. When you describe the problem, be specific and concise.

5. *PROCEED GRADUALLY.* Often your confrontations will be more effective if you *proceed gradually*. Deal with one

specific behavior or issue at a time. Those you confront have to absorb what is being said—internalize it—or it won't have an impact. If you overwhelm them with too much at one time, they are likely to feel you are attacking them and will raise their defenses.

When to Confront

Psychologists who have studied confrontations tell us that if an athlete, fellow coach, or parent behaves in a way that concerns you, you should not keep it locked up inside yourself, festering animosity. Confront these people by skillfully describing the behavior that concerns you, letting them know that you confront them only because you care about them. This doesn't mean, however, that you should become picky about every little thing either. Some uncommonly common sense is needed here.

Five Don'ts

There are some things you should avoid when you initiate a confrontation:

- Don't communicate the solution—communicate the problem when confronting others. Allow people to figure out how to stop or change the behavior that concerns you. Coaches often are too quick to tell athletes what they *must* do, which usually causes them to rebel. Only when the other person does not have a solution should you offer one.
- Don't stop communicating. As conflicts escalate, the tendency is to quit communicating; but resort to this only when neither of you are using good confrontation skills. The only way to resolve a conflict is to keep communicating about the problem in a constructive way.
- Don't use "put-downs"; they always cause alienation. Coaches sometimes use sarcasm or cynicism because they see a confrontation as yet another competition. They want to be the victors, and the recipients of their wrath are the vanquished. While coaches who use put-downs in confrontations may achieve their personal goals, they seldom maintain a positive relationship.
- Don't use nonverbal hints to communi-

cate your thoughts or feelings when you wish to confront someone. Refusing to look at someone, excluding a person, withholding feedback, or biting your lip is not good enough to communicate clearly what concerns you. Be courageous and speak face-to-face with the person whose behavior troubles you.
- Don't discuss the problem with everyone else before confronting the person. This person is likely to hear that you have been sharing the problem with others and it will cause him or her to be even more resistant to a constructive confrontation. Confront the person directly without discussing the problem first with everyone else.

Two Concluding Points

Sometimes, even though you skillfully initiate a confrontation, the other person simply won't accept any discussion of his or her behavior. The challenge to you, then, is to convince the person that you seek the confrontation only in the spirit of being helpful.

Sometimes you will be the recipient of a confrontation. When the tables are turned, will you accept the communication as you would want others to respond to you? Or will you reject the message, ignore it, or react with hostility toward the person confronting you? Johnson (1981) offers four guidelines to follow when you are confronted:

- Be certain you understand the other person's position.
- Be certain you understand how the other person feels.
- Paraphrase the other person's position and feelings.
- Now describe your position and feelings.

As you work to become more skillful in confronting others, also work to become more skillful in accepting the confrontations of others.

SUMMARY

1. The process of communicating involves (a) the decision to send a message, (b) encoding of the message, (c) sending

the message, (d) the channel through which the message is sent, (e) decoding the message by the receiver, and (f) an internal response to the message.

2. There are many sources of noise in the communication process that can lead to misunderstanding. Successful communication is enormously difficult and depends on eliminating or controlling the noise.

3. Sending messages that are accurately decoded is a vital skill for coaches. This chapter included fourteen guidelines for doing so.

4. Feedback is a special form of sending messages. This feedback can be objective descriptive, direct descriptive, and direct evaluative. Coaches should also know how to receive feedback properly.

5. Listening is a critical communication skill. You can improve this skill by developing your active listening skills and incorporating into your listening behavior the ten other tips given in this chapter.

6. Nonverbal communication involves kinesics (body language), proxemics (spatial relations), and paralanguage (the way in which words are spoken).

7. Body language involves your physical appearance, posture, gestures, touching behavior, and facial expressions. You should be cognizant of how you communicate through each of these methods.

8. Coaches interact with many people and thus need to know the appropriate physical distances (proxemics) for various relationships.

9. Paralanguage involves the pitch, resonance, articulation, tempo, volume, and rhythm of the speaker. Coaches should work to master these elements of their speech to become more effective communicators.

10. Nonverbal messages, while more powerful than verbal messages for communicating feelings and emotions, often are more difficult to interpret accurately.

11. Coaches are likely to have numerous conflicts. By learning what is involved in a conflict and various ways to approach conflicts, coaches can become more skillful at handling them.

12. Confrontations are useful for resolving conflicts. Confrontations can be handled more skillfully when you follow the five guidelines of thinking, understanding, caring, being tentative, and proceeding gradually.

Answer key Table 4.3. 1 = D, 2 = G, 3 = I, 4 = A, 5 = C, 6 = J, 7 = E, 8 = H, 9 = F, 10 = B.

PART III
Psychological Skills for Athletes

Larry Bassham said he choked terribly in the 1972 Olympic competition in shooting. "I worked very hard but I wasn't prepared mentally." Thus in preparation for the next Olympic Games, Bassham talked with other Olympic champions about how they prepared mentally, and he studied sport psychology, ultimately developing his own mental training program. He practiced this program regularly for the next four years and credits it for his gold medal performance in the 1976 Montreal Olympic Games.

The vast majority of elite athletes recognize the importance of psychological training for competition. Bassham says "athletics is 90 percent mental." Jack Nicklaus, Larry Bird, Reggie Jackson, Fran Tarkenton, and many other great athletes also credit the mental side of the game with high importance in determining the outcome. Yet these athletes know the importance of physical skill and preparation. What they mean when they credit psychological preparation with great importance is that once athletes have developed their physical skills to a high level, and when they are competing with others at that level, the winner is more likely to be the person who is best prepared psychologically.

Coaches also recognize the significance of being mentally prepared in order to compete well. Yet most coaches spend little time, if any at all, in helping athletes prepare psychologically. If the mental side of the game accounts for 90 percent of the outcome, or only 50 percent, or even only 10 percent, doesn't it make sense to devote at least some time to mental training?

Why is psychological training so neglected? Probably, in most cases, because coaches have not known *how* to help athletes learn the es-

sential psychological skills. Then, too, some coaches espouse the view that these psychological qualities are innate characteristics that cannot be taught. Athletes either have these psychological qualities, or they don't. If they don't, then competition will eliminate them as they compete at higher and higher levels. A few coaches also believe that psychological training is unimportant and that only hard physical work is necessary to prepare athletes.

The vast majority of coaches, I believe, recognize the importance of psychological training, but simply do not know how to implement such training with their teams. For those coaches, part III will be a comprehensive introduction to a highly effective *Psychological Skills Training* (PST) program. Each skill will be thoroughly explained so you understand how it influences athletes' performance. Practical guidelines will be offered to assist you in teaching these skills to your athletes. Then, in the companion *Study Guide*, you will receive even more assistance, including specific exercises, for implementing PST.

Chapter 5 is an overview of the Psychological Skills Training program, explaining what is unique about the PST approach in helping your athletes prepare mentally for competition. Then in the next five chapters you will be introduced to five basic psychological skills.

In chapter 6 you will be introduced to the power of imagery, a skill not used often enough by athletes. Through systematic practice of imagery, you will give your athletes a powerful tool for improving performance and developing all the other psychological skills.

In chapter 7 you will learn how to help your athletes manage their psychic energy. You will be shown how to find the optimal energy zone, which helps athletes perform their best. But when athletes' psychic energy gets too high, they become anxious or stressed. So in chapter 8 you will learn how to help athletes manage stress, probably the most pervasive psychological problem in sports.

Coaches are faced with the problem of athletes' poor concentration and lack of attentional skills daily. In chapter 9 you will learn the basic attentional skills and how they affect athletes' performances. Then you will be given techniques to help athletes enhance their attentional skills.

In chapter 10 the vital role of self-confidence and how it affects an athlete's performance is explained. Through a unique goal-setting training program, you will learn how to help your athletes set challenging, realistic performance goals that will improve performance by helping to develop optimal self-confidence.

Chapter 11 will help you implement the PST program by outlining how you should (a) conduct the initial orientation, (b) evaluate your athletes' present psychological skills, (c) teach the basic skills during team sessions, and (d) incorporate PST into practice and game plans. This chapter also outlines the steps for precompetition psychological preparation and how to conduct postcompetition debriefings that are psychologically healthy.

The sixth psychological skill that comprises the PST program consists of interpersonal skills, primarily communication skills. These communication skills are discussed in chapter 4 and are not considered again in part III, but they are just as beneficial for your athletes to learn as they are for you to learn. Thus be sure to add the communication skills presented in chapter 4 to your PST program.

While the emphasis in part III is on your teaching these psychological skills to your athletes, these are vital skills for every coach to possess as well. As you read each chapter, think about how skillful you are in managing stress, concentrating under pressure, and setting effective goals. A bonus for doing the hard work required to teach your athletes PST is that you yourself will master these skills.

You will find that these chapters contain considerable information and much of it may be new to you. Read slowly and study the content thoroughly. Some coaches have seen the content of sport psychology as covered by some mysterious shroud. What you will find in these chapters is that psychological preparation requires the learning of skills much like physical preparation requires the learning of physical skills. Through careful study, you will remove the shroud.

Chapter 5
Psychological Skills Training

Some athletes have more than just physical skills; they have tremendous abilities to psych themselves up for competition, to manage their stress, to concentrate intensely, and to set challenging but realistic goals. They have the ability to visualize themselves being successful, and then doing what they visualized.

Rick McKinney was among the top ten archers in the world, but he couldn't win the big meets. He finally discovered that, because he focused on the goal of winning during the contest, he was not concentrating on his own performance. He trained himself to refocus on his own performance, and then winning took care of itself as he systematically broke world records.

Kerry Dickson was a promising young miler at the University of Illinois, but because his unrealistic expectations in his first two years exceeded his abilities, he became increasingly diffident and, oddly, especially fearful of leading races. Kerry sought help and became one of the first athletes to participate in the Psychological Skills Training program that my colleagues and I offered at the University. Through a combined program of imagery, in which he practiced envisioning himself leading races while running relaxed; a systematic goal-setting program, which brought his expectations closer in line with his abilities; and much hard work, Kerry became an All-American runner his junior and senior years.

Rick McKinney, Kerry Dickson, and many other athletes have developed psychological skills. They were not born with these mental abilities; they acquired them through experience and hard work in much the same way they acquired their physical skills. In this chapter you will learn more about the basics

of PST, but before doing so, you should understand the two major functions of sport psychology.

TWO SPORT PSYCHOLOGIES

Athletes' behavior can be represented on a continuum ranging from abnormal to supernormal, with normal falling somewhere in between (see Figure 5.1). When athletes have profound psychological problems, such as neuroses or psychoses, their behavior is to the left of normal. You will likely encounter some athletes who are on this end of the continuum, for it has been said that sport serves as a kind of emotional barometer. If athletes have troubles in their personal lives, those problems will likely show up in their sport performance.

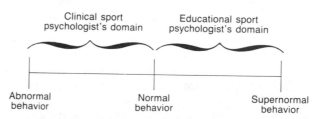

Figure 5.1 The distinction between clinical and educational sport psychology.

When athletes' behavior falls left of normal, then a *clinical psychologist* or psychiatrist or counselor are the appropriate professionals to provide assistance. When the problem behavior is related to athletes' sport participation, then a *clinical sport psychologist*—a person who understands both abnormal behavior and sport—will be the professional of choice to assist athletes.

When you have athletes with significant emotional problems, you will need to wisely counsel them or their parents to seek professional help. Such a recommendation needs to be made with the greatest of care for obvious reasons. Meanwhile, you should continue to provide these athletes with the same excellent coaching and emotional support you would provide any other athlete. Of course, if athletes' emotional problems are so significant that they are a risk to themselves or others, then you must not permit them to participate in practice or in competition.

Sport psychology also assists "normal" athletes to move further to the right, toward supernormality, on the continuum in Figure 5.1. What I mean by "supernormal" is that athletes, because they have superior physical skills, are placed into extremely demanding competitive environments that require extraordinary psychological skills to perform optimally. More "normal souls" can manage the stress of hitting a softball in the Monday night recreational league, but it takes psychologically supernormal beings to stroke a twenty-foot putt optimally in the Masters with $200,000 at stake and a viewing audience of millions.

Most of sport psychology is devoted to helping psychologically normal athletes become psychologically supernormal. Those sport psychologists and coaches who help "normal" athletes acquire psychological skills to improve their performance and enjoyment of sports are called *educational sport psychologists*.

It is very important not to confuse clinical and educational sport psychology functions with each other. PST is primarily for normal athletes who face abnormal stress from competitive sports, not for abnormal people who have trouble coping with life's normal stressors. While PST may be beneficial to those on the abnormal end of the continuum, PST should never be used to replace the psychotherapies of professionally trained clinicians. Also, "normal" athletes may experience emotional traumas, or special problems, that require the assistance of a clinical psychologist to work through.

When you have athletes with serious psychological problems, you should seek the help of a clinical sport psychologist. Even after you have mastered the contents of this book, you are *not* equipped to provide the clinical assistance your athletes may need. Remember, your role is to educate your athletes as to how they can develop specific psychological skills, and to refer those who need more psychological assistance to appropriate professionals.

Furthermore, recognize that just because a person is a clinical psychologist does not mean he or she is well prepared to serve as an educational sport psychologist. Clinical psychologists specialize in helping people achieve normalcy; educational sport psychologists help athletes build supernormal psychological skills that will help them execute their supernormal physical skills. Without special study in sport psychology, clinical psychologists do not have the knowledge or skills to perform the duties of an educational sport psychologist.

PST BASICS

PST is no magical, quick-fix program. It is a systematic, educational program designed to help you and your athletes acquire and practice psychological skills that have been shown to be useful for improving performance and enjoyment of sports. PST can give your athletes an edge, and often only a slight edge is needed. For example, a few years ago Jack Nicklaus was the leading money winner on the Professional Golfers Association tour with earnings of $230,000 and a stroke average of 70.3 per eighteen holes. Bob Charles won $50,000 with a 70.9 average—about a half-stroke difference. Could it be that Nicklaus' psychological skills made the difference?

Interrelationship of Skills

The basic skills of the PST program covered in part III are

- imagery skills,
- psychic energy management,
- stress management,
- attentional skills,
- goal-setting skills.

These psychological skills are closely interrelated; improvement of one skill helps the development of the other skills. This interdependence is depicted in Figure 5.2. One example of how each psychological skill in-

Table 5.1
Interrelationships Among
the Five Psychological Skills

1. Effective management of psychic energy avoids stress, and high stress produces high psychic energy.

2. An athlete must be relaxed to image effectively, and imagery is useful for learning to relax.

3. Through imagery athletes can practice improving their concentration, and to image effectively athletes must be able to concentrate on desired images.

4. Attending to and concentrating on specific goals are essential for goal setting to improve performance, and an important goal is to improve an athlete's attentional skills.

5. Challenging, realistic goals energize behavior, and psychic energy is more effective when properly directed through effective goal setting.

6. Too little or too much psychic energy impairs the ability to image effectively. Through imagery of previous optimal performances, athletes can identify optimal psychic energy levels.

7. As psychic energy increases, attention also increases up to a point, whereupon further increases in psychic energy impair optimal attentional focus. As the ability to attend to the correct stimuli in sports improves, athletes' ability to develop optimal psychic energy improves.

8. When stress is effectively managed, athletes are better able to focus on their goals, and when behavior is directed by clear performance goals, the stress to win is dissipated.

9. When stress is managed, attentional flexibility and concentration are greatly improved, and attentional skills help keep athletes from focusing on negative thoughts, which are the source of stress.

10. The imaging of goals is a powerful way to keep athletes committed to attaining these goals, and imagery can be greatly improved when athletes set realistic goals for practicing imagery daily.

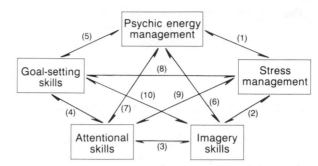

Figure 5.2 The interrelationships among the five psychological skills presented in part III.

player. But simply knowing how to pass, dribble, or shoot does not necessarily make you a basketball player. Budding basketball players must be able to combine these skills into game situations. They must, for example, be able to receive a pass, make a pivot, dribble around a player, make a fade-away jump shot with a defensive player's hand in their face, and then hustle down to the other end of the court to play defense. To be able to shoot the eyes out of the basket while alone in the gymnasium is one thing; to do it in a championship game is something quite different.

Using the PST program is similar to learning the physical skills of your sport. First you must learn the fundamentals; there is no substitute for that. Then you must be able to combine these fundamental psychological skills in competitive situations. It's quite easy to learn to relax in a quiet room with no distractions; it's something entirely different to be able to calm yourself when competing in an emotionally charged contest. Simply learning to relax or to obtain vivid images in the locker room is of little use unless you can use these skills precisely when you need them in competitive situations. Being able to do that is the objective of the PST program.

Self-Knowledge

"Know thyself" is the first of three maxims inscribed on the Temple of Apollo at Delphi; it also is a goal of sport psychology. Becoming a psychologically skilled athlete depends greatly on athletes coming to know themselves, just as becoming an excellent coach requires knowledge of self. To help athletes identify which skills they need to develop, athletes need to develop greater self-awareness,

fluences the others is presented in Table 5.1 and is number coded in Figure 5.2.

To become a basketball player, the first step is to learn the basics of passing, dribbling, shooting, and rebounding. Mastering these fundamentals is essential to becoming a good especially of their psychological strengths and weaknesses. Athletes who have been running away from their psychological deficits for some time may need your assistance to help identify what skills need developing. Cartoonist Walt Kelly put it succinctly in the comic strip *Pogo*: "We have met the enemy, and he is us."

When athletes come to know themselves, they have taken the most important step toward acquiring self-control. In chapter 1, I mentioned the importance of your helping athletes become responsible for themselves and perceive that they are in control of their lives. Psychological Skills Training assists athletes in gaining greater control over their lives. Self-control is one of the qualities that distinguish champions from the other players.

Learning Psychological Skills

PST is taught through a three step process.

1. *Educate* athletes about each psychological skill so that they can (a) recognize that these skills can indeed be learned, (b) understand how these skills affect their performance, and (c) learn how to develop these skills.
2. Help athletes *acquire* these skills through a structured training program using the best information available.
3. *Practice* these skills so that they are integrated into competition. The only way these skills can become well developed, like athletes' physical skills, is to practice them until they become habitual.

You will recognize these steps—educate, acquire, and practice—as the same steps you use to teach physical skills.

The strategies for acquiring these skills involve the following processes:

- *Self-monitoring.* Once the skill has been introduced to athletes, they are asked to keep a log that records their progress in demonstrating the particular psychological skill being developed.
- *Self-evaluation.* Here athletes compare the information obtained from the self-monitoring with the standards they have set for that particular skill.

- *Self-reinforcement.* This is the athletes' response to the self-evaluation. Many athletes fail to reward themselves adequately for making progress toward their physical and psychological performance goals; but this is an important step in helping to develop psychological skills.

Trial and Error Learning

Athletes, of course, are not totally devoid of these psychological skills; most athletes have learned these skills to a sufficient degree so that they function quite well in many day-to-day situations, or even in low-level competitive events. But when confronted with the more demanding, high-level competitive situations, they may not possess these psychological skills to the extent needed. This can be most frustrating to athletes—and their coaches—because they know that they have superior physical skills. They have displayed them time after time in practice or in less intensive competitive events, but then are unable to perform them in the big events because the psychological skills needed to complement their physical skills are not equally extraordinary.

Athletes who have developed psychological skills to a supernormal level have done so only through years of trial and error learning. Micki King finished in fourth place in the 1968 Olympic diving competition. In the 1972 Olympics she won a gold medal and credited her winning performance to being more skilled mentally. "I realized that I didn't need to work out my body as much as my head." Veteran athletes often recognize that what the years of athletic experience taught them consists primarily of strategies and psychological skills. They had acquired the physical skills early; but only as they developed the cognitive and psychological skills did they become "complete" athletes.

Some athletes never learn these psychological skills through the inefficient trial and error process. And for others, ironically, it takes so long that by the time they learn the mental skills, their physical progress has declined. (I frequently offer this as an explanation, or rationalization, for my personal athletic endeavors.) Other athletes, failing to recognize that their performance problems are due to a lack of psychological skills, train their bodies even harder, sometimes to the point of over-training.

A Positive Approach

The PST program is based on a fundamental assumption: Athletes strive to do the best they can, given their physical limitations and unique learning history, to respond as effectively as possible in every situation. When an athlete's best effort is judged to be deficient, it is presumed that he or she does not possess the skills that are needed. If athletes knew of a better, more skillful way to behave, they would. This is a *positive* approach. It focuses on the acquisition of new skills in precisely those areas where athletes demonstrate deficiencies.

Negative Approaches

So many psychological programs that have been used with athletes assume that the correct response or skill is latent, and that through some technique the hidden or suppressed response will surface. These approaches focus on what athletes should stop doing wrong rather than on what they should start doing right.

This emphasis on detecting the problem behaviors of athletes is represented by the use of personality tests designed to detect abnormality. If athletes do not score within the same range as elite athletes on such personality tests as the *Athletic Motivation Inventory*, they are labeled "problem athletes." Then recommendations are offered to coaches for changing these problem athletes' personalities on the premise that such changes will help them win.

This emphasis on the negative—on what not to do—is also present in the instructional methods of many coaches. All too often, coaches make the assumption that athletes know the correct response and thus need only be told when they do it wrong. What athletes need is not only assistance in eliminating incorrect responses, but instruction on how to acquire the correct response. Using the positive approach to teaching sport skills is dis-

cussed in the *Coaches Guide To Teaching Sport Skills* (Christina & Corcos, 1987).

Some coaches would benefit from applying the *dead man test* to their efforts at helping athletes develop both physical and psychological skills. The dead man test works this way: If a dead man could meet the directions of the coach, then the information given is incomplete in that it does not adequately specify how to do something correctly.

Consider these comments: "Stop getting so uptight." "Quit listening to the crowd." "Don't let that turkey get your goat." "Quit thinking so negatively." A dead man could do any of these—they specify only the elimination of certain behaviors without specifying positive behavioral alternatives. And, of course, vague positive behavioral alternatives are of little use either. For example, to say "Just relax," or "Concentrate!" doesn't tell the athlete *how* to relax or concentrate.

In most cases athletes recognize the debilitating effect of being overly anxious or of not being able to concentrate. They need not be told, for example, "Stop getting uptight." What the athlete needs, rather, is specific instruction on how to relax so that he or she can perform better. The coach who lacks the ability to help athletes acquire the necessary stress management skills usually does one of three things instead:

- Uses empathy, trying to provide support for the athlete to overcome this problem.

- Selects another athlete who can perform better under the pressure, even though the other player may have less physical talent.
- Aggravates the problem by placing more pressure on the athlete to begin performing up to his or her capability.

The fourth alternative, of course, is for coaches to capitalize on the advances being made in sport psychology by including PST into the athletes' training programs.

More Than Positive Thinking

The PST program is not to be confused with the "positive thinking" approach that is often espoused by motivational speakers. Positive thinking encourages people to view negative events in a positive way—to wash over their problems. Positive thinking has a very short life, because those who follow only this approach have not done what is necessary to develop alternative skills to deal with the problems that require positive thinking.

PST, on the other hand, doesn't discourage thinking positively, but goes well beyond to help athletes critically examine themselves to understand their psychological deficiencies, and then work to acquire the skills needed to eliminate those deficiencies. Coaches do not merely say "think positive about making your free throws" to their players; they also have them practice the skill of free throw shooting. They must use the same method with the development of psychological skills.

YOU AND PST

The concept of PST is not new. It was advocated by Coleman Griffith, the father of American sport psychology.

> We know that some men see better than others . . . some men have a better type of attention than others . . . some men have a better imagination than others . . . and some men have greater powers of learning. If we propose to say that we are either better or worse in these things because we are born that way, there is nothing we can do about it. But if we realize that we are what we are in all of these *psy-*

chological skills [my emphasis] mostly because of the ways in which we have trained, we shall discover that there is a great deal we can do about some of them. The coach who does nothing about them . . . cannot get very far. The coach who does know something about psychology can hope to train his men in psychological as well as in physical skills. (1930, p. 16)

Griffith wrote these words in *Psychology of Football* in 1930 and they could not be truer today. He also observed that

> The critics of football say that the game is not useful . . . because its educational value is too small. If the educational value has been small, the cause must lie in the fact that so few coaches try to make men any better in fundamental psychological skills than they were when they first came to the squad. (p. 94)

Psychological Skills for Life

Those who believe deeply in the value of sport often claim that sport can help teach young people how to be leaders, to be more self-confident, to have better interpersonal skills, and to be able to achieve difficult goals. But we know today that these potential benefits of sports participation do not just happen; coaches must teach and inculcate these psychological benefits. The PST program directs itself to this purpose.

From time to time when I teach PST, athletes will comment on how they see that the benefits of learning these skills can carry over to their planned future careers. Learning to control psychic energy, to manage stress, to keenly focus attention, to set realistic but challenging goals are skills useful not only in sport, but in any achievement endeavor.

Proper Expectations

Psychological Skills Training is in its infancy at the present time. In working with some athletes and coaches, I find they expect incredible results from minimal effort. Athletes try a little progressive relaxation training, meditation, autogenic training, or hypnosis and after a few sessions they quit because nothing miraculous happened. They would not expect to become professional basketball players after practicing only a week, or world class tennis players in a month, or Olympic champions in skiing in a year. Yet they expect a few sessions of psychological training to produce demonstrable results.

It was not that long ago that athletes did not physically train under any regimented program; they just went out and played the sport. Slowly over the last fifty years coaches and sport scientists have learned how to train the body more and more effectively. Record after record has fallen. Feats once thought impossible, such as running a marathon under two hours and twenty minutes, are now done by thousands. Coaches and athletes have learned the benefits of training systematically and intensively.

Psychological training is where physical training was fifty years ago. Coaches and athletes must become convinced that the benefits of psychological training are similar to those of physical training. They must recognize that psychological training is not a quick fix, but that they will have to work equally hard to develop psychological skills. My experience has been that it is hard for athletes, but even more so for coaches, to allocate time to psychological training. They will continue to spend 100 percent of their time training physically when, by their own admission, psychological factors are significant in determining the outcome of contests.

Today it may seem impossible that athletes will be able to regulate their autonomic nervous systems, control their physiological systems through the mind, and manage their attentional skills with such precision that they will achieve performances yet unimagined. The record-breaking performance of the future will not be achieved by athletes training harder physically, but by athletes training smarter mentally.

I believe athletes will ultimately become so committed to psychological training that they will pioneer the development of mind over matter. The major obstacle to these developments is disbelief. But the relentless competitive spirit will overcome this obstacle. Throughout the world today pioneering athletes, coaches, and sport psychologists are advancing on the psychological frontier of sport.

Your Role

The key to the success of PST is *you*. You must not only believe in the value of this type of training, you must understand it to the same extent you understand the skills and tactics of your sport. Then you must be willing to make PST a regular part of your formal training program.

You may find it beneficial to employ the services of a sport psychologist to help you launch your PST program, but ultimately you must be responsible for it. You will need to teach and refine psychological skills on a daily basis just as you teach and refine physical skills daily. Your commitment to the program will increase your athletes' commitment to the program.

Some coaches shy away from PST because they have little preparation to be educational sport psychologists. This is understandable, but you should recognize that times are changing and progressive coaches today—and all coaches of tomorrow—will be acquiring that little edge gained through PST. If you do not prepare yourself to teach PST, you will deprive your athletes of the advantage other athletes will have.

Some coaches consider PST to be too much work. They look for quick fixes. They will use PST when motivation can be injected with a syringe (and some have sought to do so), when self-confidence can be swallowed in tablet form, and when anxiety can be flushed from the system with an enema. Such magical potions don't exist and aren't on the horizon, and if they are discovered, we can hope they will be banned.

Coaches who can teach PST will help athletes avoid the frustrations of trial and error learning in acquiring psychological skills, which will increase the likelihood that physical and psychological progress will peak together. These coaches will help athletes avoid overtraining physically and undertraining mentally. These coaches will teach athletes not only the skills to win games, but the skills to win in the game of life.

SUMMARY

1. *Clinical sport psychologists* are uniquely qualified to help athletes with serious psychological problems, whereas *educational sport psychologists* are especially qualified to help normal athletes develop supernormal psychological skills.
2. Coaches are encouraged to teach psychological skills to their athletes, but should avoid attempting to function as clinical sport psychologists with athletes who have serious psychological problems.
3. The basic skills of PST are imagery skills, psychic energy management skills, stress management skills, attentional skills, and goal-setting skills.
4. All these psychological skills are interrelated; the development of any one skill helps the development of the other skills.
5. An essential prerequisite for the development of psychological skills is for athletes to come to know themselves psy-

chologically—to know their strengths and weaknesses. Thus greater self-awareness is an important objective of PST.
6. PST involves educating athletes about each psychological skill and helps athletes to acquire and practice these skills until they become habitual.
7. In acquiring these skills, athletes need to monitor, evaluate, and reward themselves.
8. Some athletes learn psychological skills on their own through trial and error methods, but PST is a much more efficient means of learning these skills.
9. The fundamental assumption of PST is that athletes attempt to do the best they can, given their physical and psychological capabilities. When these efforts are not adequate, it is presumed that the athletes do not possess the skills that are needed.
10. PST is a positive approach to helping athletes, but it is much more than just positive thinking. PST teaches athletes not only to think positively, but how to acquire the skills necessary to eliminate a deficiency.
11. PST skills are helpful not only for better participation in sports, but for any achievement endeavor.
12. Coaches and athletes must have realistic expectations of the progress that can be made in acquiring psychological skills, and they must realize that much practice is required.
13. An educational sport psychologist may be helpful in launching your PST program, but the coach must assume ultimate responsibility for this type of training.

Chapter 6
Imagery Skills

The high jumper toed his starting mark and stood poised, seemingly for hours, as the crowd apprehensively waited for his jump. Asked why he often takes so long to start his approach, the athlete explained that just before each jump he attempts to envision himself clearing the bar.

But does that take so long?

Yes, he explains, because sometimes in his mind's eye he misses—so he keeps practicing the mental jump until he clears the bar. Then and only then does Dwight Stones, U.S. Olympian high jumper, actually jump.

A long-distance runner lies on a bench in the solitude of the stadium's locker room waiting the start of the 10,000-meter race. He mentally rehearses the race, seeing potential trouble spots, visualizing how he will implement his strategy, and seeing himself cross the finish line—first, of course. He especially rehearses the finish of the race, for he has had difficulty tightening up at this point when passed by another runner. In his mind's eye he sees himself being passed, but then instructs himself to jump in behind the runner and feel himself being shielded from the wind. Then, like the draft phenomenon in auto racing, he visualizes himself "slingshotting" around the lead runner to win the race. The athlete is Dick Burkel, former record holder of the indoor mile.

Before every shot I go to the movies inside my head. Here's what I see. First I see the ball where I want it to finish in a specific small area or fairway or green. Next I see the ball going there—its path, trajectory, and behavior on landing. Finally I see myself making the kind of swing that will turn the first two images into reality. These "home movies" are a key to my concentration and to my positive approach to every shot.

The golfer is none other than the great Jack Nicklaus (1976).

A skier stands atop a mountain preparing for the most important slalom race of his life as he seeks the Olympic gold. Able to take only two practice runs on the course because of weather conditions, the skier has mentally practiced the run countless times. Moments before it is his turn, he once again runs through the course in his mind, seeing each turn, feeling his body respond to each mogul and shift in direction. The skier is Jean Claude Killy (1977), a believer in the power of imagery.

UNDERSTANDING IMAGERY

What is the magic in imagery that helps a skier skirt disaster to win gold medals, a golfer win hundreds of thousands of dollars playing subpar golf, and runners and jumpers break world records? It's no magic at all. It's a human capacity that most of us have chosen not to use. It's a skill that few athletes have developed to its potential.

Before language, the only way humans could think was through images. But as Homo sapiens became civilized through the increasing use of language, the imagery capacity of our brain atrophied. Children often reveal considerable imagery capabilities, but quickly are taught to neglect this form of thinking when they enter our educational system, which emphasizes the development of our brain's left hemisphere—our analytical and language centers.

However, the right hemisphere, our imagery center, fortunately is responsive to exercise. Much like a muscle is strengthened, imagery skills that have withered from lack of use can be regained by imagery calisthenics.

In this chapter you will learn how imagery works and the many potential applications your athletes can make of this imagery skill. I will review the evidence about the value of imagery and explain why imagery may be such a powerful aid to your athletes. I say *may be* because, like nuclear energy, your athletes' potential imagery powers can be used constructively or destructively, as they choose to direct them. They can image themselves accomplishing great feats and overcoming hardships, or they can image themselves as failures. The key to the constructive use of imagery is harnessing this power. Then in the last section of this chapter the *Sport Imagery Training* program is described, a program you can put to use with your athletes.

Imagery Defined

Imagery is an experience similar to a sensory experience (seeing, feeling, hearing), but arising in the absence of the usual external stimuli. You do not actually see a basketball or hear it bouncing on the floor, or feel its pimpled leather in your hand, or sense the movement of your body as you dribble it, but you do experience all of these within your mind. These experiences are essentially a product of your memory, experienced internally by vividly recalling and perhaps reconstructing previous external events.

Imagery is more than just visualizing (seeing) an experience in your mind's eye, although visualization is usually the dominant sense. Imagery can involve any and all of the senses. Along with the visual sense, the auditory and kinesthetic sense are most significant to athletes. *Kinesthetic sense* is the sensation of bodily position, presence, or movement that arises from the stimulation of sensory nerve endings in muscles, tendons, and joints.

When you experience reality, you learn to attach various emotional states or moods to these experiences. You feel anxiety as you anticipate playing an important game, you experience great joy when winning it, or considerable dejection when losing it. You also can experience these emotions when you vividly image certain situations you have come to associate with these states of mind. This is an important dimension of imagery that makes it such a powerful tool for developing psychological skills.

Uses of Imagery

If imagery is such a valuable psychological skill, why haven't athletes discovered it before now? The answer is that they have; athletes have been using imagery on occasion since sports were first conceived, but seldom do they use it *systematically*—and this is the key. Imagery must be practiced regularly and correctly for it to help your athletes the way it is potentially capable of doing.

One reason imagery has not been widely used in sports is that psychologists scorned it for many years. Psychology went through a period from the early 1900s until the 1960s when any nonobservable phenomenon, such as imagery, was considered illegitimate for scientific study and thus nonexistent. But scientists who studied observable behavior often found themselves unable to explain why humans behave so differently in what is seemingly the same situation. The answer, of course, is that people see their physical world differently. People have dreams—and nightmares—and they have images of the past, present, and future that shape the way they behave. The behaviorists, as the scientists were known, ignored these things. Finally in the 1970s psychologists realized that we cannot understand human behavior without understanding humankind's imagery powers. Thus imagery today is an active area of study, a major tool in many psychotherapies, and part of several sports training programs.

You will find many uses for the imagery skills your athletes will develop through the Sport Imagery Training program explained later. The primary uses emphasized in this chapter are

- to help athletes acquire or practice complex motor skills (what I will call *motor imagery*);
- to rehearse the strategies to be followed in a particular contest;
- to acquire the psychological skills discussed in part III.

This third function is achieved by helping athletes develop greater self-awareness or bring to consciousness what they really feel as they participate in sports. Imagery also helps in developing such psychological skills as psychic energy and stress management through the rehearsal of the techniques described in chapters 7 and 8. Imagery helps to focus attention and increase the capacity to concentrate (chapter 9), and it helps build self-confidence as athletes see themselves attaining their goals (chapter 10).

DOES IMAGERY WORK?

You may be rather skeptical about the value of imagery in helping athletes acquire physical and psychological skills. When first investigating imagery I, too, was skeptical. I had been trained in the tradition of American experimental psychology, where carefully conducted experimental studies that obtained statistically significant findings are the only evidence that counts.

While I subscribe to the belief that scientific research is an important source of knowledge, I do not believe it is the only source. Through experience, or what is termed *experiential knowledge*, we come to know many things about our world. In this section I will review a sample of the knowledge I have unearthed about imagery—first experiential knowledge, and then scientific.

Experiential Knowledge

The famous psychologist Dr. A.R. Luria (1968) of the Soviet Union describes in *The Mind of a Mnemonist* (a person with superior memory) a man who could alter his pulse from its normal rate of 70 beats per minute to 100 beats, then back to 70.

"How do you do it?" inquired the puzzled Luria.

"I simply see myself running after a train that has just begun to pull out. I have to catch up with the last car if I'm to make it. Is it any wonder then that my heart beat increases?" answered the man.

"But then how do you lower it?" queried Luria.

"After that I saw myself lying in bed, perfectly still, trying to fall asleep . . . I could see myself beginning to drop off."

For years reports have come from India of yogis performing remarkable feats such as walking barefoot on hot coals, lying on beds of sharp spikes, and showing remarkable control over their autonomic nervous system—the system that controls heart rate, respira-

tion, skin temperature, and a number of other bodily functions. Recently the Public Broadcasting System showed a documentary film of Swami Raja performing one of these remarkable feats, but unlike other reports, a team of scientists monitored the Swami to learn how he did it.

The Swami had electrodes pasted on his body to monitor his heart rate, respiration, skin temperature, and brain waves via an EEG. Then he was placed in an airtight tank that had a five-minute oxygen supply. Just before the door closed, the Swami's bodily functions were as follows: heart rate—68, respiration—12 per minute, skin temperature—91 °F, EEG wave—beta pattern, indicating normal brain activity.

Five minutes later the Swami's vital functions had dramatically changed: heart rate—24, respiration—3 per minute, skin temperature—68 °F, EEG waves—alpha pattern, characteristic of brain activity just before going to sleep. Incredibly, the yogi Swami Raja had slowed his bodily functions—which are normally thought not to be under volitional control—to an almost unbelievably low level. The Swami remained in the tank for thirty minutes, six times longer than the air supply would allow a normally breathing person. When the tank door was opened, his bodily functions quickly returned to normal and he emerged as healthy as ever.

How do yogis perform these feats? The remarkable mental control of the autonomic nervous system is acquired through years of imagery training.

Just how much control can a person exert over his or her bodily functions? Can the heart or other vital functions be voluntarily made to stop—to cause death? It appears so. The Murngins, a Northern Australian tribe, practice what is known as *taboo deaths*. If a Murngin is told that his soul has been stolen, and it becomes general knowledge among the tribe, he will die within several days. Scientists have found no illness present in the corpse. On the other hand, a Murngin hovering near taboo death frequently recovers if he is told that the curse or spell has been broken (Samuels & Samuels, 1975). Is it possible, if you believe devoutly a death curse will cause you to die, that your mind can cause you to die?

The annals of American medicine are beginning to report an increasing number of cases where imagery played a part in the treatment of illness. Most beginning medical doctors soon recognize that physical illnesses are often associated with psychological problems. In fact, many doctors now believe all illnesses must be considered *psychosomatic* (psychological and physical).

For centuries doctors have used placebos—sugar pills—as an effective medical treatment. For example, in one study, painting warts with a brightly colored inert dye described to patients as a powerful medicine was as effective as surgical excision of the warts. Patients hospitalized with bleeding ulcers showed 70 percent excellent results lasting over a year when the doctor gave them an injection of distilled water and assured them that it was a new medicine that would cure them (Samuels & Samuels, 1975).

How do placebos help? Dr. Jerome Frank (1961), a psychiatrist, believes that a placebo is a symbol of healing. It is as if the symbol triggers in the patient a healing visualization. The fact that a drug has been administered to the patient by a doctor lends authority to the patient's visualization of the drug's effectiveness.

One of the most remarkable uses of imagery in modern day medicine is found in the treatment of cancer by Dr. O. Carl Simonton of Fort Worth, Texas. Simonton, Matthews-Simonton, and Creighton (1978) observed in their early treatment of cancer patients that many were depressed or under enormous stress for many months prior to their illness. Over the years they have come to believe that somehow the immune system of the body is affected by stress and depression and that cancer is a response to despair experienced at the cellular level.

Simonton teaches his patients to "conjure up mental images of a sort of inner battlefield upon which healthy cells can be observed putting the malignant ones to rout." His desperate patients, many who have been given only weeks or months to live through conventional medicine, are persuasively convinced that fighting their disease with a positive attitude through vivid images is their final hope.

A number of Simonton's patients are living proof of remarkable remissions of terminal cancer. His patients are eager to defend his unconventional methods, which are frequently attacked by traditional medical practitioners. Simonton's patients, however, do not abandon conventional cancer treatment; they merely supplement it with imagery. While a number of medical authorities are skeptical of the value of Simonton's methods, and some consider them pure quackery, an increasing number of scientific studies are supporting the idea that the mind plays an important role in the prevention and healing of illness. It is becoming increasingly evident that our ability to see ourselves healthy is one step toward being healthy.

While imagery is creeping into the treatment of physical illness, it has swept psychotherapy off its feet, becoming a dominant mode for treating mental illness. There are no less than thirty-five psychological therapies that use imagery as a component of their treatment programs. Imagery is the core of autogenic training, which is widely practiced in Europe and to a lesser extent in this country. Systematic desensitization, implosive therapy, covert modeling, and hypnosis all involve imagery to a greater or lesser extent.

Yes, even hypnosis. Two leading researchers of hypnosis, Theodore Barber and Sheryl Wilson (1978), report that persons who are said to be hypnotized are indistinguishable from individuals who are fully utilizing their abilities to imagine. There is some evidence, too, that when these methods fail to be effective, the cause is the inability of subjects to develop vivid and controlled images. Too often therapists have assumed that individuals possess strong imagery skills. Now many therapists first evaluate a patient's imagery skills, and if they are weak, help patients to develop these skills as a preliminary step to therapy.

But what about sport, you say? So yogis are weird and imagery helps people with cancer and mental illness—but most athletes aren't yogis and don't suffer from cancer or mental illness, thank goodness. What's the evidence that imagery is helpful in *sport*? Give me some scientific proof!

Just because Dwight Stones, Dick Burkel, Jack Nicklaus, and Jean Claude Killy *claim* that imagery works doesn't prove a thing. And just because golfer, Nancy Lopez, or former Baltimore Oriole pitcher, Steve Stone, or the all-time leading passer in the NFL, Fran Tarkenton, say imagery helps doesn't prove it either.

Perhaps you place little significance on the fact that most great golf and tennis coaches teach players through the use of imagery. Never mind the fifty books and journal articles on golf instruction alone that recommend using imagery. You might even doubt Peter Karns, the 1976 U.S. Olympic Biathlon coach, who credited *Visuo Motor Behavior Rehearsal* (VMBR)—a relaxation and imagery training program—for making a vast improvement in his team's performance. And you probably will discount Richard Suinn's (1976) report that VMBR helped Colorado State University's *B* ski team so much that many of its members quickly won places on the *A* team.

Scientific Evidence

Well, perhaps you won't find it so easy to discount or doubt John Lane's (1980) controlled study of the effectiveness of VMBR. One group of players practiced shooting basketball free throws supplemented with the relaxation and imagery VMBR program. The other group practiced shooting, but no VMBR. The results: The players in the VMBR group improved from 11 percent to 15 percent compared to the players who did not use VMBR.

An even more impressive study was completed by Barbara Kolonay (1977), who also examined the effects of basketball free throw shooting among college basketball players. The VMBR-trained players improved *statistically* significantly over the control group. Another important finding to come from Kolonay's study is that a group who practiced relaxation training, but not imagery, and a third group who used imagery, but did not use relaxation, did not improve as much as the combined relaxation and imagery training group.

The scientific evidence in support of motor imagery is impressive when scrutinized critically. Allan Richardson (1967a & b) reported the first extensive literature review of motor imagery. It was followed five years later by an incisive analysis of the experimental literature by Charles Corbin (1972). Both of these reviewers concluded that the weight of the evidence clearly supported the value of imagery in learning and performing motor skills. This conclusion, however, was qualified with certain conditions that I will present when describing the Sport Imagery Training program.

Ten years after Corbin's review, I reviewed another thirty-four studies that were completed in the interim (Martens, 1982). Almost all of these studies found motor imagery to be helpful, although once again there were some qualifications to these results. It is the accumulated evidence from all these studies and the experiential knowledge of teaching imagery to many athletes that guided my development of the Sport Imagery Training program. Before explaining this program in detail, I will try to help you understand how imagery works.

HOW IMAGERY WORKS

It is useful to think of imagery as being analogous to a videotape system rather than a movie projector with film. Unlike movie film, actual pictures are not stored on videotape. Instead, an electronic process is stored through the arrangement of magnetic particles. A picture is reproduced only when the videotape is played back on a video recorder, which scans the particles and converts them into a picture.

A brain works much the same way, sorting sensory input as a process, not a picture, and recalling these inputs when the initial storing process is correctly rescanned. Some people have excellent capacities to store these processes; others have less, often because they have neglected to exercise this capacity. This storing and retrieving of information occurs not only for visual inputs, but for all our senses. Thus our brain's recorder is not just a video recorder, but a multisensory recorder. It is this multisensory input that we can recall and rearrange in our imaginations to create powerful internal experiences.

Motor Imagery

How can imaging the making of a free throw, hitting a golf ball, or kicking a football help athletes do these things better? Sport psychologists aren't exactly certain, but they have some theories that are useful for you to understand in the wise use of imagery. Maxwell Maltz (1960), who propelled imagery into popular use again in the 1960s through his bestseller *Pyschocybernetics* explains the use of imagery this way: Our brain and nervous system are a highly complex servo-mechanism, which Maltz describes as an automatic goal-seeking machine that steers its way to a target or goal by the use of feedback and stored information, automatically correcting its course when necessary.

Maltz asserts that this servo-mechanism can function only when it has a clear goal. Through imagery Maltz advocates "programming" the servo-mechanism by imaging the goal, whatever it may be. Then he says to let the servo-mechanism take over; it will move you toward your goal much better than you can by conscious effort or willpower.

This may be one way imagery works, but there is little scientific evidence to support Maltz's explanation. There is, however, a related and compatible explanation that does have considerable scientific support. David Marks (1977) stated in the *Journal of Mental Imagery* that substantial evidence supports the conclusion that "imagined stimuli and perceptual or 'real' stimuli have a qualitatively similar status in our conscious mental life" (p. 285).

This is an enormously significant conclusion. What it says is that normally we receive information through our senses from the external environment that we process in our brains. However, we also can generate information from our own memory, in essence creating our own environment internally, that our brain processes in essentially the same way as an actual experience. Thus imagined events can have an effect on our nervous system, on our brain, on us, identical to the actual experience. Researchers presently theorize that this may happen in one of two ways.

Psychoneuromuscular Theory

The psychoneuromuscular theory postulates that vivid, imagined events or behaviors should produce neuromuscular responses similar to those of an actual experience. That is, the images produced in the brain should transmit impulses to the muscles for the execution of the imagined skill, although these impulses may be so minor that they do not actually produce movement, or the movement may be undetectable.

The primary evidence to support this theory comes from Edmund Jacobson (1932), who reported that the *imagined* movement of bending the arm was associated with small but measurable contractions in the flexor muscles of the arm. In addition, M. B. Arnold (1946) observed that when a person is told to imagine falling forward or backward, slight movement is made in the imagined direction. To illustrate that small movements accompany vivid imagery, try the simple pendulum experiment.

Make a pendulum of a ten-inch piece of string, and put your ring on it. Now draw a circle and divide it into four quarters such as the one shown in Figure 6.1.

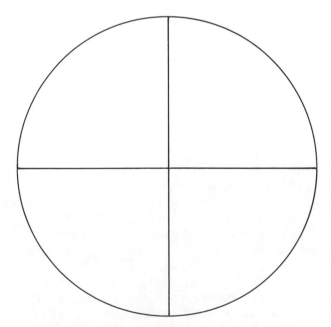

Figure 6.1 An experiment to see how vivid images can cause minute muscle action.

Hold the string with both thumbs. The pendulum will move in various directions at first, but its direction can be influenced by you. It will swing in any direction that your thoughts will it to swing. Try it. Close your eyes, concentrating on visualizing the pendulum swinging in a particular direction. Intently imagine the motion, thinking about nothing else. Keep your fingers as still as possible—do not interfere by intentionally moving your hands. Open your eyes and see if the experiment was successful (adapted from Lindemann, 1973).

Eccles, in a 1958 *Scientific American* article, presented evidence that the slight firing of neural pathways puts down a mental blueprint that helps the individual execute the movement later on. To test out the notion that vivid imagery produces electrical activity in the muscles, Richard Suinn (1980) attached electrodes to the leg muscles of an alpine skier as he imagined a downhill run. The electrodes were connected to an electromyograph (EMG), which is able to make highly sensitive recordings of electrical activity in muscles. Suinn obtained electrical patterns in the muscles of the skier during this imagery session that closely approximated the electrical patterns of the skier's muscles if he had actually been skiing.

Symbolic Learning Theory

The psychoneuromuscular theory is questioned by some, though, because not all studies have been able to obtain neuromuscular activity when individuals image motor skills. Thus an alternative theory advocates that imagery works because it helps athletes develop a coding system of movement patterns. The symbolic learning theory says that imagery helps develop a mental blueprint, not by the minute firing of the muscles during imagery, but by creating a motor program in the central nervous system. Some research supports this theory over the psychoneuromuscular theory (Feltz & Landers, 1983; Ryan & Simons, 1983), but the issue is far from decided.

Nevertheless, both theories lead us to one important conclusion: imagery works, even in studies where people spend very little time practicing or developing their imagery skills. And it works because imagery, one way or another, helps people develop a mental blueprint for executing the skills.

Controlling the Autonomic Nervous System

OK, if motor imagery works by developing a mental blueprint, how does imagery help people alter their bodily functions that are controlled by the autonomic nervous system (ANS)? How can we explain the amazing feats of yogi Swami Raja? Scientists now think there are pathways between the imagery center of the brain and the ANS, which is contrary to what they had believed for years. Today evidence abounds that shows a person can control the ANS. This evidence is the basis for the new field known as *biofeedback* (Lang, 1970). Biofeedback and imagery combined, as mentioned in chapter 8, are effective measures to gain control of the once-believed involuntary ANS.

Psychological Skills

How, then, does imagery help in the development of psychological skills? Once again the answer is that it probably works by helping you develop a mental blueprint of how to act. Whether you imagine yourself pitching horseshoes, or becoming angry as you argue with the umpire, or feeling anxiety as you prepare to perform, the *effect on the nervous system may be almost identical to the actual experience*. With this knowledge in hand, Joseph Cautela and Leigh McCullough (1978) conjectured that imagery should follow the same principles of learning as overt behavior. Their extensive research confirms their conjecture.

The implication of this finding is most significant. Consider the principle of reinforcement, which states that positive reinforcement of a behavior strengthens the possibility of that behavior recurring. Simply translated, that means success leads to more success. Imagery therefore may be a way to help athletes break out of the vicious cycle of playing badly, experiencing the negative reinforcement of losing that diminishes self-confidence and breeds anxiety, which leads to more bad play, and so on. One solution is to imagine success by having athletes vividly see themselves playing well and mentally reinforcing themselves for having succeeded. Because vivid images follow the same laws of behavior as actual experiences, if athletes can control their imagery they can "program" themselves for success.

SPORT IMAGERY TRAINING PROGRAM

The Sport Imagery Training (SIT) program represents my efforts to combine the scientific findings with the practical experience I and others have had using imagery in sport. Unquestionably the most important facet of imagery is the recognition that this capacity is a *skill*. While there are certainly individual differences in ability, all individuals can improve their imagery powers through practice. And like all skills, imagery is more effective when the skill is practiced properly.

The objective of SIT is to improve an athlete's imagery *vividness* and *controllability* through the practice of certain imagery exercises. The first step in using SIT is to assess an athlete's imagery skills using a simple imagery test. The purpose of the test is to assess the vividness or intensity of an athlete's imagery with regard to visual, auditory, and kinesthetic senses as well as the athlete's related emotional state for a series of sport situations. This test will help you determine the type and quantity of imagery training needed by your athlete. The test is included in the *Study Guide*.

It is vital to remember that imagery is more than just visualization; it is a polysensory process. The more senses the athlete can stimulate through imagery, the more vivid or intense the images are. The greater awareness the athlete has of the senses and mood stimulated by his or her images, the greater capacity the athlete has to use images to his or her benefit.

While vividness is important, it is essential that athletes have the ability to *control* their images. The productive imager manipulates, shapes, and moves his or her images toward a desired goal. Vivid but uncontrollable images are counterproductive; they debilitate performance. For example, a basketball player attempted to image making free throws, but each time she did, she saw the ball sticking to the floor in her preshot dribble. Her inability to get the ball off the floor in her mind disrupted her concentration and thus did not help her put the ball in the hoop.

Imagery control also involves the perspective taken when imaging—whether it is *internal* (seeing it through your eyes as you are doing the activity) or *external* (seeing it from the perspective of a camera filming you). Although the research evidence is not conclusive, in my judgment the internal perspective is usually desired because it more closely approximates the way athletes actually perform activities. On occasion, however, it may be valuable to take the external perspective. If an athlete is having a problem doing a task, it may help to analyze the error by taking an external perspective. In general, though, it is my experience that most athletes prefer and benefit more from the internal perspective.

To be skilled in the use of imagery also requires another type of control. Athletes need to develop the ability to turn their imagery center on and off as required. As you can readily imagine, there are appropriate and inappropriate times for an athlete to use imagery skills. The inability to turn images on and off may find athletes unable to practice mentally when they need to, or mentally rehearsing when they should be analyzing or just playing.

The SIT program for motor imagery consists of three phases:

1. Sensory awareness training
2. Vividness training
3. Controllability training

Phase One: Sensory Awareness

The images athletes use in sport are formed from their experiences. The athlete's goal is to take these experiences, which are stored in memory, and use them to create images that he or she can shape and control. That is, the athlete mentally wants to manipulate past experiences first to experience internally what he or she wants to do in the future and then to do it.

Thus the athlete's first step to improving imagery skills is to become more aware of his or her experiences in sport. The more the athlete sees, feels, and hears, and the more the athlete is aware of his or her emotions and moods, the more likely he or she will be able to create vivid images of these experiences.

Many athletes, of course, feel they are aware of their experiences. They know what they have done; they remember what they saw, felt, and heard. But many times we really are not aware of some of the things we do. For example, as you walk toward your car, you automatically reach in your pocket and get the key out to unlock the door, yet you really are not consciously aware of this action unless you turn your attention directly to it. Someone is talking to you and you acknowledge what they said, but you may not have really heard them because you were thinking about something else. As you read a book you turn the pages, but you are not really aware of turning the pages because you are attending to the ideas being expressed.

The same thing happens in sport skills. They become so automated that athletes can go through the motions without really attending to what they are doing. As actions become automated, or when attention is on something else at the same time another event is experienced, the athlete loses awareness of these experiences. Automating sports skills is desirable, but sometimes, when actions become so automated, athletes may lose awareness of some of the critical elements involved in performing the skill.

The point here is that an important first step for improving athletes' imagery skills is for them to become more aware of all of their senses as they experience sport. Athletes need to take notice of the position of their bodies, the footwork, the timing, the flow of movement, the change of direction, the preparatory movements to the actual striking or hitting of an object. And of course they need to become more aware of their own visual, kinesthetic, and auditory senses as they play sport.

The best technique I have found to create greater awareness is known as *mindfulness* (Goleman, 1976). This program essentially directs athletes' attention toward those events where greater awareness is desired by asking them to slow down and become more mindful. The mindfulness procedures are explained in the *Study Guide*.

Phase Two: Vividness

The next step is to practice vividness through a series of exercises involving those senses that are important in the sport. Remember, vividness does not mean vivid *visual* images

only; vividness refers to vivid images for all the senses. The athlete, coach, or sport psychologist can quite easily design such exercises. It just takes a little imagination, and to help stimulate your imagination you will find several examples in the *Study Guide*. I also recommend that you obtain a copy of *Put Your Mother on the Ceiling* by Richard DeMille (1973). It is full of interesting images to help develop vividness.

If athletes have very poor imagery skills, then I begin with some simple exercises such as the bedroom exercise (see *Study Guide*). This exercise asks athletes to recall their bedroom when they were twelve years of age. It almost always results in vivid images. Thereafter, I strive for variety in exercises and to make them specific to the sport of the athlete. Also, I quickly encourage athletes to develop their own vividness exercises, to take responsibility for their own psychological training.

Phase Three: Controllability

Controllability exercises involve learning to manipulate images to produce the desired outcome. I usually take athletes through a series of nonsport exercises first, such as manipulating a wooden cube, experiencing arm heaviness, or placing a foot in a bucket of ice water (see *Study Guide*). Then the athlete is guided to designing his or her own sport-specific controllability exercises. For example, a basketball player may image dribbling, shooting certain shots, or improving specific defensive skills.

Preparing to Practice

Imagery research has revealed that vividness and controllability are best practiced under the following conditions:

- The right setting or environment
- Relaxed attention
- The motivation to train
- The right attitude or expectancy
- Systematic practice

The Setting

Those highly skilled in the use of imagery, such as yogis, can practice and perform their skill in almost any setting. Few athletes possess such skill, however, and therefore need initially to practice imagery in a setting that has no distractions. As athletes' imagery skills develop, they will learn to use imagery even when they are in the midst of all the distractions of a competitive contest. They will be able to let these distractions recede from their consciousness while they focus on their internal images.

Relaxed Attention

Relaxation skills are an important part of imagery training. Before each imagery exercise athletes should become completely relaxed, but not so relaxed that they fall asleep. They want to quiet their mind and muscles, but at the same time be attentive to what they are about to do—in other words, athletes want to be in a state of *relaxed attention.*

Relaxation is important because if athletes have a lot of left brain activity going on—analyzing past mistakes, thinking about the day's events, worrying about an examination, stewing over something their girlfriend said—little will emerge from the right side, the imagery center. Relaxed attention releases imagery; tension supresses it.

Furthermore, as long as the body is physically tense or active, attention is distracted from what's going on inside you. A quiet state permits imagery to have a greater effect on the nervous system because it need not compete with other events. Research supports this, showing that imagery is most effective when the brain waves are in the alpha phase, indicating a quiet mind (Wallace & Benson, 1972). In addition, several other researchers have found that relaxation *and* imagery combined are more effective in imagery training than either one separately (Kolonay, 1977; Weinberg, Seabourne, & Jackson, 1981).

Motivation

As you have already learned, the best athletes are those who are intrinsically motivated, which keeps them practicing for months and even years in preparation for the big event. Athletes must have that type of motivation to develop both their physical and psychological skills. Quite frankly, the single biggest problem with PST is getting athletes to make the commitment to practice the skills on a system-

atic basis—and this is true for imagery training. Because this type of practice is not yet widely recognized as being beneficial, few athletes have the motivation to make the long-term commitment to practice regularly. That's why it is so important that you help your athletes structure their imagery training and all of their PST program.

Expectations

Imagery training, like most things, is more successful when athletes expect it to be helpful. Images always are more vivid and stable when athletes believe in them.

Yet some athletes quickly reject such non-traditional activities as imagery training. Hard physical work and dedicated practice have gotten them where they are, not such mumbo jumbo as movies of the mind. "Just leave me alone man, and I'll do my thing!" is the attitude of some athletes exposed to imagery training. Negativism and doubt neutralize images, just as they doom an athlete's performance. Athletes should avoid evaluating the imagery experience while they are experiencing it.

On the other hand, some athletes are eager to use imagery, but expect to achieve the feats of yogi Swami Raja overnight. Of course, this is unreasonable, but athletes often can improve their imagery skills remarkably in a few weeks because these skills are usually quite underdeveloped. After the initial spurt, however, progress is likely to slow to a snail's pace, in much the same pattern as when athletes first learned the sports skills they now possess. Thus athletes must be realistic in their expectations of imagery. Imagery will not transform a forty-three-year-old man who is 5'6", weighs 140 pounds, and is confined to a wheelchair into an explosive middle linebacker for the Pittsburgh Steelers. Imagery is not magic; it is a useful skill when properly used.

Practice

Every athlete knows the importance of practice. But not every athlete knows or remembers that it is not the quantity of practice, but the quality of practice that is more important. Just going through the motions when practicing sports skills will not accomplish what athletes want, and may even hurt their performance by introducing errors into the skill because they are not fully concentrating. Just going through the motions with imagery exercises also will not achieve what athletes want.

MOTOR IMAGERY: SOME ADDITIONAL OBSERVATIONS

Both research and experience in using imagery have taught us some useful lessons. In this section, we consider what we know about the role of imagery in learning new motor skills and what you can do to enhance the use of motor imagery with your athletes.

Imagery in Learning New Skills

It is uncertain how much motor imagery helps athletes learn an entirely new motor skill. We do know that people cannot learn to play quarterback or the piano by motor imagery alone. Evidence indicates that motor imagery is most helpful for complex sports skills once athletes have a reasonable idea of what the skill looks and feels like—once the blueprint is at least roughly etched into their brains.

By observing skilled performers or listening to a coach's instructions, athletes can acquire this blueprint in part. But they cannot develop the vital kinesthetic sense this way. It can only be developed through the actual performance of the skill. Once athletes have a faint blueprint of what the skill looks and feels like—then they can benefit from motor imagery.

Motor imagery is analogous to a vitamin supplement. It does not replace the basic need for nourishment, but supplements it. It is a compact, efficient way to practice once the blueprint is established; it helps to refine the blueprint and etch it in.

This process of etching in the blueprint is what every athlete knows to be the hard work of practicing a skill to the point that it is overlearned. When the skill is overlearned, the performance of it can take place automatically. The process of taking a poorly developed skill and developing it into a smooth, well-coordinated, highly automated skill can be greatly helped through imagery.

And there are advantages to this form of practice. It is efficient. Athletes can practice quickly, without physical fatigue and without risk of injury. Some athletes have told me they have relied heavily on imagery when they were injured to keep their game skills sharp.

Imagery can be practiced without equipment, when weather conditions are adverse, or when physical practice is not permitted. Imagery can be practiced almost any place and any time.

Imagery has another advantage not often recognized. The repeated practice that is required to make a skill highly automated is often exceedingly boring. As athletes practice over and over, their minds may begin to wander as their bodies go through the motions. When this occurs, athletes are not strengthening the blueprint because they are not concentrating on what they are doing. This is when errors or bad habits are introduced into their blueprint. Thus motor imagery offers a change of pace from the tedium of physical practice.

An important practical question, then, is this: What ratio of physical to motor imagery practice should be used at each stage of skill development? While we lack experimental evidence to answer this question precisely, from the information already presented you can deduce a reasonable answer.

When first learning a skill, athletes should use imagery to keep vivid in their minds someone doing the skill very well. Imagery practice at this point should be minimal until the athletes have acquired a good feeling for the movement through physical practice and coaching. Once they have the "feel," then imagery practice should become a much greater part of their total training.

As the skill becomes well-learned, physical practice may be decreased slightly, with emphasis on the quality of practice rather than the quantity. Motor imagery practice can then be increased to benefit from the several advantages mentioned above. At this stage mental and physical practice may occupy virtually equal amounts of practice time.

Additional Refinements

Athletes tell me it is helpful to image not only the execution of the skill, but the outcome as well. For example, in baseball, pitchers should not only visualize and feel the windup and delivery of the ball, but see it going exactly where they want it to go. And when athletes succeed in their imagery, they should tell themselves they did a nice job in having controlled both their image and the pitch (positive self-reinforcement).

A useful technique some athletes have developed is slow motion imagery. When they wish to analyze their performance to make improvements or etch in a particularly weak part of their skill, they will visualize it in slow motion and then isolate on that component. Once they are able to image it clearly in slow motion, then they mentally practice speeding up the action.

While it makes sense to have athletes focus on the positive and, especially, image performing a skill successfully (Powell, 1973), there is benefit in using imagery as a self-awareness tool to look at mistakes being made. When athletes are having difficulty with a skill and keep making an error, I ask them to do this: Imagine themselves making the mistake, seeing and feeling the error. Then think about what it would take to make the correct response. (The athlete may need some assistance here either from you or from watching a highly skilled performer execute the skill properly.) Then immediately imagine performing the skill correctly. Now repeat the correct image several times, perhaps switching back and forth between practice and the actual observations of a skilled performer. I recommend that athletes immediately follow several repetitions in imagery with physical practice.

I suggest that athletes try this entire routine as soon after their performances as possible so that their mistakes are vivid in their memories. But I do not recommend doing it if they are emotionally upset from a loss. It is better if they wait until they are calm and relaxed.

Just as imagery can be valuable to correct errors, evidence indicates that imagery can be very helpful to strengthen the blueprint of those skills performed well. Thus I recommend that, after a contest, athletes find a quiet place and think about their good performances. They are instructed to recall vividly their best performance several times to help strengthen their mental blueprint for future performances.

Some athletes find their imagery enhanced by using what are called triggers—some prop or object involved in the sport, or a word or phrase to help them concentrate on the activity. Chess players, for example, find the use

of a blank board helpful when they play mental chess. Bruce Jenner, winner of the 1976 Olympic decathlon, kept a hurdle in his living room. When asked why, he said he would mentally jump over it whenever he was lying on the couch.

Videotape-Augmented Motor Imagery

One of the difficult problems in the development of sports skills is acquiring the initial blueprint, or getting enough of an idea of how to do the skill so that an athlete can come reasonably close to performing it. The long trial and error learning process, the repeated instructions from coaches, the countless hours to try to get the exact blueprint—the perfect movement—recorded in memory can often be frustrating. Then the problem becomes one of etching it in or strengthening that perfect blueprint and not the other less skillful movements. The challenge is to capture that one perfect shot, pass, kick, or routine and lock it in so that the athlete can practice it mentally and perform it consistently.

A method that appears to be helpful is the use of videotape or film to capture those few perfect movements for later playback. What several psychologists have tried with athletes is to make a movie or recording of the athlete practicing the skills of the sport. The film is carefully edited, usually in consultation with a coach or the athlete, to identify the perfect, or near perfect movements. These movements are then duplicated repeatedly on the film and shown over and over to the athlete. The athlete observes his or her own skilled movements in the same relaxed state that is prescribed for imagery training. After viewing the film for several minutes, the athlete closes his or her eyes and images the skill.

From the information presented in this chapter, it should be clear how the use of the tape or film may enhance the development of a blueprint for the perfect movement. A training program called *Sybervision* (DeVore & DeVore, 1981) has made use of this principle and has reported excellent results with the Stanford University's tennis team. Also James Loehr (1978), a sport psychologist, reported good results with this method.

The approach, however, still awaits scientific scrutiny; but based on the mechanisms we have described here, there is every reason to believe that the use of visual prompts of a skilled performance will be helpful. With the increasing availability of videotape units, which are highly portable and can readily be edited, this technique holds much promise for assisting athletes in their skill development. One cautionary note, however. To the extent that the key ingredient of the skill is kinesthetic and not visual, this approach may be less helpful, unless in some way the observation of the movement makes it easier for the athlete to reexperience the kinesthesia associated with the movement when mentally practicing.

PSYCHOLOGICAL SKILLS TRAINING THROUGH IMAGERY

So far I have discussed the Sport Imagery Training program only with regard to the practice of motor skills. Now let's look at how we use imagery to help athletes acquire such psychological skills as controlling anxiety, improving attentional skills, and using goal setting to develop and maintain an optimal self-confidence level.

Vivid and controlled images are important for the use of imagery in the development of psychological skills just as they are for the practice of motor skills. Rather than emphasize *sensory awareness*, however, for the development of psychological skills, we emphasize *self-awareness*. The objective of self-awareness training is to help athletes feel the mood or emotional states they experienced when playing sports and to recall these experiences vividly.

Sometimes athletes run away from their negative emotional experiences in sport. They never face up to their anxiety or loss of concentration. Consequently, they never develop the ability to deal with these powerful emotions when they most need to—during the more important contests.

I help athletes develop self-awareness by using regression imagery exercises (see *Study Guide*) and other exercises in which I ask them to recall previous sport experiences, including anxiety- and anger-provoking events. I also ask athletes to recall previous positive experiences, those joyous moments of sport. It is useful to help athletes recall those days when they played very well, when concentration was automatic, when events flowed easily, when self-doubts were unknown.

The PST program then uses imagery, first to help athletes face up to their emotions, next to help them acquire the basic skills of PST, and finally to provide them with a way to practice these psychological skills in self-simulated competitive situations. Although there is far less evidence in sport about the use of imagery in this way, there is abundant evidence for its use in helping nonathletes deal with psychological problems (Singer & Pope, 1978).

SUMMARY

1. Imagery is a skill that most athletes have not sufficiently developed through systematic training.
2. Imagery is an experience, similar to a sensory experience, but arising in the absence of the usual external stimuli.
3. Imagery is polysensory, involving not only the visual sense, but the auditory, olfactory, tactile, and kinesthetic senses.
4. Imagery is useful in practicing motor skills and developing the psychological skills presented in part III.
5. Both experiential and scientific evidence demonstrate the power of imagery in helping athletes develop physical and psychological skills.
6. We are not exactly certain why motor imagery works—whether through minute neural firings in the muscles or symbolic coding of patterns in the central nervous system—but it does work

by helping to develop a mental blueprint.

7. The Sport Imagery Training program involves three phases: sensory awareness training, vividness training, and controllability training.

8. Athletes should initially practice imagery in a distraction-free environment.

9. Athletes will benefit more when practicing imagery in a relaxed but attentive state.

10. Coaches play a vital role in helping to motivate athletes to practice their imagery program.

11. Coaches and athletes need to have reasonable expectations about how fast imagery skills can be learned and what imagery can do to help athletes.

12. The most important element of imagery training is to practice *systematically*.

13. Imagery appears to be less helpful in learning new motor skills than in helping to refine developing motor skills.

14. Imagery offers advantages for practicing sports skills in that motor imagery training can be practiced when athletes are physically fatigued, when facilities or equipment are inaccessible, or when athletes are injured. In addition, motor imagery training provides a change of pace from physical practice.

15. Athletes should image not only the performance, but the outcome of the performance, rewarding themselves when they are successful.

16. Using slow motion imagery may be helpful in refining skills.

17. Triggers may be useful to stimulate vivid imagery.

18. Videotape augmented motor imagery is recommended to improve the performance of complex sports skills.

Chapter 7
Managing Psychic Energy

Excellent coaches are skillful managers of their athletes' energy. As an energy manager, you help athletes condition their bodies to increase their physical energy reserves. You plan a tapering-off period from heavy training in preparation for an important event in order to conserve energy. You develop a race or game strategy to use energy in a certain way. You appreciate that running a marathon challenges the athlete's skills in managing energy, and that a two-day decathlon is an extraordinary feat of energy management. You obviously recognize the importance of managing *physical* energy, but do you recognize that these events, and all sports participation, also require the management of *psychic energy*?

Just as athletes can condition their bodies to increase their physical energy, they also can condition their minds to increase their psychic energy. Physical energy is produced more efficiently by proper exercise of the body and good nutrition, which increase the body's ability to release the energy stored as muscle glycogen, carbohydrate, and fat. Psychic energy is produced more efficiently by proper exercise of the mind and a good diet of realistic, constructive thoughts.

As an energy manager, you need to recognize that physical energy influences psychic energy—that a fit body is an important part of a healthy mind, and that physical fatigue can weaken the will to win. You also need to know that psychic energy influences physical energy. When the mind is energized the body will follow, and when the mind is calm and in control it can demand the same of the body. As an energy manager, then, you strive to achieve a union of physical and psychic energy—an optimal psychophysical state. When your athletes have insufficient psychic energy, you seek ways to psych them up—to motivate them. When they have too much psychic energy in the form of anxiety or anger, for example, you try to calm them.

Highly trained and experienced athletes become very skillful at perceiving their physical energy reserves and at discerning their energy expenditure. Long-distance runners are capable of setting paces precisely, to within a few tenths of a second; they are capable of feeling their anaerobic threshold and running at a pace just to that point. Slightly above that point, they know they are using their physical energy less efficiently. In much the same way athletes can learn to manage their psychic energy. Athletes can be taught to feel their mental tension and to pace the expenditure of psychic energy in competition.

In this chapter you will learn what psychic energy is and how it is related to stress. You will learn how to identify the optimal energy zone. I'll explain how to "psych up" your athletes and how they can avoid being "psyched out." You also will learn about the inverted-U relationship between performance and psychic energy, and how to help your athletes reach the optimal energy zone more often.

UNDERSTANDING PSYCHIC ENERGY

Psychic energy is harnessed by teaching athletes how to gain control of their thoughts—their minds—which is what Psychological Skills Training is all about. Too often coaches function as if the athlete's mind is not within the coach's realm of influence, but to be an effective energy manager, you must help athletes acquire control over both physical and psychic energy.

When I say athletes must learn to control their thoughts, I am referring to their consciousness—those inner activities of which the person is aware. All of us have a tendency to believe that only what is observable is real, but our inner life is just as real. All our actions are manifestations of our inner experiences. We don't just behave or perform; we think, we plan, we image, and then we decide in our minds what action we will take. It is when athletes harness the much more powerful energy source of the mind that they achieve their best performances.

Human energy—physical and psychic—must not only be controlled, it must be directed. You coach your athletes to avoid wasting physical energy with unnecessary actions. Thus you direct their energy by teaching them to run efficiently and skillfully, or to go to the exact spot on the court to return the opponent's shot rather than chasing the ball around the walls.

Psychic energy also needs to be directed because it can be constructive or destructive, positive or negative. You help athletes direct their psychic energy by teaching them how to focus on task-relevant matters and avoid distractions, and how to think about what can be done rather than what cannot be done. When performing, athletes need to learn to think about *now*, not what was or might be; and they need to learn when to analyze themselves or their performance and when to avoid doing so.

Athletes take the first step toward controlling their psychic energy through greater self-awareness—by coming to know their own minds and bodies and knowing how they respond to various situations. (Recall how imagery can be used to enhance self-awareness.) They take the second step by exercising their minds in learning the psychological skills described in part III, and by assuming greater responsibility and control for themselves.

Psychic Energy Defined

In psychology, psychic energy is typically referred to as *drive*, *activation*, or *arousal* of the mind *and* body. But these terms confuse psychic energy with physical energy, and that is the reason the more popular term *arousal*

is inadequate for our purposes.[1] *Psychic energy* is, rather, the vigor, vitality, and intensity with which the *mind* functions and is the bedrock of motivation. Psychic energy also is either positive or negative, and thus is associated with various emotions such as excitement and happiness on the positive end and anxiety and anger on the negative end.

As with most psychological qualities, psychic energy falls on a continuum, as shown in Figure 7.1—people have more or less of it at different times. Where on the continuum would you place yourself when watching television? Moments before your team is to play an important game? Right now as you are reading this book?

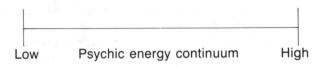

Low   Psychic energy continuum   High

Figure 7.1 The psychic energy continuum.

Some tasks require relatively low psychic energy, such as watching television, taking out the garbage, and raking the leaves. Other tasks require high psychic energy—giving a speech, confronting an athlete, or performing a gymnastics routine in competition. The sport world has its own vocabulary for psychic energy. When athletes go from low to high, they are getting *psyched up*, and when the psychic energy is too high, they are *psyched out*. Athletes speak about wanting to "get up, but not uptight," meaning they want to find the right level of psychic energy for the situation at hand.

---

[1]I prefer the term *psychic energy* for several reasons when discussing the practical application of this concept and those related to it. It is helpful in the development of Psychological Skills Training to focus on the activation of the mind separately from the activation of the body, although this in no way applies a mind/body dualism perspective. Of course activation of the mind may cause activation of the body, but it also may not. In addition, I prefer the term *psychic energy* because it is more closely associated to other terms coaches are familiar with that are related to this phenomenon, such as *psyching up* and *psyching out*. Finally, I hope the analogy to physical energy helps make the management of psychic energy more understandable and rememberable.

Stress Defined

Psychological stress is closely associated with psychic energy, but they are not the same. Psychological stress occurs when athletes perceive that there is a substantial imbalance between what they perceive is being demanded of them and what they perceive they are capable of doing, and the outcome is important to them. Don't let this rather academic definition put you off, but you need to understand it to work through this chapter and chapter 8, "Stress Management." The concept is not that complicated and Figure 7.2 will help you understand it.

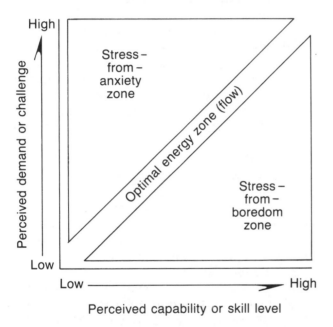

Figure 7.2 Psychological stress arises from an imbalance between perceived demand and perceived capability. When perceived demand and capability are in balance, the optimal energy zone, or flow, is more likely to occur.

What this figure suggests is that when athletes look at a situation, such as an athletic contest, they have some perception of what will be demanded of them, and they compare it to what they perceive they are capable of doing. If they perceive that *more* is being demanded of them than what they believe they are capable of doing, then they will experience stress arising from anxiety, which is shown in the upper left triangle. In addition,

the more important they perceive the outcome to be, the more stress they are likely to experience. On the other hand, when athletes are in a situation where they perceive that their ability is well above what the situation demands, then they may experience stress arising from boredom, which is shown in the lower right triangle. Although it is not common for boredom to be so great that it becomes highly stressful in sports, being deprived of all stimulation for an extended period of time can be extremely stressful and has been a common method of psychological torture. In between these two zones of stress, as shown in Figure 7.2, is an *optimal energy zone*, which is called the *flow* state. This state will be discussed shortly.

Relationship Between Stress and Psychic Energy

Now that you understand what stress is, just how is it related to psychic energy? Most coaches would tell you that high stress is associated with high psychic energy and low stress is associated with low psychic energy. So would most sport psychologists, for many treat stress and psychic energy as synonymous concepts. But they are not, and the failure to understand the difference between the two has hindered both coaches and sport psychologists in helping athletes find the optimal energy zone where the chances of performing optimally are maximized.

You can see in Figure 7.3 that stress and psychic energy are two independent dimensions. This idea is supported by research (Kerr, 1985). In quadrant *A* we see the typically expected relationship between high psychic energy and high stress, which manifests itself in such emotional states as anxiety and anger. However, as you just learned, athletes can be bored or mentally fatigued, which is also stressful, yet at the same time their psychic energy can be low (quadrant *B*). In quadrant *C* athletes are relaxed or drowsy, but neither stressed nor high in psychic energy. Finally, in quadrant *D* athletes are high in psychic energy, but not stressed. This can occur when they are in a state of excitement or happiness, or in the flow state.

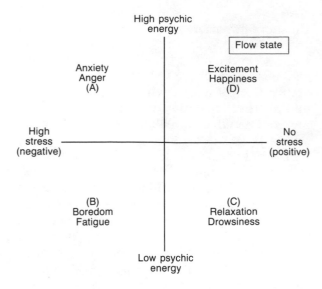

Figure 7.3   The relationship between psychic energy and stress.

Anxiety

Anxiety is another term bandied about indiscriminately. It is important to distinguish between two types of anxiety: trait and state. Some people have a tendency to "get uptight" more readily or frequently than other people and are referred to as having high *trait* anxiety. Low trait anxious people also may experience anxiety, but not as readily or frequently as high trait anxious people. Whenever low or high trait anxious people perceive that what is being demanded of them is greater than what their capabilities can manage, then they are said to have *state* anxiety. Thus trait anxiety is a person's *tendency* to experience state anxiety, and the actual experience of state anxiety occurs when the person perceives stress and is high in psychic energy (quadrant *A* in Figure 7.3).

CONTROLLING PSYCHIC ENERGY

Can athletes learn to control their psychic energy just as some do so skillfully with their physical energy? The answer, of course, is yes. All of us learn to control our psychic energy to some extent, but some people learn to do so to a much greater extent. The evidence to demonstrate—the encouragement to believe —that athletes can learn to control their psy-

chic energy is found in both science and experience.

Jacques Mayol

For years people thought that the deepest one could dive unassisted by any breathing apparatus was about 100 feet. In 1956 two Italian divers, Albert Novelli and Ennio Falco, set a depth record of 134 feet. Twelve years later U.S. Navy diver, Robert Croft, topped that record with a breath-hold dive to 240 feet. But the present-day record is held by Jacques Mayol, who shattered Croft's record with a 110-meter, or 359-foot, dive.

Mayol accomplished this remarkable feat not only by managing his physical energy well, but by exerting amazing control over his psychic energy. A student of yoga, Mayol, who was raised in the Orient, believes that the key to his remarkable diving ability is "to know yourself, to be at peace with yourself," as he himself states it. Mayol, in preparation for his record-breaking dive, studied dolphins, which are breathing mammals like humans, to see how they were able to hold their breaths so long and to dive so deeply.

During Mayol's physical training, his red blood corpuscle count doubled, giving him increased oxygen-carrying capacity. Only after months of preparation, physically and psychologically, was Mayol ready to dive. As he approached his record-breaking dive, eight safety divers were stationed in the water below, but Mayol knew they would not be able to help him at great depths. Below 150 feet he would be unable to draw a breath from a regulator because of the pressure squeezing his epiglottis shut and compressing his lungs.

First, Mayol went through a pre-dive routine of heavy hyperventilation using his yoga techniques. Then he became very focused and his concentration became inwardly directed, as he asked his mind to take control of his bodily functions. Mayol, holding on to a sixty-six-pound sled attached to a cable, began his headfirst descent. During the 105 seconds that he descended, he concentrated intensely on asking his body to slow down. On the surface Mayol's heart rate was sixty-eight beats per minute; at 100 feet it was forty; at 200 feet it was thirty; and at 110 meters, Mayol's heartbeat was an incredible twenty-four beats per minute. At 110 meters Mayol took a marker from the cable, while his body fought the pressure of approximately 160 pounds per square inch—a total weight on his body in excess of 100 tons!

Mayol's return to the surface was accomplished by slow kicks and steady pulls with his hands up the cable. If fear or panic struck, his body would need more oxygen quickly—oxygen his body no longer had. As he slowly made his way to the surface, his mind fought with his oxygen-depleted body to keep from becoming disoriented or blacking out. And finally, after three minutes and fifty seconds, Mayol broke the surface. While a remarkable example of controlling his physical energy, Mayol's dive is an even more remarkable example of controlling his psychic energy.

Jacques Mayol managed to lower his heart rate dramatically to conserve energy, but it has been suggested that this is merely the *div-*

ing response, an oxygen-conserving condition found also in marine mammals. Mayol, however, contends that it is not; he has learned to control his heart rate, and that is why he is able to dive more deeply than any other human. Other evidence also indicates that people can control their heart rates, even though for years we have thought this impossible.

Elite Shooters

Daniel Landers (1985) conducted a series of studies with elite shooters, discovering that the very best shooters had learned through experience to pull the trigger between heartbeats so that the vibration of the beat would not affect their aim. Elite shooters did not know they did this, nor how they did it, but the very best of them all did it.

Landers then trained less skillful shooters to see if they could learn this skill without the years of trial and error that the elite shooters had needed. He attached an electrode to the skin near the heart and fed back the beat to the shooters through headphones, instructing them to pull the trigger between beats. They quickly learned to do so. Then they were gradually weaned from the external feedback until they became able to monitor their own heartbeats.

If a shooter's heart is racing, though, it is almost impossible to shoot between beats. Thus shooters must learn to slow their heart rates to a level where they can shoot between beats. Landers found shooters and archers could learn to do this quite readily through *biofeedback*—monitoring the person's heart rate and feeding this information back to the person. By willing it with their minds, asking their hearts to slow down, shooters were able to manage their psychic energy.

What Landers demonstrated with elite shooters has been demonstrated in hundreds of biofeedback research laboratories and clinics around the world. Biofeedback is widely used today not only to feed back heart rates, but also muscle tension, blood pressure, electrical activity in the brain and on the skin surface, skin temperature, and other activities of the body that are not readily observable to the individual. Biofeedback is simply a way of enhancing self-awareness, the first step to managing psychic energy.

Sport Parachutists

Athletes' ability to control their psychic energy was demonstrated in a fascinating study of the stress response among novice and experienced sport parachutists, which was conducted by Walter Fenz and Seymour Epstein (1967). Using various measures of psychic energy, Fenz and Epstein found a pattern indicating that novice jumpers' psychic energy increased steadily right to the moment they jumped, as shown in Figure 7.4. The experienced parachutists, on the other hand, underwent high psychic energy at the time they arrived at the airport, with their energy levels then steadily declining till they reached a near normal level when they jumped.

Based on discussions with the experienced jumpers, Fenz and Epstein concluded that they energized themselves well in advance of the jump, and then used self-taught coping techniques to rid themselves of negative psychic energy while focusing on and intensifying the positive psychic energy. The experienced jumpers would focus on how they would handle the impending stressful situation, while the novice jumpers focused on the stress source itself, and the consequences if the jumps were unsuccessful.

Fenz and Epstein also found that not all of the experienced jumpers were equally adept at managing their psychic energy. Those who were skillful managers of psychic energy performed well in their jumps; those who were not performed less skillfully. Thus this study demonstrates not only that some jumpers were able to learn to manage their psychic energy, but that those who did performed better. It also indicates that even highly experienced jumpers were not without greatly increased psychic energy; however, through their experience they learned to manage this energy by getting rid of the negative thoughts and self-doubts and focusing on the positive elements of the jump—the excitement and exhilaration.

My own experience corroborates what Fenz and Epstein discovered. When I first began giving speeches at conferences, I would become so nervous that it was hard for me to think while speaking. Thus I would prepare my talks to such an extent I almost had them memorized, and always had a complete written copy of the talk before me at the podium. The psychic energy that I expended prior to and during a speech was enormous, and consequently the enjoyment of speaking was nonexistent.

As I learned more about the subject matter of this book, I actually began taking some of my own medicine. In an identical way to the experienced parachutists, I would find a quiet place thirty to forty-five minutes before my talk, during which time I would get very charged up about the speech. Disastrous images and negative thoughts would leap out at me from every direction, but I would challenge each one with constructive thoughts that generally dealt with "I have something important to say, and although I may not say it perfectly, the audience needs to hear my message."

This routine worked well for me. I had my panic attack now thirty minutes before, rather than during, the speech, and I survived it. Soon I needed my notes less, and speaking be-

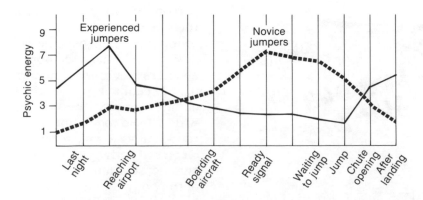

Figure 7.4 A comparison of the psychic energy levels of experienced and novice sport parachutists as jump time approached.

came an enjoyable activity, an opportunity for me to perform. I had learned how to manage my psychic energy.

THE OPTIMAL ENERGY ZONE

To perform their best, athletes need to find their optimal energy zones. The more you know about how athletes feel in this zone, the more you will be able to help them achieve this level of psychic energy. And the more you know about what may prevent an athlete from reaching this zone, the more you can do to remove these obstacles.

The optimal energy zone is shown in Figure 7.2 as lying between the two stress zones of anxiety and boredom. It is a zone in which athletes have very high psychic energy and no stress whatsoever. According to Mihaly Csikszentmihalyi (1975), this zone is reached when athletes are in a state of flow. *Flow* is the ecstatic feeling that everything is going just right. Whatever you are doing so engrosses you that your actions "flow" almost effortlessly, although what you are doing may be very hard work. Flow has been described as the "fun" in fun. One of the joys of coaching is that it can easily be so engrossing that you readily experience flow.

John Brodie, the former quarterback for the San Francisco 49ers, described achieving the flow state in football. He said that at times when he would drop back to pass, even with 1,200 pounds of animals charging toward him, he was able to concentrate on the receivers very intensely. When he threw the pass it felt like the ball was guided by an "energy streamer," which effortlessly directed the ball into the receiver's hands thirty yards downfield. He felt fully in control and was totally involved in the game.

From his study of many rock climbers, surgeons, artists, pianists, and athletes, Csikszentmihalyi (1975) found five qualities common to the flow state. They are described here as they pertain to athletes:

- Athletes are aware of their actions when playing, but are not aware of the awareness itself. When athletes in flow are asked what they are doing, they can readily tell you. But when in flow they never think about it from this perspective; they simply do it.

- Athletes' attention is centered completely on the activity, and concentration is vastly increased.
- Athletes lose their self-consciousness or egos. The activity so involves them with its demands for action that there is no evaluation of doing well or poorly. There is no concern with results while playing the game.
- Athletes feel in control of their actions.
- The activity provides athletes with clear, unambiguous feedback.

The flow state is achieved when athletes are totally involved in the activity; there is no room for self-praise or self-criticism. Flow is the complete absence of stress—no anxiety, no boredom. The flow experience is so exhilarating that it is intrinsically rewarding; that is, it is its own reward. Flow is the optimal energy zone. It is this zone you want to help your athletes reach to perform optimally.

Psyching Out

Only after I learned about flow, did I come to understand what *psyching out* really meant. Being in flow is being *psyched up*, and you cannot psych out someone unless they are first psyched up. Thus psyching someone out is simply disrupting that person's state of flow. It's causing them to shift from quadrant *D* in Figure 7.3 to any of the other three quadrants.

Psyching out techniques typically are designed to get the other person to think about what he or she is or is not doing. It is an attempt to shift the attention of the person from the activity being performed to how the performer is doing the activity. It's explained beautifully in this verse:

A centipede was quite happy
Until a frog in fun
Said, "pray which
leg comes after which?"
This raised her mind to such a pitch, she
lay distracted in a ditch,
Considering how to run.
Author Unknown

You are playing tennis with a highly competitive friend who is playing superbly and is clearly in the flow state. When you change sides, as you pass at the net, you comment,

"Lori, you really are hitting the ball well to-day. That's not like you." If Lori thinks about the comment and begins analyzing how well she's hitting the ball, she'll be out of the flow state. You psyched her out, you rascal!

Typically, athletes psych themselves out through their own analytical minds, which we will consider in detail in chapter 8, but coaches also can psych out or disupt the flow state of their athletes, often unwittingly. Listed in Table 7.1 are seven things coaches can do to disrupt athletes' state of flow. Read each item and then rate yourself on the scale that follows.

Psyching Up

If disrupting flow is psyching out, then psych-ing up is enhancing the likelihood of your ath-letes experiencing flow. We know far too little about how to do this well, and it certainly is not possible to offer a proven prescription for achieving the flow state every time, but here are some things that increase the chances of your athletes experiencing flow.

- *Athletes are more likely to experience flow when they perceive that the diffi-culty of the competition matches their skill levels.* As shown in Figure 7.2, flow, or the optimal energy zone, occurs in that thin area between the two stress zones.

You can help athletes match their skill levels to the challenge of the competition in several ways. When possible, you can attempt to enter athletes in contests that are closer to their own skill levels. You can, of course, help them improve their skills so that they can compete success-fully at the level of competition in which

Table 7.1
Coaches' Self-Evaluation for Influencing Athletes' Flow State

1. You constantly talk to the athletes during practice or competition, preventing them from centering their attention on the activity.

1	2	3	4	5
Never	Seldom	Sometimes	Often	Always

2. You frequently offer evaluative comments (positive or negative) about how athletes are playing while they are playing. This increases the chances of the athletes keeping their egos in the game, thus evaluating themselves.

1	2	3	4	5
Never	Seldom	Sometimes	Often	Always

3. You so control the flow of events in practice and contests that the athletes are unable to feel in control.

1	2	3	4	5
Never	Seldom	Sometimes	Often	Always

4. You provide instructions or feedback that are inconsistent, confusing the athletes and causing uncertainty in their minds.

1	2	3	4	5
Never	Seldom	Sometimes	Often	Always

5. You place a great deal of emphasis on the outcome of winning in your communication with your athletes. This distracts them from becoming absorbed in the process of playing.

1	2	3	4	5
Never	Seldom	Sometimes	Often	Always

6. You call time-outs when your team is in flow, decreasing the likelihood of them reentering flow when the game resumes.

1	2	3	4	5
Never	Seldom	Sometimes	Often	Always

Total your responses. If your score was 18 or more, you are not giving sufficient recognition to helping your athletes achieve the flow state. Now that you are cognizant of how you might be unknowingly helping to psych them out, you can take steps to change.

your team participates. And the most powerful option available to you is to help athletes perceive the challenge not as winning the game, but as achieving their own performance goals. When these goals are realistically set, then the challenge is always near the athlete's present skill level. This powerful goal-setting strategy is the theme of chapter 10.

- *Help your athletes focus their attention more on the activity itself.* Let them get absorbed in the game. Give them an opportunity to do this in practice by avoiding overcoaching and remaining a silent partner during the competition. You will find more useful information about how to improve athletes' abilities to focus their attention correctly in chapter 9.
- *Help your athletes focus on the present.* Teach them to put aside thoughts about the past or future. Too often athletes get caught up in the past, thinking about an error just made, or they project ahead, worrying about the outcome. Gaining control of these distracting thoughts is discussed in chapter 8 and exercises for developing this skill are in the *Study Guide.*
- *Athletes need to learn to stay relaxed physically and alert mentally.* If athletes are too relaxed, the mind wanders; if they are too tight, it becomes worried. The relaxed body and alert mind are the ideal conditions for experiencing flow. You will learn more about helping athletes achieve these states in all the remaining chapters.
- *Develop routines or rituals in preparation for performing.* They increase the ability to center the athletes' attention and are a source of confidence. Develop routines for putting on equipment, warming up, getting ready to execute the skill, and so on. Athletes with whom I have worked find pre-event routines very helpful in achieving the optimal energy zone.
- *Use the imagery techniques described in chapter 6 to reexperience previous flow states.* Then transfer these feelings to the forthcoming competition.

Pelé, the great soccer player, would lie on the floor of the locker room before games with his feet elevated on a bench. A towel would be neatly folded under his head, and another would shield his eyes. Then he would image pleasant scenes of playing barefoot on Brazilian beaches and

moments from his finest games—which he intended to emulate. The more important the game, the longer his imaging.

- *Flow is possible only when an athlete lets it happen rather than attempts to make it happen.* A power game won't work; flow requires finesse. When your athletes try to force their minds to flow, they surely won't.

As you can see from the list, psyching up is no simple, pre-event gimmick for putting athletes into the optimal energy zone. There is no psych vitamin that can be swallowed or injected shortly before game time to achieve flow, although a few athletes try to find their psychic energy in pills of one type or another. Psyching up is a long-term program, based on the same type of hard work required to develop the physical skills to perform well.

You will more likely help athletes reach the optimal energy zone by having the right coaching philosophy, applying the motivational guidelines presented in chapter 2, and using the leadership and communication skills described in part II. When you apply these skills, and when your athletes use the psychological skills that you teach them, as presented in part III, then you will have done all you can. Now it is the athletes' responsibility to find their optimal energy zones.

THE PSYCHIC ENERGY-PERFORMANCE RELATIONSHIP

Most coaches are interested in psychic energy as it influences performance, and rightfully so. They know from experience that not having enough psychic energy produces lethargic and inferior performance and experiencing too much psychic energy in the form of stress also hurts performance. So if you are going to be an energy manager, you need to know what the right amount of psychic energy is for superior performance. In this section you will learn what is known about the relationship between psychic energy and performance.

Inverted-U Principle

Think of the highest psychic energy you ever experienced—perhaps you were extremely stressed, angered, or grieved over some event, or you were jubilant and enthused with anticipation. Would you have been able to perform your best in any sport with that level of psychic energy? Not likely. Instead, while you want to be energized, you do not want to be overenergized. If this is what your common sense tells you, it is consistent with the widely recognized inverted-U principle, shown in Figure 7.5.

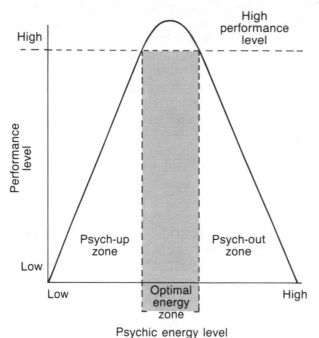

Figure 7.5 The inverted-U principle, showing the relationship between psychic energy level and performance. The optimal energy zone, the psych-up zone, and the psych-out zone are also identified.

This principle states that as psychic energy increases from very low levels, performance improves until some point or zone at which the person performs at the best of his or her capabilities. Then, with further increases in psychic energy, performance deteriorates. This range, where performance is very high, is what I have termed the *optimal energy zone* and is indicated by the shaded area in Figure 7.5.

This inverted-U principle is one of the best established principles in sport psychology and is generally known by most coaches. However, its practical implications are poorly understood and thus seldom utilized by coaches. You can be a much better coach, a skillful energy manager, by gaining a better understanding of this important principle and put-

ting it to use. That is the objective for the remainder of this chapter.

The Lowe Study

A fascinating study that looked at the relationship between psychic energy and batting performance in baseball is very instructive about the inverted-U principle. Randy Lowe (1971) sat on the bleachers for every game of a four-team league of eleven- to twelve-year-olds, recording their batting performances. At the same time, assistants obtained measurements of heart rate and subjective ratings of the players' fidgetiness when standing in the on-deck circle prior to batting. Lowe hypothesized that the psychic energy that hitters experienced in baseball was a consequence of both the criticalness *of the game* in the league standings, and the criticalness *of the situation in the game* when the young hitters actually batted. *Game criticality* was regarded as highest when the two teams at the top of the standings played each other late in the season. *Situation criticality* was highest when it was the last inning, the score was tied, the bases were loaded, and the count was full. Both of these indices of criticalness were quantified by Lowe so that he could assign a score to them.

Each time a player batted, the situation criticality score was recorded and the player's performance rated, but not in the conventional way. When the player hit the ball solidly, regardless of the outcome in terms of singles, doubles, and so on, the performance was given a high rating. The better the ball was contacted, the higher the rating. Thus a sharply hit line drive that was snagged by a diving third baseman received a high performance score, but a low outcome score. In turn, a swing that produced a dribbler in front of the plate, but resulted in the player being on third base because the catcher overthrew first base, received a low performance score and a high outcome score.

The study's results are enlightening. First, the relationship between all the players' performances as batters, and the outcome in terms of the bases they advanced to, was zero. In other words, poor performances resulted in getting on base just as often as good performances did, which suggests that for this age group luck is a big factor in who wins the game!

Next, Lowe looked at the relationship between the combined game and situation criticality scores, and the measurements he took of psychic energy level. His study was based on the premise that as these combined criticality scores increased, players would see the situation as more demanding; therefore, their psychic energy level would increase. His results supported this premise.

Then Lowe looked at the relationship among all the players' performances and the combined criticality scores of the game and situation. The expected inverted-U relationship was obtained, as shown in Figure 7.6. The players hit the best in games of moderately critical situations, and less well in low critical situations and extremely high critical situations.

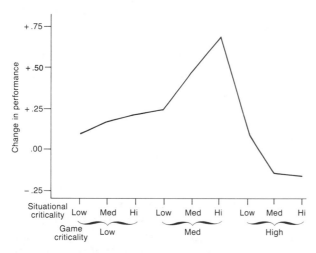

Figure 7.6 Performance of batters for the combined game and situation criticality ratings in the Lowe (1971) study.

But these were the results when all the players were averaged together. When Lowe looked at each player individually, he found the players differed widely in the level of psychic energy at which they performed best. Some hit best under low levels of psychic energy, others at moderate levels, and still others at very high levels of psychic energy. Some hit best at low *and* high psychic energy levels, and still others demonstrated no pattern at all. So although the combined results for all the players supported the inverted-U principle, there were wide variations in optimal energy zones among individual athletes.

Lowe also found that in the more critical games, teams tended to have their best pitchers pitching which made the task of hit-ting more difficult. Thus task difficulty was an important factor in influencing players' optimal energy zones. We will look more closely at this relationship shortly.

In summary, Lowe's study is instructive for the following reasons:

- It provides support for the inverted-U principle in sport when considering all the players together.
- It clearly demonstrates that each player's optimal energy zone differs.
- It indicates that the difficulty of the task influences the inverted-U relationship.

Individual Differences

The Lowe study, along with much additional research and common sense, all indicate that the optimal energy zone for each athlete is unique, as shown in Figure 7.7. Note that the shape of the curves is not symmetrical as shown in Figure 7.5, nor is the height of the curves the same for each player. These three players not only have different optimal energy zones, the width of the zone varies as well. Thus Julie, for example, has a much wider optimal energy zone than Diane.

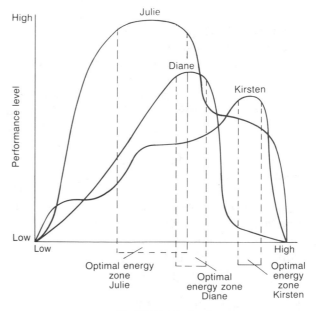

Figure 7.7 The relationship between psychic energy and performance among three athletes, showing differences in the width of the optimal energy zone and the level of highest performance.

Note too that the optimal energy zone lies in quite different regions of the psychic energy continuum for each athlete; Kirsten performs her best at a much higher psychic energy level than Julie. Also, not all players have the same ability, so what is a high-level performance for Kirsten is a lower level performance for Julie and Diane. In the final section of this chapter, you will learn how to help each athlete find his or her own optimal energy zone, despite these significant individual differences.

The Misunderstood Inverted-U Principle

In reading this chapter carefully, you may have discovered an enigma about the inverted-U principle. The riddle is this: The inverted-U principle says the best performance occurs when athletes have a moderate degree of psychic energy, regardless of whether this psychic energy is from moderate levels of excitement or from stress. In fact, many coaches and sport psychologists believe, based on the inverted U-principle, that moderate levels of *stress* produce optimal performance. On the other hand, the research and personal reports of the flow experience indicate that optimal performance occurs when athletes are very high in psychic energy but are stress free. You need to know which position is correct if you are going to help athletes manage their psychic energy correctly to optimize performance.

The answer is that both positions are true, but the inverted-U principle is not true for the reasons commonly given. Our riddle is solved by recognizing that people do not experience changes in psychic energy without assigning some cause to the changes. Typically the change in psychic energy is assigned to some emotion or motivational source—you are happy or sad, relaxed or anxious, excited or bored, and so on. These emotions are either positive or negative, and thus any changes in your psychic energy level are perceived by you as being positively or negatively directed.[2] You

may recall from chapter 2 that motivation is defined as having both an intensity and direction dimension. The intensity dimension is the degree of psychic energy and the direction is either positive or negative. To understand the motivated behavior of people, you must know about both these dimensions, not just one.

How psychic energy influences performance, then, is not determined only by the level of psychic energy, but also by the source of the psychic energy, be it positive or negative. It is my contention that positive psychic energy always facilitates performance, and that you cannot have too much of it. Negative psychic energy, on the other hand, always hurts performance and any of it is too much. The evidence to support this position is found both in scientific sources and in logic.

Let's first consider the question from a logical point of view. Stress is a negative emotion. It is an aversive state we seek to avoid. Not only does it hurt performance, it is among the leading causes of physical and mental illness. We place ourselves in stressful situations only when we need or want to achieve other positive goals.

Stress is known to hurt athletes' performances by creating unnecessary muscle tension and causing attention to become overly narrow. Under high stress, attention also begins to jump around so that athletes cannot concentrate intensely as is required for superior performance. A major reason that athletes are unable to concentrate is that they have negative thoughts associated with the stress. They worry about how they are performing, or what the coach is thinking, or about their chances of getting hurt. When athletes are in flow, their minds are fully focused on the task; when athletes worry, their mind's attention is divided between the task and the subject of their worry. The highest levels of performance are achieved only when athletes are in the worry-free state that exists between the two stress zones—anxiety and boredom—shown in Figure 7.2.

The scientific research is extensive indicating that worry consistently hurts performance, whether it is in sports, the arts, or academics. Scientific evidence and personal accounts of the flow experience also consistently report that the best performances occur in a stress-free state. It is virtually unheard of for athletes to report that they performed their best when they were filled with moderate

---

[2]Others have recognized the need to distinguish between positive and negative psychic energy. Harris and Harris (1984) refer to both kinds of energy as "good arousal" and "bad arousal," and the famous stress researcher, Hans Selye (1956), called positive energy *eustress* and negative energy *distress*. But to call one component of stress positive is a non sequitur; stress is a negative emotion replete with harmful effects.

levels of worry. And yet this is what is asserted by the inverted-U principle when no consideration is given to whether the psychic energy is positive or negative.

Clearly, the inverted-U curve shown in Figure 7.5 is not correct, but should look as it is shown in Figure 7.8. The difference in these two figures is that in Figure 7.5 psychic energy is shown on the horizontal axis as moving from low to high with the best performance occuring when the psychic energy is moderate, be it positive or negative. In Figure 7.8 the horizontal axis takes into account whether the psychic energy is positive or negative. It shows that as positive psychic energy increases, performance improves, and any negative psychic energy hurts performance. The more negative psychic energy experienced, the more performance suffers. The best performance, the very apex of the inverted-U curve, is a state of maximum positive psychic energy with absolutely no negative psychic energy.

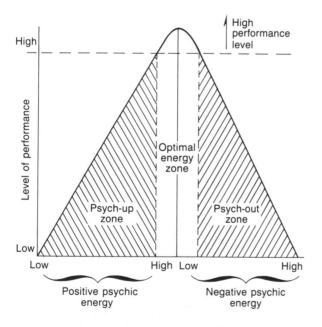

Figure 7.8 The inverted-U principle, showing positive psychic energy facilitating performance and negative psychic energy debilitating performance.

In Figure 7.8 I have also identified two other zones besides the optimal energy zone. The zone to the left of the optimal energy zone is the *psych-up zone*, the area where athletes need more positive psychic energy to perform better. The zone to the right of the optimal energy zone is the *psych-out zone*, the area

where athletes' negative psychic energy hurts their performance.

The ideal state of maximum positive psychic energy with no negative psychic energy is rarely achieved. Furthermore, athletes typically experience multiple emotions when competing. They may have high positive psychic energy arising from the challenge of the task, the joy of playing the sport, the determination to demonstrate competence, and the anticipation of extrinsic rewards. They may also experience high negative psychic energy in the form of anxiety or anger, for example. The negative psychic energy fights the positive; the positive psychic energy facilitates performance and the negative psychic energy inhibits performance.

Athletes certainly may still perform well, and even be in the optimal energy zone, when experiencing some negative psychic energy, as you can see in Figure 7.8—mostly because they have a great deal more positive psychic energy. But to whatever extent they have negative psychic energy, it detracts from them performing as well as they are capable.

If only negative psychic energy existed, there would be no motivation to perform the task. When athletes perceive that there is no possible way that anything beneficial can come from participating in a contest, and only negative consequences will result, they will not play. Thus, unless the existing negative psychic energy is exceeded by more positive psychic energy, an athlete would not want to participate. Fortunately, the positive sources of psychic energy usually overshadow the negative, but not always. When the negative is greater than the positive, those people drop out of sports.

A major reason that the inverted-U principle has not been correctly interpreted is that stress was treated as synonymous with psychic energy. It was assumed that some stress was good in motivating athletes up to the optimal point, and only when the stress became too great did it hurt performance. But as you saw when we discussed the relationship between psychic energy and stress, these two concepts are not identical. Reexamine Figure 7.3 and consider how it fits into Figure 7.8. In Figure 7.3 both quadrants *A* and *B*, the two types of stress, are conditions under which athletes will not perform optimally. Both quadrants *A* and *B* put athletes in the psych-out zone of Figure 7.8, quadrant *A* more so than quadrant *B*. When athletes are in quadrant *C*, they will not perform optimally either, but the reason is that they lack sufficient positive psychic energy and thus are in the psych-up zone. Only when athletes are experiencing no stress and high psychic energy (quadrant *D*) will they perform optimally.

Is it possible for athletes to have so much positive psychic energy that it hurts performance? Can athletes want it too much, try too hard? Yes they can—but "wanting it too much" and "trying too hard" are disguised forms of stress that produce negative psychic energy. Athletes change their thinking from "I'll do the best I can," to "I *must* do well or else." Trying too hard is not an uncommon source of stress among many otherwise positively energized athletes. Thus *positive psychic energy can never be too high when the energy is directed to the task being performed.* Such psychic energy contains nothing that would pollute performance. No research evidence of which I am aware has ever shown that too much positive psychic energy is harmful to performance or health.

Now that you understand what causes the inverted-U principle to work, it casts a new light on the practical applications of this principle. According to the old view, you wanted to help your athletes increase their psychic energy any way you could—positive or negative. Many coaches thought that by placing some stress on athletes they would become psyched up. But now we see why this is the wrong approach. You want to rid athletes completely of any negative psychic energy in order to maximize the possibility of reaching the optimal energy zone. Second, you want to enhance positive psychic energy in any way possible. The more positive psychic energy, the better.

Task Differences

Typically athletes will experience a combination of positive and negative psychic energy, so with these two sources present, let's learn how they influence the inverted U for different kinds of tasks. Although it is not possible to tell you exactly what level of psychic energy is desirable for any one sport or task, or for any

one athlete, you can gain some insight by knowing how positive and negative psychic energy influence performance on three different task categories:

- Simple versus complex tasks
- Fine versus gross muscle tasks
- Short-term versus long-term events

Simple Versus Complex Tasks

The major difference between a simple task and a complex task is that simple tasks generally require a lower level of performance to execute them successfully. Consequently, as shown in Figure 7.9, a simple task has a wider optimal energy zone than more complex tasks. Furthermore, the amount of negative psychic energy that can be tolerated when positive psychic energy is at its maximum is greater with simple tasks (the distance from *A* to *C*) than with complex tasks (the distance from *A* to *B*). As you can see in Figure 7.9, the optimal energy zone for complex tasks is very narrow, and very little negative psychic energy can be tolerated to perform at a high level. Because most sports tasks are complex, the implications should be clear.

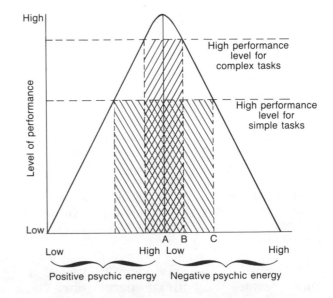

Figure 7.9 The inverted U and optimal energy zone for simple and complex tasks.

Fine Versus Gross Muscle Tasks

Convention has it that tasks requiring fine muscle control are performed better at a lower psychic energy level than tasks demanding gross motor activity. The example is often given that if a golfer had the psychic energy of a middle linebacker or a weight lifter when attempting to make a thirty-foot putt, he or she would surely hit it in the trees.

The error in this example is that physical energy demands are confused with psychological energy demands. The psychic energy demands of playing golf are no less than those of playing middle linebacker. Both benefit equally from maximum positive energy. You cannot have too much *positive* psychic energy for a fine motor task or for a gross motor task.

One difference may exist, though, between fine and gross motor tasks. Gross motor tasks are generally measured less precisely than fine motor tasks, so the standard that marks high performance is lower (there is more room for error) than with fine motor tasks. Consequently, in exactly the same way differences exist between simple and complex motor tasks: Fine motor tasks tolerate less negative psychic energy than gross motor tasks.

Study Figure 7.10 for a moment. You should be able to reach the following conclusions from this figure:

- Both fine and gross motor tasks benefit equally from positive psychic energy.
- The optimal energy zone for gross motor tasks is wider than the optimal energy zone for fine motor tasks.
- Gross motor tasks can tolerate more negative psychic energy than fine motor tasks, which require extreme precision for superior performance.

Task Duration

Another task difference that you need to consider is the length of time required to perform the task. Some events require a few seconds to execute and others take hours or even days. The optimal energy zone for these two types of events most likely differs significantly. Consider long-term events, be they running, skiing, walking, or bicycling. The highly automated tasks in these events are relatively easy

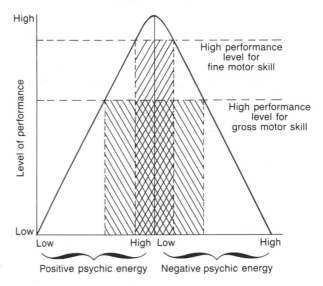

Figure 7.10 The inverted U and optimal energy zone for fine and gross motor tasks.

to execute, and can be executed successfully within a very wide psychic energy range as indicated by the simple tasks section of the inverted U in Figure 7.9. But the challenge in long-term events is to execute the skill as efficiently as possible over the distance to be covered, meaning with minimum expenditure of physical energy. As a coach of these events, you emphasize good technique because you know it conserves physical energy.

Just as athletes want to conserve physical energy, and yet complete the event as fast as possible, they also should conserve their psychic energy because long-term events are psychologically very demanding. Especially as they fatigue physically, athletes will need psychic energy to maintain their concentration on good form, to monitor the physical energy being expended, and to adjust their pace accordingly. Psychic energy is also needed for pushing through the pain barrier, maintaining the will to excel, overcoming self-defeating thoughts, and avoiding apathy and distractions. Because of the length of time involved, and because the task does not demand all their attention, negative thoughts can fester in the mind. Thus athletes in long-term events need especially good psychological skills.

Short-term events require positive psychic energy to be sharply focused for the few moments the athletes perform. Then the positive psychic energy can be turned down. For athletes who participate in short-term events that are repeated, such as in certain track-and-field events and tennis tournaments, they must become adept at turning the psychic energy up and down as required. Athletes who attempt to maintain a high psychic energy level while waiting between events, trials, or contests are more apt to suffer psychological fatigue.

Brief episodes of momentary negative psychic energy are less harmful to athletes in long-term events because there is time to get rid of the negative psychic energy and continue to perform well. If negative psychic energy exists to any extent at the moment of performance in short-term events, it will hurt performance substantially.

EBB AND FLOW OF PSYCHIC ENERGY

Psychic energy is never fixed, but constantly changing as athletes respond not only to their external environment, but to the internal environment that they create through their thoughts. We know far too little about what factors cause psychic energy to change prior to, during, and after participation in sport. At present the best you can do is become a close observer of changes in both positive and negative psychic energy among your athletes.

One of the more fascinating phenomena in sports occurs when the *momentum* of the contest changes. What causes the momentum to shift within a contest between two individuals or between two teams? It is my opinion that changes in momentum occur because of the ebb and flow of psychic energy among the individuals or teams playing.

Consider the example in Table 7.2 of Harry, a 9-to-2 favorite to defeat Stan in a racquetball game.

Harry had the momentum at 12-0, but backed off and gave Stan a chance to get his game together and grab the momentum. Often athletes will let go of their negative psychic energy, which may be a result of their concern about winning, when they see they are almost certain to lose. Stan began his comeback when he shifted his goal from winning to trying to perform well. When Harry saw Stan's comeback, he began to worry and to press harder, resulting in the negative psychic energy that hurt his game.

Many factors, most of which we can only speculate about from our own experiences, can change psychic energy during a contest. Some things that are likely to affect psychic energy are physical fatigue, mental fatigue, how well one is playing, how well the opponent is playing, officials' calls, fan reaction, injuries, anticipating impending defeat or victory, and receiving positive or negative feedback from fellow players or the coach. For athletes to manage psychic energy successfully, they must become familiar with all these events and countless others that may cause positive and negative psychic energy to change. Then they must have developed the psychological skills to keep their minds on the right course.

HELPING ATHLETES FIND THEIR OPTIMAL ENERGY ZONE

In this section we'll first consider a traditional way coaches have helped athletes find their optimal energy zones—the pep talk. Then

Table 7.2
An Example of Changes in Momentum

Score Harry	Stan	Energy Report
0	0	Harry is full of self-confidence, knowing he is the favorite. He has high positive psychic energy and very low negative psychic energy.
		Stan has high positive psychic energy, but knowing he is the underdog, has moderately high negative psychic energy.
12	0	Harry sees this as an easy match now, lowers his positive psychic energy to a moderate level, and has no negative psychic energy.
		Stan feels he is out of it, deciding he cannot win, but trying to play well to improve his game. He experiences moderately high positive psychic energy and lower negative psychic energy.
14	6	Harry's psychic energy is unchanged.
		Stan is encouraged by his play. Positive psychic energy is now high, with very low negative psychic energy.
15	11	Harry begins to get concerned. He shifts his positive psychic energy to moderately high, but also has moderate negative psychic energy as he entertains the possibility of Stan making a comeback.
		Stan now feels his game is flowing—high positive psychic energy, no negative psychic energy.
17	17	Harry realizes he is struggling to get back into the game and tells himself to fire up. He has high positive psychic energy and moderately high negative psychic energy.
		Stan feels in full control of his game, experiencing high positive psychic energy and no negative psychic energy.
19	21	Harry has very low positive psychic energy and very high negative psychic energy, for he is angry at himself for letting the game get away from him.
		Stan continues to have high positive psychic energy and no negative psychic energy. He's ready for the next game.

we'll look at how the optimal energy zone can be found using the PST program.

The Pep Talk

Many coaches continue to use the team pep talk as a traditional means to motivate athletes to achieve the optimal energy zone. At this point you should be able to see why this is such a foolish practice. First, in giving the pep talk, the coach assumes the athletes are not already high in positive psychic energy. Second, the coach assumes that the entire team needs to increase their psychic energy level to the same degree. Third, the coach at least

hopes that the increased motivation is positive, not negative, psychic energy. Now if the coach exhorts the team to win, implies negative consequences if they lose, and causes athletes to focus on their weaknesses rather than on their strengths, then the athletes may begin to worry and thus increase their negative psychic energy. It is far better to help athletes understand how psychic energy relates to performance as discussed here, and then to teach them how to manage their own psychic energy. No one can find the athletes' optimal energy zones as well as the athletes themselves. It seems to me, then, that the coach's responsibility is to help athletes acquire the skills needed to manage their psychic energy levels.

The PST Approach to Managing Psychic Energy

Now how do you do this? Your objective is to help your athletes find the optimal energy zone every time they play, but you know it is not possible to prescribe exactly the optimal energy zone for athletes. We know what it feels like to be in this zone—to flow—and we know when we are not in flow. But how to reach it every time we compete is beyond our present knowledge, although this book has provided some useful general guidelines for increasing the chances of your athletes finding the optimal energy zone more often.

One of the major problems in helping athletes find the optimal energy zone is that a simple and accurate instrument for measuring positive and negative psychic energy does not exist. Researchers have been searching for years for such an instrument without success. The problems in measuring psychic energy are complex (and a full description is beyond the scope of this book), but the primary difficulty is that there are no scales that have anchor points to which much meaning can be affixed. A thermometer, in contrast, is an accurate scale for measuring temperature. We know that 32 degrees Fahrenheit represents the point at which water freezes; 98.6 degrees Fahrenheit is the human body's normal temperature; and 212 degrees Fahrenheit is the point at which water boils. The best we can do in measuring psychic energy is to have each person indicate if he or she is experiencing more or less psychic energy than at some other previous time. Unfortunately, that strategy does not tell you exactly how much more or less is needed for achieving the optimal energy zone. The problem, too, is that you cannot make comparisons readily among your athletes.

But don't abandon ship yet; there is a solution, although not as simple and accurate as the thermometer. The approach for you to help each athlete find his or her optimal energy zone must be a method in which each athlete makes comparisons between his or her own psychic energy levels, not one in which comparisons are made among athletes.

The procedures, then, for helping athletes find their optimal energy zones are subjective but achievable by taking the following steps.

1. Athletes must attain greater self-awareness with respect to their psychic energy levels. They must become sensitive to their emotional states without being distracted by them. They must perceive the psychic energy they have in practice and in games; in easy games and in difficult games; when they have performed well and when they have performed poorly; when they have experienced flow and when they have experienced high stress. (I highly recommend Terry Orlick's book *In Pursuit of Excellence* [1980] for helping athletes develop greater self-awareness.)

2. Next you need to initiate the Psychological Skills Training program described in part III. You especially need to educate your athletes about

   - psychic energy management as a concept analogous to physical energy management;
   - what the state of mind is when athletes experience flow;
   - the inverted-U principle and how positive psychic energy always facilitates performance and negative psychic energy always debilitates performance;
   - the principles for psyching up;
   - how to avoid being psyched out;
   - how to manage stress when it is encountered (see chapter 8).

3. Develop a psychological training log that athletes can use to record their changing energy levels. A sample log is found in the *Study Guide*. This log shows the psychic energy rating, the time when the psychic energy level is rated, the performance during that time period, and any observations of the causes for a certain psychic energy level or performance level. The log is also useful to record any personal recommendations to oneself regarding how to change psychic energy in the future.

4. Athletes may find useful a subjective scale that has been developed for rating psychic energy levels. This scale is found in the *Study Guide*.

5. Meet with each athlete personally to implement the keeping of the log and

to set up a schedule for periodically reviewing the log.

6. Reinforce the value of managing psychic energy by adopting coaching practices that are consistent with the content of this chapter.

SUMMARY

1. Athletes need to manage their psychic energy, just as they do their physical energy.

2. Psychic energy is the vigor, vitality, and intensity with which the mind functions and is distinct from arousal, which refers to the activation of the mind and body.

3. Psychic energy and stress are two independent concepts and should not be regarded as synonymous terms.

4. There is both experimental and experiential evidence to show that psychic energy can be managed.

5. The optimal energy zone is defined as a stress-free state of flow in which the person feels fully in control, concentration is intense and well focused, and the psychic energy level is high and positive.

6. Psyching out someone is disrupting their flow.

7. Psyching up is achieved by increasing an athlete's positive psychic energy.

8. The inverted-U principle is widely held to be true. It states that performance improves as psychic energy increases to some optimal point, but with further increases in psychic energy performance decreases. Evidence supports this principle, but not for the reasons commonly given.

9. Psychic energy, just like electrical energy, is both positive and negative. The positive psychic energy facilitates performance, while negative psychic energy debilitates performance.

10. Rather than performance deteriorating because of too much psychic energy per se, it deteriorates because of negative psychic energy in the form of stress. Therefore, rather than try to find some middle-range psychic energy level, you want to help athletes acquire a state of mind where positive psychic energy is as high as possible, and negative psychic energy is nonexistent.

11. Complex skills compared to simple skills demand a higher level of positive psychic energy to perform the skill optimally, have a narrower optimal energy zone, and can tolerate less negative psychic energy for successful performance.

12. Similarly, fine motor skills, compared to gross motor skills, demand a higher level of positive psychic energy to perform the skill optimally, have a narrower optimal energy zone, and can tolerate less negative psychic energy for successful performance.

13. Long-term events, such as endurance running, require sustained psychic energy, which athletes must condition themselves for, while short-term events require athletes to focus their positive psychic energy very well for the brief moments when they execute the skills.

14. Psychic energy is never fixed, but constantly changing as athletes respond to both their external and internal environments. These changes are thought to explain the phenomenon of momentum in sports, something that is not yet well understood.

15. The team pep talk is an ill-advised means to increase athletes' psychic energy.

16. The PST approach to managing psychic energy is based on increased self-awareness, combined with the acquisition of all the psychological skills presented in part III.

Chapter 8
Stress Management

Psychological stress has robbed more athletes of physical energy, victory, and enjoyment in sport than any other factor. Stress can destroy self-confidence by leading athletes to believe they are incompetent. It can deny athletes the joy of demonstrating skills they have mastered through countless hours of practice. And it can deprive athletes of experiencing the ecstasy of flow. Stress causes interpersonal conflict, induces physical injury, and drives athletes to early retirements. Stress is an insidious disease and when sustained, manifests itself in the form of burnout—an affliction not only of athletes but of coaches as well.

The purpose of this chapter is to help you understand stress so you can help athletes manage their stress—and manage your own in turn. In this chapter you will learn about (a) the causes of stress, (b) the role of the brain's right and left hemispheres in experiencing stress, (c) the techniques for helping your athletes manage stress, especially to eliminate unproductive, negative self-talk, and (d) what you, as a coach, can do to avoid being a burnout victim.

CAUSES OF STRESS

In chapter 7 stress was defined as occurring when there is a substantial imbalance between what you *perceive* is being demanded of you from the environment and what you *perceive* your capabilities are, when you *perceive* the outcome to be important. Stress, then, contains three elements: your environment, your perceptions, and your responses to these in the form of arousal (which is the activation of the mind and body).

Typically, when people experience stress they try to discover the cause, and usually blame the environment. "The coach pressured me too much," or "When I looked at all those people, I panicked," are examples of identifying the environment as the cause of the stress. It was the coach or it was all those people. We all tend to blame the events in our environment for causing our stress; it becomes an automatic way of thinking, but it's wrong.

You probably noticed in the definition of stress how important perceptions are in experiencing stress. It is not the environment entirely that causes us to experience stress, but how we *perceive* these events. One athlete, when seeing a stadium full of people, can think, "What a great opportunity this is to show all these people how well I can play," while another can think, "How embarrassing it will be if I make a mistake in front of all these people." Of course, it's the same stadium full of people, but one athlete perceives the situation positively and the other negatively.

The third element of stress is the response of individuals to the environment in the form of *arousal*, the intensity dimension of behavior. The term *arousal* is used here rather than psychic energy because arousal refers not only to the psychic energy, or mental activation, of the person, but also to the physiological and behavioral activation of the person. Table 8.1 summarizes many of the physiological, psychological, and behavioral changes that occur in people when they are stressed. When seeking to understand how to manage stress, we need to consider all of these manifestations of stress.

Table 8.1
Common Changes Associated
With Increased Psychic Energy

Physiological (A)	Psychological (B)	Behavioral (C)
Increased heart rate	Worry	Rapid talking
Increased blood pressure	Feeling overwhelmed	Nail biting
Increased sweating	Inability to make decision	Foot tapping
Increased brain wave activity	Feeling confused	Muscle twitching
Increased pupil dilation	Inability to concentrate	Pacing
Increased respiration	Inability to direct attention	Scowling
Decreased blood flow to the skin	Not feeling in control	Increased blinking
Increased muscle tension	Feeling "different"	Yawning
Increased oxygen uptake	Narrowing of attention	Trembling
Increased blood sugar		Broken voice
Cotton mouth		
Frequent urination		
Increased adrenalin		

The definition of stress tells us that stress is a result of a person's negative thoughts and changes in arousal in response to the environment. However, there are two types of stress, depending on whether the negative thoughts or the changes in arousal occur first (McKay, Davis, & Fanning, 1981). These two formulas of stress are shown in Figure 8.1.

Stress Formula 1

You visit the locker room of your alma mater where you had prepared for many important games (E—an environmental stimulus). As you enter, you suddenly feel increased muscle tension, your heart beats faster, your palms

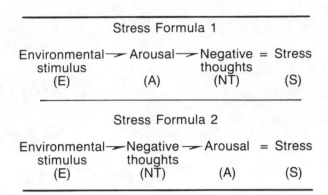

Figure 8.1 The two formulas for stress.

become clammy, a few butterflies flutter in your stomach, and your mind races with thoughts of the past (A—arousal). You explain these feelings by remembering how stressed you used to become moments before a game (NT—negative thoughts). You experienced increased arousal in this example, not because the locker room itself was threatening to you, but because you had made a strong association between increased arousal and this place years ago. When you returned for a visit 15 years later, the stimulus of the locker room triggered the surge of arousal automatically. Uncertain why you felt this increased arousal, you sought an explanation, which was your recollection of the enormous stress you experienced and how you disliked it. It would have been just as possible for you to have experienced the arousal, but interpreted it positively as the exhilaration and excitement of playing the game.

Stress Formula 2

It's moments before the game and you are watching your opponent warm up (E). You think it will be impossible to beat her and you imagine how humiliated you will be in front of all these people (NT). Then you feel your heartbeat speeding up, the adrenalin flowing, the knees wobbling, the muscles tensing in your neck and upper back, and your mind leaping from thought to thought as it intensely analyzes the situation (A). In Stress Formula 2 the negative thoughts precede the increased arousal, while in Stress Formula 1 the surge of arousal occurs first and negative thoughts follow.

The Role of Perceptions

Notice that in both examples the environment itself was not the cause of stress, but the *interpretation* of the environment—the negative thoughts—that made the environment stressful. It is our *perception* of the world, not the world itself, that causes our emotions. This is not to say that the environment does not play an important part in a person experiencing stress. Certainly some environmental events are more likely to produce negative thoughts than other environmental events. Regardless of the event, however, it does not become stressful unless it is interpreted negatively by you.

The interaction between arousal and negative thoughts, whether in Stress Formula 1 or 2, leads to an often devastating negative feedback loop. For example, experiencing Stress Formula 2, you say to yourself, "Oh, oh! I could be in trouble here" (negative thought). Then you experience the rush of arousal that reinforces your perception of trouble, leading you to further negative thoughts about the situation, which lead to greater arousal. And so it goes, until you are thoroughly bummed out.

Stress Formula 1 occurs far less frequently in sports than Stress Formula 2. Thus the emphasis in this chapter will be on managing stress when negative thoughts precede and lead to increased arousal.

Worry

Negative thoughts that lead to stress typically take the form of worry. Worry occurs when there is a discrepancy between what you hope will happen and what you perceive is occurring or will occur. You hope your team will perform flawlessly when they play, but based on what you observed in practice, you worry about their capability to attain such perfection. You hope to be able to control your anxiety prior to the game, but you worry about your ability to do so. (This is not an uncommon source of stress—the work of worrying is mentally fatiguing.)

Worry in itself is not necessarily stressful. When you identify a problem (a discrepancy between what you wish for and what you perceive may occur), worry may help you find a solution to the problem. If you have sufficient information, the work of worry will be productive; however, if you do not have sufficient information, the mind for some reason seems compelled to continue trying to solve the problem. Worry becomes stress, then, when problem solving resulting from reasonable worry becomes unproductive and frustrated—when the worry turns negative.

People also differ in their tendencies to worry. High trait anxious people have acquired a tendency to perceive more events as negative, to worry more, and to respond more negatively to a particular event than other people. For complex reasons, based substantially on the types of explanations people make to themselves about the experiences in their lives, high trait anxious people see the seamy side of almost everything while in pursuit of the elusive "silver lining." These thought patterns are difficult to change because they are highly automated. Thus it is very difficult for these people to see that it is their perceptions of the environment, not the environment itself, that cause their stress.

THE TWO-SIDED BRAIN

Tremendous progress has been made in the last twenty years toward a better understanding of how the two hemispheres of the brain work, and especially how they function in the stress response. The brain, it seems, has organized itself to deal with different types of functions. The left hemisphere is the analytical center where information is processed sequentially, and where the mathematical and language centers are located. The right hemisphere is where more integration occurs in the form of spatial functions, parallel processing of information, and imagery. In Figure 8.2 you can see the functions of the two hemispheres. I recommend reading Thomas Blakeslee's *The Right Brain* (1980) for more information about the functions of the brain's two hemispheres.

Although recent research suggests the division of labor as shown in Figure 8.2 may be somewhat oversimplified, the distinction between right and left brain functions is still very useful. In sport, the left hemisphere—the *Analyzer*—is used to learn new skills, correct flaws in technique, and develop strategy when competing. The Analyzer, which processes information one step at a time, is guided by verbal self-instructions that help cue an athlete's body about the type and sequence of movements to be performed. When first learning to throw a ball, the Analyzer determines what muscles must be contracted at what time. Slowly, clumsily, the Analyzer begins the arduous process of constructing a mental blueprint of how the skill should be executed. Then as the athlete practices, the Analyzer detects and helps correct the blueprint.

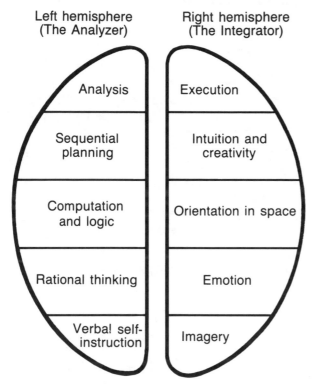

Figure 8.2   The functions of the brain's two hemispheres.

The right hemisphere, the *Integrator*, controls the way an athlete integrates individual components of a skill into a complex whole. The Integrator takes the Analyzer's blueprint of step-by-step instructions and converts it into a single, complex image. Now the brain need process only a single image rather than a series of complex verbal instructions. Thus imagery guides the Integrator in the same way that verbal self-instructions direct the Analyzer. The Analyzer, then, is the specialist for developing skills, and the Integrator is the specialist for controlling the performance of well-learned skills. Given this hemispheric specialization, it seems that coaches would do well to use fewer words and rely on images

more when coaching athletes to combine the components of a skill.

When the Analyzer is in control, attention is focused inwardly, comparing past performances and planning future performances. When the Integrator is in control, attention is on the present execution of the skill. When an athlete is *learning* skills, the Analyzer should be used, but when the athlete is *performing* skills in competition, the Integrator should be called upon. Even during a competition, though, there are appropriate times to analyze, such as between plays or during time-outs.

Analyzer-Integrator Teamwork

When athletes are in flow, their Analyzers and Integrators know their roles and control of performance switches smoothly between the two as the situation demands. The Analyzer helps to correct errors and develop strategy; the Integrator then executes those well-learned skills automatically, and sometimes in new and creative ways.

Theoretically, once athletes have the correct blueprint, they should perform flawlessly every time. If athletes can perform well in practice, why can't they replicate that performance in competition? If they perform well in one game, why can't they perform well in every game? One problem is that the Analyzer and Integrator often compete rather than cooperate for control. Athletes may analyze when they should be just playing, and far less frequently, athletes "just play" when they should be analyzing their performance.

This latter type of hemispheric insolence tends to occur in practice when athletes are fatigued or bored. They tend just to go through the motions, letting the Integrator totally dominate; but without analysis, no improvement in the skill will occur. Only through analysis can the mental blueprint be perfected. This is why the old adage "practice makes perfect," is invalid and has been replaced by the new adage, "perfect practice makes perfect."

One reason the Analyzer tends to dominate the Integrator so often is that our society puts so much emphasis on the development of logic and reasoning, causing the Analyzer to become strong while the Integrator weakens.

Parents and teachers reward their children for being logical and analytical, not for daydreaming or playing creatively. By the time young people graduate from high school, the Analyzer is much stronger than the Integrator. Therefore, when there is a struggle for control of performance, the powerful Analyzer usually wins out.

A crucial skill for athletes in all sports is to know when to analyze, when to integrate, and how to switch between the two effectively. Analysis is best done before the game, after the game, and during the game when there are time-outs and transitions between plays. Through greater attention to this skill, you can coach athletes on when they should analyze and when they should integrate. Also, be cautious about making analytical statements while they are attempting to integrate.

Mistakes Versus Flaws

Mistakes are a good example of how the dominant Analyzer interferes with efficient performance. *Mistakes* are occasional errors that occur in almost anyone's performance, whereas *flaws* are systematic errors that develop because of a problem in the performance blueprint. Mistakes are the occasional bad throws, catches, or kicks that happen even in the best learned, highly automated skills because the athlete lacks concentration or motivation to perform the skill. Flaws, on the other hand, are systematic "glitches" in the performance blueprint causing repeated errors. To eliminate flaws, the glitch must be totally erased from the blueprint and replaced with the correct program through practice. Mistakes simply require more concentration or motivation to execute an already well-learned skill.

When a mistake is made, the Analyzer should recognize that more concentration is needed and turn the job over to the Integrator, but all too often the powerful Analyzer tends to say, "I performed poorly. I have a problem, but I can correct it." The Analyzer treats the mistake as if it were a flaw, and begins changing the blueprint when it should have left it alone. This, I suspect, is a major cause of "slumps."

A baseball player, for example, has one of those games where his mind is elsewhere. The poor concentration leads to poor hitting, and the Analyzer jumps in, changing the blueprint by altering his stance or the position of the bat. Now the player has to relearn the hitting skill because of these changes, which lower his batting average even further until he learns the new skill.

Stress and Analyzer-Integrator Teamwork

Timothy Gallwey, in his innovative *Inner Game* books (e.g., Gallwey, 1974), introduced the concepts of Self 1 and Self 2, which have considerable similarity to the Analyzer and Integrator respectively. Self 1 is the voice in your head doing all the talking, worrying, judging, and self-doubting, says Gallwey, and Self 2 is the body that performs the action. The "inner game" is to quiet Self 1 and trust Self 2 to perform the whole skill. Gallwey also observes that children learn skills so much easier than adults because their Self 1 has not had a chance to become so powerful. It is Self 1, the Analyzer, that is the source of negative self-talk and worry and must be quieted for athletes to perform in the optimal energy zone.

What is even more unfortunate is that when athletes are stressed, the Analyzer is even more domineering. Thus, when athletes enter competition and want the Integrator to control performance, the stress of the competition increases the likelihood that the Analyzer will take command. The Analyzer, being the self-critical, judgmental self that it is, only causes the athlete to experience more stress, which further interferes with performance by making it more difficult for the Integrator to gain control. Flow, of course, is nowhere to be found. Branch Rickey, the great baseball coach, recognized the problem when he observed, "A full mind is an empty bat." Only by learning to control stress (our mission in this chapter), and by developing a stronger Integrator (the mission of chapter 6, "Imagery Skills"), is it likely that performance can be improved.

SELECTING A STRESS MANAGEMENT TECHNIQUE

Stress can be managed many different ways. Some of the popular fads among athletes these days are the use of massage, listening to special music tapes, and lying in tanks of warm water, all of which can be effective. Athletes have used hypnosis, yoga, autogenic training, visualization, and transcendental meditation for managing stress as well. Sport psychologists use such techniques as progressive muscle relaxation, systematic desensitization, biofeedback, stress inoculation, sybervision, implosive therapy, and covert modeling. Which of these techniques are best for helping your athletes manage stress? Which techniques can you teach them? Which techniques are better for different types of stress? In this section, you will learn the answers to these questions.

As you study this section and the remaining sections of this chapter, keep in mind that the techniques described here have been selected for use with athletes who are not suffering from severe stress to the point where they are dysfunctional. The techniques presented are especially useful for "normal" athletes who wish to improve on their present stress management skills for coping more successfully with pressure in competitive sports. Athletes who show signs of profound stress, depression, and such physical ailments as ulcers and headaches, which are commonly associated with stress, should be referred to a mental health specialist. The techniques presented here are not dangerous to use. Instead, they are valuable psychological skills from which anyone can benefit.

It is my strong recommendation that you study these techniques and learn them yourself first. Then you will be comfortable teaching them to your athletes—and you will be a better and happier coach!

How Well Do You Recognize Stress?

To help your athletes manage stress, you should be skillful in recognizing the symptoms of stress. You can review some of the common symptoms in Table 8.1 (p. 112). How skillful are you?

A few years ago my students and I investigated this question with high school basketball and volleyball coaches. Toward the end of the season, when the coaches knew the players well, we asked them two days before a game to predict each player's state anxiety as they thought it would be moments before the game. Then we measured the players' state anxiety just before the game using a special scale validated for this purpose. The results indicated that, collectively, the coaches were very poor in predicting the players' state anxiety, although a few were excellent. From our follow-up analysis, those coaches who were excellent were high in empathy. This is one reason why in previous chapters I have emphasized the importance of this quality.

By the way, we also asked the athletes to predict the coaches' state anxiety, and then we measured the coaches' state anxiety moments before the game began. Much to our surprise the athletes in general were much better at predicting the coaches' state anxiety than the coaches were in predicting the players' anxiety.

If you suspect that you are not skillful at judging your players' stress symptoms, you have taken the most important step. You recognize the problem and the need to become more skillful. Now work on developing greater empathy, and by thorough study of this book and the *Study Guide* you should be better at detecting the symptoms of stress.

Three Ways to Manage Stress

All stress management techniques use at least one of three approaches to reducing stress. You can see, by looking at Figure 8.1, that only three things can be changed: the environment, the arousal level, and the negative thoughts. In the next section, you will learn what you can do to become a behavioral engineer and change the environment to decrease stress. Then in the following section, you will learn how to decrease stress by lowering physical arousal through various body relaxation techniques—*somatic* (body) *stress management* procedures. The next section will discuss *cognitive stress management*, or how to reduce or eliminate negative thoughts and worry. Before you study these techniques, however, it will be helpful to consider which of these methods is best for which type of stress.

Obviously, changing the environment, to the extent this can be done, will help any type of stress. So the biggest decision you will need to make is whether to use a somatic technique or a cognitive technique for the athlete you are helping. If stress occurs by Stress Formula 1 ($E \rightarrow A \rightarrow NT = S$), then somatic techniques are thought to be better. If the stress occurs by Stress Formula 2 ($E \rightarrow NT \rightarrow A = S$), then cognitive techniques are considered better. You can see this by looking at Figure 8.3, which shows the two stress formulas, and the point where intervention by the stress management technique takes place.

In Stress Formula 1, arousal occurs first because these arousal responses become conditioned to, or linked with, the environmental stimulus through repeated occurrences. Thus, before any negative thoughts occur, arousal increases and the athlete searches for explanations. If these explanations take the form of negative thoughts, then the athlete feels stressed. When stress occurs by this formula, somatic techniques are thought to be more effective. All these techniques, in one way or another, teach the athlete to relax physically so that when they are in the presence of the event that initially produces the increased arousal, they can substitute the relaxation response. Relaxation is the opposite response to high physical arousal, so the athlete is deconditioning him- or herself to the environmental stimulus → arousal link.

In Stress Formula 2, the negative thoughts precede the increase in arousal. Thus it is more effective to reduce the stress by stopping the negative thoughts before they increase arousal. While somatic techniques are helpful to those experiencing stress by Formula 1, and cognitive techniques are helpful to those experiencing stress by Formula 2, neither procedure is as effective as selecting the techniques that attack the stress earliest in its development and most directly.

Because Stress Formula 1 occurs far less frequently in sport, the use of somatic techniques alone is seldom appropriate. Yet many coaches and well-intentioned sport psychologists teach athletes only physical relaxation techniques. When stress is caused by Stress Formula 2, and most often it is in sports, then somatic techniques alone attack the stress only indirectly and are far less likely to be

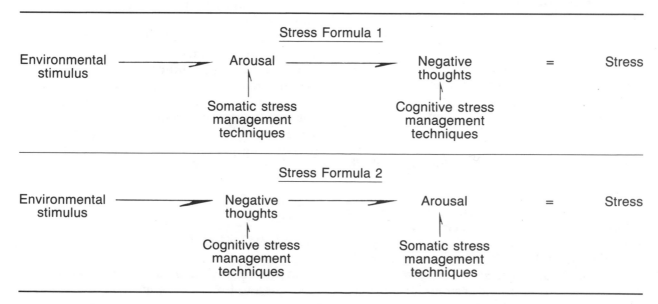

Figure 8.3 The use of somatic and cognitive stress management techniques in Stress Formulas 1 and 2.

effective. This is why so many athletes have been turned off by the sole use of simple relaxation techniques. They quickly recognize that it is one thing to learn to relax using these techniques in a quiet room, and it is quite another to apply them when competing in highly important competitions. When stress is caused by Stress Formula 2, athletes intuitively know they need assistance in quelling those insidious negative thoughts. From my observations, in highly competitive situations the powerful Analyzer takes over and worry is so pervasive that somatic techniques often do not even come to mind.

ENVIRONMENTAL ENGINEERING

What aspects of the environment increase the likelihood of athletes experiencing stress, and what can you do to change both the physical and the social environments? The answer to these questions comes by reconsidering the cause of stress. Stress occurs when athletes are *uncertain* that they will be able to do what is expected of them and when the outcome is *important* to them. Thus the two elements that you can engineer in the environment are to reduce *uncertainty* and decrease *importance.*

Reducing Uncertainty

In Table 8.2, in the left-hand column, is a list of events that can increase uncertainty and over which you may have some control. In the right-hand column is a recommendation about how you may decrease the uncertainty. The list is only illustrative, intended to stimulate your thinking. If you will think in terms of what exists in the athletes' environment that may cause uncertainty and what you might do to alleviate it, then you will be effective in engineering the environment.

Some uncertainty, of course, is inherent in sport. Generally it is the uncertainty about the outcome of the competition that makes sport challenging and fun. You cannot, and should not, remove this uncertainty—athletes need to learn to develop sufficient psychological skills

to cope with it. It is the unnecessary uncertainty, which adversely affects certain athletes, that you want to eliminate.

Reducing Importance

The other cause of stress is the importance the athlete assigns to the outcome of the event. The outcomes a person values may be intrinsic or extrinsic, as you learned earlier. The intrinsic rewards are not directly available to you to engineer, but the extrinsic rewards of an event—such as money, trophies, praise, getting to play more or practice less, advancing to a higher level of competition—are within your control. Table 8.3 is an incomplete list of what makes events more important and what you may be able to do to decrease that importance for those athletes who are experiencing inordinate stress.

An important aspect of environmental engineering is trying to change the reactions of those people who are important to the athlete in terms of the social support they provide. For example, a parent orientation program to educate parents about their child's participation, particularly about the importance of winning, may be very useful in reducing an athlete's stress. You may be able to convince parents not to emphasize winning to their son or daughter.

Many environmental events that can potentially increase uncertainty and importance are not easily or realistically within your power to change. Thus this approach to stress management is limited. But it is especially useful, as the above examples illustrate, when you, as coach, are responsible for increasing uncertainty or importance. Remember, then, when you identify an athlete who is experiencing substantial stress: First ask what can be changed in the environment to reduce the uncertainty or the importance of the outcome. When these changes have been made, you are ready to proceed to the next step.

SOMATIC STRESS MANAGEMENT

The procedures introduced in this section are intended to help reduce arousal or tension in

Table 8.2
Reducing Uncertainty in Athletes' Environments

Source of Uncertainty	Action to Reduce Uncertainty
1. Waiting to announce the starting line-up until only moments before the game.	Let athletes know well in advance of game time whether or not they will be playing.
2. Not letting athletes know their status on the team in terms of their permanence or the role you perceive for them.	Let athletes know what contributions you think they can make, what strengths they have, and what weaknesses they need to improve upon.
3. Sending vague, nonverbal messages that are generally interpreted negatively, but that leave the cause of your disapproval unclear.	Send clear messages, using good confrontation skills, if you have an expectation of the athlete that differs from the behavior he or she demonstrates.
4. Telling athletes one thing and then doing another, or telling them one thing today and doing another tomorrow.	Be consistent in what you say and do. This does not mean to behave exactly the same way toward each athlete, but instead behave consistently in similar situations and behave in a manner consistent with your philosophy.
5. Creating uncertainty among the athletes about their physical well-being because of hazards on the playing field or poor equipment.	Remove the hazards and obtain better equipment, of course. But also discuss with the athletes the objective risks of physical injury in the sport and what you can do to minimize the chance of injury—training, safety precautions, equipment, skill improvement, observation of rules, avoiding mismatching athletes of different sizes and skill levels. Avoid using injury as a threat to athletes in hopes of motivating them.
6. Humiliating endurance athletes, who often are quite uncertain about their abilities to endure the pain of completing a race, when they drop out.	Avoid using humiliation and help athletes develop their skills to manage both their physical and psychological energy, thereby reducing their chances of dropping out.
7. Coach, players, or spectators threatening an athlete's self-worth with negative evaluations or comments.	Take any action within your control to avoid threatening an athlete's self-worth.

the body. If the tension is reduced, then the mind has no reason to search for an explanation of why the body is energized. Among athletes, the most common somatic complaint is that they cannot relax, their muscles are tense, and thus it is difficult to make the skillful movements needed to perform well. Almost everyone has experienced unwanted muscle tension, causing even simple movements to be awkwardly executed. As a coach, you may also have experienced this type of tension in your vocal cords when you were called upon to deliver a speech.

Other somatic symptoms of stress certainly exist as listed in columns A and C of Table 8.1. Fortunately, the methods that reduce muscle tension also help relieve these symptoms as well. Thus, in this section and in the *Study Guide*, various methods of relaxation will be reviewed, giving you enough information so that you can teach them to your athletes.

When you introduce somatic techniques to athletes, begin by asking them if they have any techniques of their own that work. If they are happy with a technique, build on it by having them practice it more systematically and incorporating it into the complete Psychological Skills Training program. As with most psychological skills, believing that the procedure works is an important prerequisite to it working.

Rule 1, then, is, if it works for an athlete, use it as long as it is safe. If athletes are interested in alternatives, then teach them several tech-

Table 8.3
Reducing Importance in Athletes' Environments

Source of Importance	Action to Reduce Importance
1. Parents offering their children financial rewards for winning or for achieving certain performance levels (e.g., hitting a home run).	Ask parents to discontinue the practice, explaining that you think it may be stressful for the athlete.
2. The presence of important others, be they parents or friends, making the outcome more important.	Ask those spectators who come to practice or games who are important to the athlete not to attend until the player has improved his or her skills and acquired greater confidence. Be sure to explain why you are making this request.
3. Initiating a scheme for recognizing outstanding play, causing some of the athletes to press too hard because they value the recognition.	Eliminate the recognition scheme or discuss with athletes how to keep the recognition in its proper perspective.
4. Certain athletes seeking your approval because it is important to them and because they fear losing your approval if they play poorly.	Explain to these athletes that you value them as people, not just as players who perform well. Then act consistently with this belief.
5. The league wanting to initiate an all-star team to identify those athletes who are superior in ability, thereby increasing the importance of playing well for some athletes and placing added pressure on them.	Encourage the league not to initiate an all-star team.
6. The parents or booster club wanting to develop all types of awards and recognition—such as most improved player, best offensive player, best defensive player, best sportsperson—thus increasing the importance of the games to the players.	Discourage parents and the boosters from offering these types of recognition, explaining why.

niques, emphasizing that they should choose the one that suits them. The simplest method should be taught first, then more advanced techniques can be added. Letting them know there are a variety of methods, none that work for everyone, will reduce the likelihood of their trying a technique unsuccessfully and feeling they are failures or concluding that PST is just so much hot air. Instead, it is a matter of finding the right technique for them.

Four somatic stress management procedures are explained next. The simplest is introduced first and the others follow as they become progressively more complex. Almost all athletes find one of these to be effective, with approximately 90 percent finding one of the first two procedures beneficial. The techniques reviewed include the following:

- Imagery Relaxation
- Self-Directed Relaxation
- Progressive Relaxation Training
- Biofeedback Relaxation

Imagery Relaxation

This procedure involves athletes imagining themselves in some environment or place where they always feel very relaxed and comfortable. For example, they may be lying on the beach under the warm sun as cool breezes blow intermittently and ocean waves create a rhythmical, pulsing beat. Or they may be strolling through the woods, or sitting before a warm fire in a remote cabin, or . . . you get the idea. What is important is that they imagine a place with which they have learned to associate feelings of relaxation.

The premise behind this technique is this: If you can't change the actual environment, change the environment in the person's mind. The ability to do this is one of the magnificent things about our minds; yet it is used so rarely.

The initial steps for preparing to do Imagery Relaxation are those for doing any imagery exercise:

- Select a setting that is quiet and comfortable.
- The athlete should be alert and not overly excited about some recent event. When athletes are either fatigued or over-energized, the atmosphere is not conducive to learning relaxation skills. Eventually, when the skill is mastered, it can be used to relax the overly tense person.
- Create the right attitude about learning this skill. Some athletes find PST so foreign to their thinking that they fail to take it seriously. Others develop unrealistic expectations, believing that a few minutes should produce some magical change in their psyche. Dispel both myths by establishing a relaxed, but serious, environment for practicing.
- Have all athletes find comfortable positions, preferably lying on the floor, arms to the side, feet uncrossed, and eyes closed.

Now ask the athletes to think of their favorite places for relaxing—someplace where they always feel comfortable and safe. Give them a few moments to do this. Now instruct them to become as relaxed as possible, inhaling deeply and exhaling slowly. Ask them to let go of any tension in their muscles, inhaling deeply, exhaling slowly. Now have them visualize themselves in this place. Instruct them to picture themselves there as vividly as they can—not only picture, but "feel" themselves there—hear the sounds, smell the air, feel the sand, or whatever. Urge them to notice the relaxation, to bring on the feeling of deep relaxation.

The better they can put themselves in this place through imagery, the more relaxing it will be. The athletes should regularly practice imaging this place without your guidance, until they can create the place in their mind's eye quickly and feel the associated relaxation. Then they should practice using the technique in their daily lives, whenever they are confronted with stressors, and where there is an opportunity to retreat in their mind to their special place. Initially they should use this technique with minor stressful events, and then gradually use it with increasingly stressful events, both in sport and in their nonsport life.

My relaxation place is a "camp" located on Hancock Point, Maine, where I am writing this book. As I glance up, I see Mount Desert Island, Frenchman's Bay, the loons and sea gulls, and two lobster boats. It's beautiful and peaceful; it's my place where I come to relax—and work, too. When I feel muscle tension and other somatic stress symptoms, I come to "my place" through imagery for a quick relaxation. It works well for me, and so I use it. Many athletes to whom I have taught this simple procedure also subscribe to the method.

Jackie Stewart, former world champion auto racer, used imagery to relax in a slightly different and novel way. He would sit in the car moments before the race and imagine his body inflating like a balloon. Then he would let the air out and feel himself relax. This, he contended, helped him prepare physically and mentally for the race.

The keys to using Imagery Relaxation successfully are these:

- To have a place clearly in mind with which one strongly associates feelings of relaxation.
- To have reasonably good imagery skills so the place can be seen vividly in the mind's eye.
- To practice the technique initially in nonstressful situations, and then gradually use it in increasingly stressful situations.

Self-Directed Relaxation

This procedure, an abbreviated form of Progressive Relaxation Training, is easy to use as well. Initially you guide your athletes through relaxation of the body's muscle groups while emphasizing slow, easy breathing and visualization of the tension flowing out of the body.

After a few practice sessions under your guidance, the athletes are asked to practice the relaxation on their own. If they have difficulty doing the procedure without your guidance, you may want to tape a session in which you provide these instructions or give them a script, such as the one that follows from which they can make their own tape.

The objective of Self-Directed Relaxation is to be able to reduce gradually the time needed to achieve complete relaxation of the entire body. While initially it may take athletes ten minutes to go through these instructions, with practice, greater and greater relaxation should be achieved in less and less time. The athletes should require fewer self-instructions to relax each muscle group, and the muscle groups should be combined, so that eventually only a few seconds are needed to achieve full body relaxation.

An example of Self-Directed Relaxation as I would do a session with athletes is included on the next page. First have the athletes prepare for the session by following the same four steps listed for Imagery Relaxation. As you read this, and use these instructions with your athletes, speak the words slowly and softly, pausing where appropriate. Try to be as unobtrusive in giving the instructions as possible, helping the athletes focus on the muscles and on the feeling of relaxation.

A Final Comment

This technique is especially effective when athletes are able to keep their attention focused on the muscle groups and can turn off the tension when directed to do so. Many athletes, because they are quite aware of tension and relaxation in their bodies, are readily able to do this when directed to do so. However, when athletes constantly find themselves distracted (although improving their concentration may be helpful), they are better candidates for the more active Progressive Relaxation Training procedure described next.

Some athletes find it useful to combine Imagery Relaxation with Self-Directed Relaxation. For example, one athlete visualizes a little man with a broom sweeping away the tension in the appropriate muscle group. Another visualizes tension as autumn leaves and each breath, like a strong autumn wind, causes the tension to fall off the muscles.

Progressive Relaxation Training (PRT)

Progressive Relaxation Training (Jacobsen, 1932) is a much more elaborate, and therefore much more time-consuming, procedure for learning to relax. Because the procedures for using this technique are extensive, I will describe only the basics here. You can learn how to implement PRT from the complete description in the *Study Guide*.

PRT, developed by Edmund Jacobsen in the 1930s and considerably modified over the years, is a skill for learning to feel tension in the muscles and then learning to "let go" of this tension. You can appreciate the basics by trying it.

With your dominant arm, contract your forearm and hand up toward your dominant shoulder, developing as much tension in the biceps and forearm as you possibly can. Hold this tension for about five seconds, and concentrate fully on what that tension feels like. Now bring your forearm down and quickly and completely relax the muscles. Keep your attention focused sharply on what the relaxation feels like. Now try to relax your arm even more, letting all of the tension go. Do you feel the tension leaving your muscles? Feels good, doesn't it?

Were you able to achieve "deep" relaxation when you let the tension go? Probably not, unless you have practiced PRT. You can learn to achieve even deeper relaxation not only by returning the muscle to the pretensed state, but by asking it to relax even more.

Try it this way. Imagine that the tension in the muscle is like the speedometer in your car. Maximum tension is 100; complete relaxation is 0. Now tense the arm, slowly bringing it to 50, then 75, and finally 100. Focus on the tension as you hold it for five seconds. Now release the tension quickly, trying to drop to 0 as quickly as you can. Is the muscle now fully relaxed? Or is it perhaps still idling at 20 or so? Can you let the rest of the tension go? Can you shut off the engine completely? When you can, that is deep relaxation.

PRT is based on this principle of neuromuscular relaxation. The athlete is initially taught how to tense and deeply relax sixteen different muscle groups. With practice, the athlete then learns to combine the muscle groups, first into seven groups, then four, and

Self-Directed Relaxation Script

Take a deep breath and slowly exhale. Think "relax" (pause). Inhale deeply . . . exhale slowly . . . inhale deeply . . . exhale slowly. Now focus all your attention on your head. Feel any tension in your forehead. Just relax the tension in your forehead. Relax . . . (pause). Relax even deeper . . . and deeper . . . and deeper.

Feel any tension in your jaw or other facial muscles. Just relax the tension in these muscles. Feel the tension flow away.

Inhale deeply . . . exhale slowly. Feel the relaxation in your facial muscles. Relax . . . (pause). Inhale deeply . . . exhale slowly (pause). Relax even deeper . . . and deeper . . . and deeper.

Now feel any tension in your arms, fore-arms, and hands. Just relax the muscles in your arms. Relax . . . (pause).

Feel any tension in your hands, fingers, or arms, and just relax the tension in these muscles. See the tension flow out your body.

Inhale deeply . . . exhale slowly. Feel the relaxation in your arms and hands. Relax . . . (pause). Inhale deeply . . . exhale slowly (pause). Relax even deeper . . . and deeper . . . and deeper.

Now focus your attention on your neck and upper back. Feel any tension in the muscles of your neck and upper back. Just relax the tension in these muscles. Relax . . . (pause).

See the tension flow out of your body. Inhale deeply . . . exhale slowly. Feel the relaxation in these muscles. Relax . . . (pause). Inhale deeply . . . exhale slowly (pause). Relax even deeper . . . and deeper . . . and deeper.

Remember to keep your facial muscles relaxed. Keep your arms and hand muscles relaxed. And keep your neck and upper back muscles relaxed. Keep all these muscles relaxed. Inhale deeply . . . exhale slowly. Feel the relaxation in all these muscles. Feel the relaxation even deeper . . . and deeper . . . and deeper.

Now feel any tension in your lower back and stomach muscles. Focus all your attention on these muscles and ask them to relax. Relax these muscles fully. Feel the tension flow away.

Inhale deeply . . . exhale slowly. Feel the relaxation in your lower back and stomach muscles. Relax . . . (pause). Inhale deeply . . . exhale slowly (pause). Relax even deeper . . . and deeper . . . and deeper.

Now feel any tension in your upper legs, both the front and back. Focus all your attention on these muscles and ask them to relax. Relax these muscles fully. Feel the tension flow away.

Inhale deeply . . . exhale slowly. Feel the relaxation in your upper legs. Relax . . . (pause). Inhale deeply . . . exhale slowly (pause). Relax even deeper . . . and deeper . . . and deeper.

Remember to keep your facial muscles relaxed. Keep your lower back and stomach muscles relaxed. And keep your upper leg muscles relaxed. Keep all these muscles relaxed. Inhale deeply . . . exhale slowly. Feel the relaxation in all these muscles. Feel the relaxation even deeper . . . and deeper . . . and deeper.

Now feel any tension in your lower legs and your feet. Focus all your attention on these muscles and ask them to relax. Relax these muscles fully. Feel the tension flow away.

Inhale deeply . . . exhale slowly. Feel the relaxation in your lower legs and feet. Relax . . . (pause). Inhale deeply . . . exhale slowly (pause). Relax even deeper . . . and deeper . . . and deeper.

Now relax your entire body. Relax it completely. Feel all the tension flow away from your facial muscles . . . your arms and hands . . . your neck and upper back . . . your lower back and stomach . . . your upper legs . . . and your lower legs and feet.

Inhale deeply . . . exhale slowly. Feel the relaxation in all your body. Relax . . . (pause). Inhale deeply . . . exhale slowly (pause). Relax even deeper . . . and deeper . . . and deeper.

finally the entire body at one time. (I find that most athletes can start with the seven muscle groups, therefore learning the procedure more quickly.) The objective with PRT, as with Self-Directed Relaxation, is to be able to achieve complete relaxation in a few seconds. Typically it takes four to six weeks to learn PRT when practicing three to four times per week.

PRT is helpful for athletes who have trouble achieving the right level of tension in specific muscle groups, for example, in letting the hamstrings relax sufficiently when sprinting. However, when athletes are unable to identify specific muscle groups that are too tense, PRT won't do the job. Then biofeedback becomes useful.

With the information in the *Study Guide*, you can learn to be a very effective instructor of PRT. Also, there are several useful audiotapes for providing PRT instructions; a few are listed in the *Study Guide*. Research has shown, however, that PRT is more effectively taught by a live instructor than from a tape. Furthermore, if you teach PRT, it shows your athletes that you believe in the program and are committed to it.

Biofeedback Relaxation

When athletes have not developed sufficient self-awareness to monitor the tension in their own bodies, providing supplementary feedback can help them develop such self-awareness. Biofeedback is used to accomplish this. The person's own biological responses are fed back to the athlete in one form or another. In the last chapter you read how heart rate was fed back to elite shooters to help them improve their performances. Now we will consider how other types of feedback can help athletes relax.

Three types of biofeedback are useful for learning to manage muscle tension—skin temperature, electrical activity of the skin surface, and electrical activity in the muscles. Skin temperature is useful for indicating a general level of tension in the body: It increases when more blood flows to the skin, which occurs when the muscles are relaxed, and decreases as the muscles tense up because less blood flows to the skin. This explains why people's hands become cold when they are stressed.

Many different methods are used to measure the electrical activity of the skin, but the most common is called galvanic skin response, or GSR. When the body is more tense the sweat glands are more active in order to dissipate the heat generated by the tensed muscles. Now you know why people get not only cold hands, but clammy hands as well when they are under stress. When there is

moisture on the skin, electricity flows from one point to another more readily. GSR is simply a method of measuring the ease with which a minute electrical current flows between two points on the skin.

A simple GSR device is shown in Figure 8.4. A person places two fingers on the metal bands, and the ease with which electricity flows between them is measured. This information is fed back auditorially or visually to the athlete. Without a great deal of practice, athletes can learn to increase or decrease the sweating on their skin by learning to relax or tense the muscles.

Figure 8.4 A simple galvanic skin response (GSR) device.

The third type of biofeedback measures the minute electrical activity in the muscles, which can be detected on the skin surface with an electromyograph instrument as shown in Figure 8.5. This information can then be fed back to the athlete who can practice reducing excessive muscle tension. Electromyography or EMG, is especially useful when athletes have *specific* muscle groups that they have difficulty relaxing properly when executing a skill. Skin temperature and GSR are better for helping athletes deal with *global* muscular tension in the body.

This may all sound too complicated and time-consuming for you to bother with, but it's not. If you really want to be a "professional" coach, isn't it worth as much energy on your part to help athletes maintain their psychic energy at optimal levels—at least, as impor-

Figure 8.5 An electromyograph (EMG) used in biofeedback.

tant as having their bodies trained so that their physical energy is optimal? Furthermore, it is a lot easier than you think.

Biofeedback is like teaching sports skills. You identify the skill to be learned (general relaxation or relaxation of specific muscle groups). Then you explain the basics of how to do the skill (explain what the specific type of biofeedback does). And then you practice. I teach biofeedback by first bringing athletes to a quiet room where I explain the equipment and how they can use it. Then I demonstrate the equipment by showing them how I can change my skin temperature or GSR by simply "willing" it with my mind. Next I attach them to the EMG because it is easier for athletes to learn to increase and decrease the tension in a specific muscle group, even with minor voluntary tension.

Then it is time to go to work. If I am trying to help them combat general muscle tension that they have been unable to reduce using the other procedures, I will select either skin temperature or GSR and ask them to use the Imagery Relaxation procedure to try to change the reading to indicate greater relaxation. Then it is a matter of practice.

A more advanced technique I use is to ask athletes to imagine themselves experiencing stress moments before an important game while they receive skin temperature or GSR feedback. Usually this imagined stress produces moderate increases in muscle tension that they can observe or hear. Then I ask them to use any one of the three previously discussed relaxation procedures to try to reduce the tension.

The electronics revolution has made biofeedback equipment very portable and much less expensive. It is now built to be readily used by coaches and athletes. Autogenics, a company that specializes in making biofeedback equipment for sports, offers a kit that measures the three types of feedback discussed here as well as heart rate. The kit includes written and audiotape instructions on how to use the biofeedback equipment.

The portability of this equipment permits it to be used in practice and prior to competitive events. A small ring is also on the market (Future Health, Inc., Bensalem, PA, 19020) that measures skin temperature in one-degree increments and has useful application. I recall wearing the ring once at an important meeting where there was some serious conflict negotiation taking place. When I'm relaxed, my skin temperature (as opposed to core temperature) is about 91-92 degrees. When I looked at my ring as things were heating up in the meeting, my skin temperature was 78 degrees. So when people say someone is cool on the outside, but hot on the inside, it is true not only figuratively, but literally as well.

Other Relaxation Techniques

Several other popular techniques are used to achieve a reduction in somatic stress or induce relaxation. Meditation techniques, including zen meditation, hatha-yoga, and transcendental meditation, all are intended initially to quiet the mind. However, a common ingredient in all these forms of meditation is an emphasis on breathing control. These procedures have been found to be effective in diffusing global muscle tension.

Autogenic training is another relaxation procedure developed in the early 1900s by J.H. Schultz that is based on self-suggestions and imagery to create feelings of warmth, heaviness, and control in different body parts. This technique has had a strong following in Europe, but has been less popular in North America.

Hypnosis is another widely used relaxation technique that has been shrouded in a cloak of mysticism. Actually hypnosis involves simply focusing all of a person's attention on only one thought at a time—it is nothing more than that! It is a cooperative venture between the hypnotist and the person being hypnotized. A person cannot be hypnotized against his or her will as has been portrayed in movies.

When people cooperate fully with the verbal suggestions of a hypnotist, they may discover things about themselves and experience things of which they were previously unaware. This occurs because the hypnotist helps them focus intensely on something that they may not have been willing to focus on previously. The imagery techniques discussed in chapter 6 have been shown to produce exactly the same mental effects as hypnosis.

Hypnosis, when used to help individuals relax, has been found to be very effective, but I do not recommend its use generally because the athlete assigns the responsibility for becoming relaxed to the hypnotist, not to him- or herself. By using the techniques presented in this section, which are equally effective, athletes learn that they can produce the relaxation whenever they want to and that relaxation is something within their control.

Use any or all of these techniques and others not mentioned if they work and are not dangerous. The four techniques I have described have been widely studied, used, and found to be effective. Furthermore, they form a logical, progressive program of somatic stress reduction that moves from the simple to the more complex. Significantly, they are skills that increase athletes' control over their environments.

Using Relaxation Techniques

You will want to use somatic techniques when an athlete appears to experience stress via Stress Formula 1. Of course, the objective is to get rid of all the stress, but not all the muscle tension. As you learned in chapter 7, the right level of muscle tension is very useful for optimal performance. Simply to teach athletes a relaxation program by itself is useless and may be even a disservice. The objective is to combine the control of somatic responses with the control of negative cognitions in order that athletes can reach the optimal energy zone.

Relaxation techniques are useful, therefore, in two ways:

- They help to create a state of being in the athlete that is useful for *practice* of cog-

nitive stress management skills, as well as imagery, attention, and goal-setting skills. Research, for example, has clearly shown that imagery training is more effective when preceded by relaxation. And as noted above, relaxation occurs more readily when imagery skills are well developed.

- They can be used in conjunction with the cognitive stress management techniques. That is, in some cases, stress may best be managed by using both somatic and cognitive techniques.

COGNITIVE STRESS MANAGEMENT

What we *believe* determines our emotions and strongly influences our behaviors. Our beliefs come from how we interpret the events in our lives, and are revealed by the things we say to ourselves. Thus self-talk is very important and has become a much-studied topic by psychologists. As you have learned, it is the negative self-talk in reaction to an event that causes stress in Stress Formula 2 ($E \rightarrow NT \rightarrow A = S$). So now our objective is to find ways to change these destructive ways of thinking. This is no easy task.

Our purpose here is not to eliminate thinking. Remember, there are times when it is valuable for the Analyzer to function. However, when it *is* time to analyze, the analysis should be constructive. We want to be able to help athletes rid themselves of "stinkin' thinkin'," "dumb talk," and "the little twerp inside" as various writers have referred to negative self-talk. Negative thinking, the opponent within, is a much more formidable opponent than any individual or team will ever be.

Read the thoughts of one athlete observing another warming up before they compete:

Oh my, is she smooth. I don't play nearly so smoothly. She is so in control; she doesn't make a mistake. I can't see any weaknesses, and I have so many. I could get annihilated in this match. Oh, gosh, how am I ever going to get through this. Why did I ever take up this game!

Whether this athlete castigated herself aloud, mumbled under her breath, or just had these

So many self-help psychology books—sport psychology books too—have written about the destructive nature of negative thinking, and offer "positive thinking" as the logical alternative. These books feed a litany of, "If you think you can, you will. And if you think you can't, you won't." I'm all for positive thinking, and it will be advocated here too. But let's be realistic about positive thinking. We cannot be anything we want to be. There *are* limitations.

In the world today, there may be 1,000 gymnasts who are serious hopefuls to be the next all-around Olympic champion. Only one will reach this goal. Will it be the one who thinks the most positively about achieving this goal? I doubt it. It just isn't that simple. Thinking positively is a vague, overgeneralized remedy that lacks substance. Thinking realistically and constructively, and then working exceedingly hard to develop the physical and psychological skills needed to achieve the goal is more substantive. Such thinking will maximize the possibility of athletes reaching their goals. Still, there is no guarantee. Athletes should understand this. They also should understand that when they have given their best, they should feel satisfied with their accomplishment, regardless of whether they were first, fifth, or fifty-fifth.

In this section you will learn (a) how negative thoughts become automated and therefore difficult to detect, and (b) three procedures for changing negative thinking.

Awareness of Negative Self-Talk

You are sitting with a friend watching a basketball game, and as a player on the other team prepares to shoot a free throw the coach calls his guard over to the sideline. You can't hear what is being said, but the coach tells him something in a highly animated way. Your friend is angered by the coach's action, commenting: "He's always ridiculing his players and taking center stage during the game. I wish he'd leave the players alone." But you saw the situation differently; you were praising the coach for observing that the guard was not getting back on defense fast enough and that this was letting the other team fast break.

Your friend's response was negative; your response was positive. You both saw the same

fleeting thoughts without verbalizing them, it is this type of negative thinking that creates stress, impairs performance, and deprives an athlete of enjoying sports.

event, but you each interpreted, judged, and labeled it differently; and these thoughts created your emotions. Our unending flow of thoughts determines how each of us sees our world; some of these thoughts become highly automated. They represent a type of self-talk that can be rational and productive or irrational, negative, and very unproductive. The difference is often very subtle, occurring when we take a normal wish or desire for approval or success and turn it into a compulsive demand for others to approve of us or for things to be as we want them to be. Negative thoughts tend to be specific, discrete messages that often appear in shorthand and are almost always believed, no matter how irrational. They tend to occur spontaneously, just popping into our heads, and are hard, very hard, to turn off. These negative thoughts are learned through life's experiences, and fortunately can be changed.

People differ in their abilities to notice their own negative thoughts. When individuals become stressed, negative thoughts become less definable, more believable, and the focus of attention. An important step in athletes overcoming the stress produced by negative self-talk is learning to become aware of these thoughts.

Chronic negative self-talk often stems from frustration at trying to change situations or people—both being difficult or impossible to do. Another major source of negative thinking comes from difficulties in developing and maintaining a task-focused, problem-solving approach. Five general categories of negative thinking often interfere with athletes' abilities to perform well.

- Worry about performance, especially about how one is performing compared to others.

- The inability to make a decision because athletes keep turning alternative responses over in their minds.
- Becoming preoccupied with the physical symptoms associated with stress.
- Ruminating about possible consequences of performing poorly, including disapproval, punishment, loss of self-worth, and damage to future participation opportunities.
- Thoughts of inadequacy, which may include active self-criticism or self-blame.

It is impossible to eliminate negative thinking until an individual recognizes that it exists. While most of our self-talk is either innocuous or rational, negative thinking can be identified by looking for the thoughts that precede the feeling of stress. These negative thoughts, however, are often lightning fast because they are so automated.

You can help athletes detect their negative thoughts by having them keep a log of the type shown in Table 8.4. If athletes are aware of the situation and of the responses they made to it, then they can work out what their thoughts were that led to the negative emotion. In the *Study Guide* you will find a complete protocol for helping athletes monitor their negative thoughts and replace them with constructive thoughts.

Thought Stopping

When athletes recognize that they are engaging in unproductive negative thinking, then Thought Stopping can be an effective technique. Thought Stopping is just what it implies: When you catch yourself having negative thoughts, you "flag" yourself, internally

Table 8.4
A Sample Log for Identifying Negative Thoughts

Time	Emotion	Situation	Negative Thoughts
7:15	Anger	Roommate making noise	No respect for my privacy. This is awful . . . I need more sleep.
10:50	Stress	Preparing for an examination	Didn't study enough . . . I must pass or else . . .
2:30	Stress	Coach to announce the travel squad	He's got to pick me. It won't be fair otherwise.

yelling at yourself, "STOP!" You disrupt the stream of negative drive, and then replace it with constructive thinking. Thought Stopping doesn't work well *unless* you have prepared constructive thoughts to replace the destructive thoughts.

Does it sound too simple to work? It's not—when athletes receive assistance in increasing awareness of their own negative thinking. For example, I worked with a member of the U.S. Olympic Cross-Country Ski Team who would engage in a flood of negative thinking whenever he heard the sounds of another skier coming up behind him. (Cross-country ski races have staggered starts, so when someone comes up behind the skier, he or she knows that at least the amount of time of one start interval has been lost.)

"Oh, my. I'm down thirty seconds already. My skis must be slow. I missed the wax. I'm not feeling good today. Coach will be pissed," and on and on he would go. Once he recognized that these negative thoughts overwhelmed him and caused him to tighten up, then it was easier for him to use Thought Stopping. The steps I used with this athlete illustrate how you can use Thought Stopping.

1. Help the athlete identify the event that triggers the negative thoughts.
2. If necessary, help the athlete recognize that the negative thoughts are disruptive.
3. Identify a clear signal that the athlete can use to signal "stop" to the negative thinking. Yelling "STOP," snapping your fingers, or visualizing seeing a red flag waving in front of your face are some examples of such signals. Tell athletes to park the negative, distracting thought until later when they are ready to deal with it. Then be sure they deal with it later.
4. Help the athlete identify realistic, productive thoughts to substitute for the negative thoughts.
5. Practice Thought Stopping using imagery to re-create the event, first permitting the negative thoughts to develop, then stopping them with the signal, and finally substituting the productive thoughts.
6. Use the technique in competition.

This skier used the "red flag" as his signal for Thought Stopping. The productive thoughts were all related to focusing his attention on the technical aspects of his skiing—kicking, poling, and gliding correctly. He also was instructed to use Imagery Relaxation at the same time whenever he felt his body tensing.

Thought Stopping was successful for this skier because he was highly motivated to improve in the event in which the negative thoughts were triggered. However, several weeks of practicing the technique were required before he fully mastered it, and he always had to be on guard for the negative thoughts to rear their ugly heads.

Rational Thinking

Rational Thinking is a useful technique for when athletes are unable to "let go" of negative thoughts and replace them with constructive ones. In such instances the negative thoughts are firmly believed to be true, and thus must be disputed. Irrational thinking tends to take the form of the following examples.

- Good athletes perform flawlessly.
  I just made an error.
  I'm not a good athlete.
- All criticism is meant to hurt.
  My coach just criticized me.
  He was trying to hurt me.
- Winning is the ultimate goal in sport.
  I just lost.
  I'm a failure.

Take Vic, for example, who thinks, "I must win this race, or I'll be a total failure in the eyes of my friends." This irrational thought could be disputed by pointing out to Vic that while it would be great to win the race, losing it is not likely to make his friends think of him as a total failure. Furthermore, if his friends *were* to conclude that he is a total failure, they wouldn't be very good friends. And even if he lost his friends, life would still go on, and there are many other good people to befriend. Thus, while it would be *nice* to win, it would not be *awful* or horrible if he lost. Getting these points across often requires intense discussion and debate to convince athletes of the irrational nature of their thinking.

The techniques for identifying irrational thoughts and for disputing them so that a person learns to think more rationally have been lifted to an art and a science by Albert Ellis (Ellis & Grieger, 1977). The basic procedures developed by Ellis are described here, and exercises for practicing and using Rational Thinking are found in the *Study Guide*.

The five most common irrational beliefs that lead athletes to stress are:

- I *must* be loved or approved of by virtually every important person in my life, and if I'm not, it is awful.
- I *must* not make errors or do poorly, and if I do, it's terrible.
- You *should* blame people who act unfairly or unkindly and see them as bad or rotten.
- If something once influenced your life in the past, it *has to* keep determining your feelings and behavior today.
- People and events *should* always be the way I want them to be.

To combat these irrational beliefs, Ellis suggests changing the basic facts to conform to more rational statements such as:

- It's definitely nice to have people's love and approval, but even without it, I can still accept and enjoy myself.
- Doing things well is satisfying, but it's human to make mistakes.
- Even though I feel I was treated unfairly, it doesn't help me improve my performance to blame others. I have to be responsible for my own behavior.
- That may have been a bad experience in the past, but I can change things if I am willing to work hard.
- People are going to act the way they want, not the way I want.

The first step to dealing with irrational thinking is to detect those corrosive thoughts. As discussed earlier, this is often not easy, and requires you to assist your athletes in identifying such thinking. Irrational thinking can be identified more readily by looking for one of four basic types of thinking:

- Someone or something should, ought, or must be different from the way it really is.
- It is awful, terrible, or horrible when things aren't different.
- You can't stand, bear, or tolerate things that are not the way they should be.
- You blame yourself or others for acting in

a way you believe is wrong and conclude that this bad behavior deserves nothing but contempt and damnation.

Notice that at the root of these problems is the attempt to control situations or people when such control is not likely to be possible. The key to combating or disputing such thinking is recognizing that some things are beyond a person's control.

Ellis, after helping individuals recognize their irrational beliefs, shows them how to dispute these beliefs using a self-questioning process. The disputing is intended to rid the athlete of the irrational thoughts by discovering them to be just that, irrational, and replacing them with rational ones.

For example, have you ever gotten angry at an athlete for making a dumb play? (Your answer is "yes" so I can continue this example.)

Why did you get angry?

"I told him how to do this correctly ten times and he keeps making the same mistake."

But why does this make you angry?

"Because the kid must be stupid. He's uncoachable!"

But you still haven't told me why you are angry. You have only told me how you feel about the player.

"Well, it's frustrating to keep telling the kid over and over again."

So your anger is because *you* are frustrated?

"Yes, the kid *should* be able to learn the skill by now. I *ought* not to have to keep teaching the same thing over and over. The kid *must* get this right if we hope to win Friday."

In this example, you have stated the irrational beliefs that the player *should*, *ought*, and *must* do certain things. You insist, in your irrational thinking, that a situation (the player's action) must conform to your wishes, and that if it doesn't the consequences will be terrible or horrible. Yet these events are beyond your control, and thus you set yourself up for a great deal of stress.

In this example, you became angry because the player didn't learn the skill according to your timetable. You may normally expect athletes to learn the skill faster, but some do not. It may be frustrating to have to teach the skill over and over, but isn't this the patience that is essential for being a coach? And think how frustrating it must be to the player to keep getting it wrong. Also, it will be nice to win, but the world won't end if you lose the game. And who knows? Maybe with more patient instruction rather than anger, the player will learn the skill before game time.

Rational Thinking is a very helpful technique for identifying and changing negative thinking. However, you will need to become more familiar with it through the exercises in the *Study Guide*. I also recommend Albert Ellis and Robert A. Harper's *A New Guide to Rational Living* (1975) as an excellent source for you to learn how to dispute ten common irrational types of thinking.

Smart Talk

There are several other cognitive stress management techniques that have been used with athletes. Stress inoculation (Meichenbaum, 1977) is perhaps the best known of these techniques and received rave reviews when it was first introduced in the late 1970s. It is a technique that helps develop a *stress hierarchy*, consisting of ten to fifteen specific events that stress them to various degrees. These events are ranked from the least stressful to the most stressful, with the athletes then identifying the kinds of negative thoughts they have when experiencing each event. They are then asked to develop positive self-statements as substitutes for these negative statements and to study them thoroughly.

The athletes start with the least stressful event on the stress hierarchy by imaging it and attempting to feel some of the stress, both cognitive and somatic. Then they practice physical relaxation techniques as well as substituting the positive thoughts for the negative thoughts. They continue this step until they experience no stress by imaging this event. Then the athletes proceed to the next event on the stress hierarchy and repeat the procedure until none of the imagined events cause stress.

Several of my former students and I have used stress inoculation with athletes over the past several years, and quite frankly have not found it very successful. More recently, Damon Burton (1986, personal communication) has developed a program that appears to be more effective based on preliminary testing. This technique places greater emphasis on helping athletes detect dumb, negative, or irrational self-talk and replace it with smarter, constructive thoughts. Thus I have dubbed it the Smart Talk program.

This program incorporates some of the techniques of stress inoculation, Rational Thinking, and imagery and relaxation techniques, but places greater emphasis on "deprogramming" the athlete who is plagued with chronic, highly automated self-talk. Unlike stress inoculation, there is a period of time during which the athlete monitors his or her negative self-talk to create greater awareness of this negative thought pattern. Then positive self-talk, or "smart talk," is taught and practiced to reprogram the athletes. The full procedures and an exercise for using Smart Talk are presented in the *Study Guide*.

Use of Cognitive Stress Management Techniques

The techniques that have been presented in this section also progress from the simple to the more complex. If the negative thinking tends to be specific to a few situations, then Thought Stopping is a good place to begin. If the negative thinking is more pervasive, more generalized, and tends to become irrational, then use Rational Thinking or Smart Talk to help athletes manage their cognitive stress.

BURNOUT AMONG COACHES

Some of America's best known coaches have burned out—Dick Vermeil, Ara Parseghian, Jack Hartman, John Madden, Al McGuire, and Earl Weaver—as have untold numbers of lesser known coaches. The pressure of coaching, the constant expectation to win, the relentless public scrutiny, the long hours and myriad of details, the travel in some cases, and the variety of interpersonal relationships that must be maintained are all probable causes of burnout. And burnout is not an ailment confined to coaches in the highly visible sports; it affects coaches of both sexes, at all levels, and in most sports.

In 1986 Jack Hartman, Kansas State's veteran coach, resigned because the game had lost its fun. Oklahoma coach Billy Tubbs, commenting on Hartman's resignation, said, "The game's just not as much fun as it used to be, as it should be . . . You're a warden, you're a lawyer—hey, coaching is almost immaterial now."

Sonja Hogg, the women's basketball coach at Louisiana Tech for eleven years stepped down, saying, "It got to the point where I was on the road so much recruiting, I really felt like I was living out of a suitcase. I had no time for myself. I was tired of the hassles." And Hogg did not quit because she was a losing coach. Her teams won the NCAA National Championships in 1981 and 1982.

Jerry Tarkanian, the highly successful University of Nevada-Las Vegas basketball coach, says big-time college coaching can be reduced to one word: *pressure*. "It's like having a gun pointed at your head for four months."

Just how stressful can coaching be? Several studies have monitored coaches' heart rates, indicators of stress, before and during competition. In one study (Gazes, Sovell, & Dellastatious, 1969), football and basketball coaches had a resting heart rate average of 68 beats per minute, but during the contest had an average heart rate of 132 beats per minute. In another study among basketball coaches (Kolbenschlag, 1976), the average heart rate just prior to the game was 150, and one coach had an average heart rate of 166 throughout the contest, reaching a peak during one intense part of the game of 188. That's heavy cardiac output for individuals who are on the sidelines rather than playing the game.

But is it the pressure to win that causes stress? Walter Kroll (1982) studied ninety-three coaches to determine the things that stressed them most. The quite surprising results appear in Table 8.5.

Table 8.5
Factors Creating Stress Among Coaches

Category	Frequency
Disrespect from players	47.8%
Not being able to reach players	20.7%
Unappreciated by administrators	14.0%
Incorrect strategy	9.0%
Unappreciated by public	6.5%
Being outcoached	4.0%
Unappreciated by players	3.0%

The two most frequent causes of stress were problems with the players. Coaches quit most often because of poor player/coach relation-ships and the inability to motivate players. These reasons were given four times more frequently than any lack of technical expertise.

So it is not the pressure to win as much as it is the problem of interpersonal relationships with athletes that leads to burnout. These findings clearly signal the immense importance of coaches developing excellent leadership and communication skills to work with all types of athletes to build a motivated and cohesive team. Also, coaches who lack the psychological skills they should be teaching their athletes are more likely to experience stress, and over the long term are more likely to burn out.

Who Is Likely to Burn Out?

Stress and burnout are similar, but they are not the same. Burnout is when you feel fatigued or frustrated because your devotion to coaching and the relationships with the athletes and others involved have failed to produce the rewards you expected. While this feeling is certainly stressful, burnout occurs when coaches feel they have no "out," no buffers, and no support system.

When people burn out they feel physically, emotionally, and mentally exhausted. Burnout arises from a sense of distress and discontent, and a perception of failing to achieve the ideals or goals that the person has set for him- or herself. After repeated efforts to attain these goals, and after working as hard as possible without complete success, feelings of helplessness and hopelessness develop along with negative attitudes towards work, life, other people, and oneself.

Burnout is especially high in the helping professions—and as I mentioned before, coaching is a helping profession. People more susceptible to burnout are empathic, sensitive, humane, dedicated, and idealistic. They are people-oriented, and tend to base their own self-esteem too exclusively on attainment of their career goals, which may be unrealistic. They also tend to be anxious, introverted, and overenthusiastic.

As you would expect, and very characteristic of those in the coaching profession, burnout victims are "workaholics." They are type A persons—a personality profile of aggressiveness, competitiveness, intenseness, and especially rigidness. Type A people don't tolerate frustrations well, and are much more subject to the risk of heart attacks.

From research on burnout victims in the helping professions, a number of work-related conditions within coaching can be identified as potential causes of burnout. Long hours, public pressure to win, public misunderstanding of a coach's program objectives, and insufficient resources are common complaints. Other factors include the constant time pressure associated with getting ready for the next practice or the next game and administrative indifference or interference. As Kroll (1982) found, though, the most prominent cause is the failure to develop rewarding relationships between coaches and their players, with coaches feeling the players were disruptive and unmotivated to achieve the coach's goals of success.

Coaches who are rigid and inflexible in adjusting to changing times are especially susceptible to burnout. For example, poor player relationships and failure to motivate athletes may be due to a coaching philosophy—and the associated coaching objectives and coaching style—that is incompatible with the attitudes of the athletes being coached. Consequently, when coaches' expectations about these matters are not met, they question the integrity of the people being coached, the value of coaching as a profession, and even their own self-worth.

Do any of these personal qualities and work-related factors apply to you? Are you experiencing burnout now, or are you a candidate to burn out later? Evaluate yourself on the *Coaches' Burnout Scale* below. Answer the ten questions by thinking back over the last six months. Write the number to the left of the item that best describes how you feel according to the following scale.

Table 8.6
Coaches' Burnout Scale

1	2	3	4	5
No or very little		Somewhat		Yes, or very much

_____ 1. Are you becoming increasingly frustrated with coaching-related responsibilities?

_____ 2. Are you feeling there is more and more to do and you cannot see the end to it all?

_____ 3. Do you have less physical energy than usual?

_____ 4. Are you more easily annoyed by those people with whom you work and coach?

_____ 5. Are you experiencing thoughts about whether or not this is really the profession for you?

_____ 6. Are you experiencing less positive psychic energy and more negative psychic energy?

_____ 7. Do you feel increasing pressure to succeed?

_____ 8. Are you thinking more often that others misunderstand you and what you are trying to do as a coach?

_____ 9. Are you too busy to do even routine things such as make and return telephone calls, read magazines or books, maintain the house, and so on?

_____ 10. Do you feel that you don't have friends or family who you can talk to about your problems?

Now sum your score and place yourself on the scale below.

0-20 You are doing fine.
21-30 You should be alert to further changes.
31-40 You are a burnout candidate.
41-50 You have it. Take action now.

Remember the scale is only an approximation, intended to increase your self-awareness. If you are experiencing some of the symptoms of burnout, then consider the recommendations that follow.

Dealing With Burnout

Burnout begins slowly, something a coach has been working towards for weeks, months, or even years. When coaches are burned out, they tend to be cranky, critical, angry, and resistant to suggestions. In short, they are not very pleasant to be around.

Burnout doesn't get better, though, by ignoring it; it's not likely just to go away. Coaches should realize that burnout is not a disgrace; it is a problem born of good intentions. It develops among coaches who begin with great expectations, perhaps unrealistic expectations, and do not compromise along the way.

While coaching is a profession vulnerable to burnout, there are many aspects of coaching that decrease the likelihood of burnout, depending on how you approach your work. Burnout is less likely to occur when you feel you are learning and understanding more about the sport and coaching. This suggests it is important for you to become involved in coaching organizations and to continue to strive for greater understanding of this enormously challenging profession.

Burnout is less likely to occur when you find meaning and significance in your work. Because coaching offers infinite variety and challenge, it should not be hard to find meaning in what you do, if you will only look for it. Unquestionably, coaches need to feel a sense of achievement and success from coaching, but this need not be in the form of games won. Instead, success can be seen in the development of better human beings and experienced in bringing enjoyment to those who participate and observe the team.

Coaches are less likely to burn out when they experience flow in their work. When they are able to become totally absorbed in coaching, to feel in control, to lose their egos, they will find the fun in coaching. And coaches are unlikely to burn out when they see themselves moving toward their own potential and growing as a person.

Dealing with burnout begins when you first recognize the problem. You have heard this over and over in this book. The biggest single gift you can give yourself is *self-awareness*. Next, if burnout is something you recognize happening to yourself, you must decide to take responsibility for doing something about it. Then think through the following issues, and make the changes in your life that you deem appropriate.

- Reassess your goals and look at your philosophy of coaching and life. What do you really want? Are these reasonable, realistic goals for you? Is there a conflict between what you value in coaching and what society values? What is the best way for you to resolve that conflict so that it does not irritate you further?

- Develop and maintain a strong support group of friends and family. Research has shown that the best defense against burnout is having others with whom you are comfortable in sharing your problems. Look at your relationships and friendships. Have they deteriorated? Why? What are you bringing to the relationship? If you don't have the satisfying relationships you would like in your life, what can you do to improve them?

- Acknowledge time constraints and your humanness. Use time wisely to complete your work as efficiently as possible (see the *Time Management Course* in this series). But also take a day now and then for yourself. Delegate responsibilities when it is possible—and find ways to make it possible.

- Balance your life with some alternative activities. Have you let your social life deteriorate? Have you tried any new activities lately? Do you devote a reasonable amount of time to your family, or are you a stranger in your own house?

- Acknowledge your vulnerabilities. You are human, not a god. You cannot do everything, behave perfectly, be all knowing. You must shed the unrealistic expectations that others place upon you, and that you place upon yourself.

- Are you taking care of yourself physically? Are you a model of fitness for your athletes, or are you only a preacher of fitness? Improving your fitness can be a big step to increasing the vitality in your life. Apply the knowledge you have about physical conditioning to yourself, and don't let the excuse of "no time" deny you this.

- Apply the stress management skills that

you have learned in this chapter to your own stress. Work hard, play hard, but relax, too, and have fun.

In the event you feel your burnout has progressed to the point where you cannot make the changes by yourself or with the help of your support group, by all means do not hesitate to seek the help of a psychologist. Coaching is a great profession, and it is a tragedy when dedicated people get derailed because of their overcommitment and intensity. Burnout is preventable and correctable. Take the actions necessary for you to maintain good mental and physical health so that you can continue to practice the wonderful profession of coaching.

SUMMARY

1. Stress occurs when there is a substantial imbalance between what individuals perceive is being demanded of them and what they perceive their capabilities are, when they also perceive the outcome to be important.

2. It is not the environment per se, but a person's perception of the environment, that causes stress according to one of two stress formulas: $E \rightarrow A \rightarrow NT = S$ or $E \rightarrow NT \rightarrow A = S$.

3. The left hemisphere of our brain is the Analyzer, where worry takes place, and the right hemisphere is the Integrator, where components of a skill are integrated into complex wholes.

4. The Analyzer and Integrator work together smoothly when athletes are in flow, but when athletes are stressed, the Analyzer tends to dominate, hurting performance.

5. Stress can be reduced by three methods: environmental engineering, somatic stress management techniques, and cognitive stress management techniques.

6. Environmental engineering is effective for stress that arises from either Stress Formula 1 or 2. Somatic stress management techniques are preferred for stress arising from Formula 1 and cognitive stress management techniques are preferred for stress arising from Formula 2.

7. Environmental engineering involves reducing uncertainty and importance created by either the physical or social environment.

8. The four somatic stress management techniques recommended for use with athletes are (a) Imagery Relaxation, (b) Self-Directed Relaxation, (c) Progressive Relaxation Training, and (d) Biofeedback Relaxation.

9. The three cognitive stress management techniques presented in this chapter are (a) Thought Stopping, (b) Rational Thinking, and (c) Smart Talk.

10. Burnout occurs when coaches feel fatigued or frustrated because, despite their devotion to coaching, their work has failed to produce expected rewards, and they perceive that there is no "out" and no support system.

11. Burnout is generally caused by the accumulation of many specific factors. Avoiding burnout involves recognizing these factors and taking action appropriate to each. A list of suggestions for avoiding burnout was provided in this chapter.

Chapter 9
Attentional Skills

How much attention do you give to attention in your coaching? When you teach skills, do you consider the attention span of your athletes? Do you teach them what to attend to before the game, during the game, and after the game? Do you recognize mental errors as errors of attention?

And how do you help athletes with attentional problems? By demanding they attend? This may help a little, but demanding attention and nothing else is neglecting your coaching responsibilities. It assumes that athletes know how to attend but are choosing not to, which often is a false assumption.

Knowing what to pay attention to, how to shift attention as needed, and how to intensify one's attention, or concentration, are skills essential for performing optimally. Athletes can be taught these attentional skills, and the responsibility for doing so is yours. You also help your athletes attend better by using good principles of attention when coaching them. Thus the objectives of this chapter are (a) to provide you with information about how to teach attentional skills to your athletes, and (b) to provide you with information about attention that will improve your coaching.

And, by the way, how *are* your own attentional skills? Do you attend to all the right things during the contest? Are you able to keep your attention on the game—deciding the next play, making a tactical move, bringing in a substitute—in the face of a bad call, a serious error, or with time running out? Do you give attention to your athletes when they talk to you? In this chapter you will learn how to improve not only your athletes' attentional skills, but also your own. So pay attention!

IMPORTANCE OF ATTENTION

Attentional skills are another vital psychological skill for successful performance and enjoyment. Superior performance occurs when athletes are in the optimal energy zone, characterized by attention being directed totally at the process of performing the skill and nothing else. Csikzsentmihalyi (1975) states that flow occurs only when attention is focused totally on the relevant factors for executing the skill. Negative thoughts, as you have learned, and other forms of distraction hurt performance.

When attention is riveted on the activity and positive psychic energy is high, athletes sometimes report experiencing altered states of consciousness—time seems to slow down or stand still, movements appear in slow motion, and the athlete has a sense of omnipotence. When such intensification of attention, or concentration, is voluntary, it is a source of enjoyment. It is experiencing flow and it can occur in two ways. The most frequent way is when the task demands the athlete's attention, such as in high-risk sports where the mind seems to know that failing to attend can be a fatal error. The second way is when athletes control the attentional process so well that they can direct their psychic energy totally into the task.

Because most athletes have not actively sought to develop their attentional skills to this level, they seldom experience flow by skillfully directing themselves to this state. Instead, flow is more likely to occur by participating in tasks that demand athletes' attention such as rock climbing, sky diving, auto racing, hang gliding, and other similar high-risk sports.

But many other sports are also engrossing. So athletes should experience flow when playing these sports, too—and they do. However, as athletes practice and practice to improve physical skills, the skills become more and more automated. The more automated, the more easily the skill can be performed without fully attending, permitting distractions to occur and negative thoughts to develop. While athletes need to automate the skill, they must stay fascinated with the sport. The best way to retain this fascination is not to compete primarily to defeat others, but to discover one's own potential. Although seeking one's potential is an endless pursuit because it can never be known, the process of pursuing it is fascinating because it is challenging and self-actualizing.

ATTENTION DEFINED

Attention is the process that directs our awareness as information becomes available to the senses. It is through our senses that we receive information from our environment. At any moment, your senses are bombarded with stimuli from the environment. As you read this book, if you are paying attention, then you are not aware of other sensations. If you redirect your awareness from this book, you will notice other visual, auditory, olfactory, and kinesthetic stimuli. When you become aware of what your senses are experiencing, you perceive it. *Perception* then is the process of knowing objects and objective events. Perception occurs only when you attend to your senses as shown in Figure 9.1.

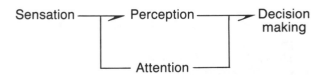

Figure 9.1 The role of attention in perceiving and decision making.

Once you have perceived the objects or objective events, then you must make a decision about whether or not you will continue to remain aware of them. The process of making this decision requires attention to what you are perceiving. Thus attention is a cognitive

process whereby a person directs and maintains awareness of stimuli detected by the senses. Attention is influenced by the person's level of alertness and capacity to process the incoming information.

Your senses are constantly exposed to countless stimuli in your environment, but if you do not attend to them, you do not perceive them. Therefore you do not experience them. What you experience, then, is limited entirely by where you direct your attention. Attentional mechanisms, therefore, exert ultimate control over your ability to manage psychic energy by regulating the stream of events that makes up your consciousness. If you can avoid attending to negative thoughts, you will not experience stress. If you can attend to all the relevant stimuli for the task you are performing, and not attend to any irrelevant stimuli, then you are more likely to perform optimally and experience flow.

We are a long way from understanding the attentional mechanisms in the brain completely and knowing how to control them fully, but we have learned much that is useful. In the next sections we will look at what we know about

- selecting the correct stimuli,
- shifting attention to the correct stimuli, and
- improving the intensity of attention, especially concentration.

SELECTIVITY OF ATTENTION

An essential attentional skill is the ability to select the correct stimuli or cues to which athletes should attend from countless irrelevant and competing stimuli. For a runner in football to be able to take the ball from the quarterback, watch the blocking develop, determine if the planned hole is open, see all the opposing tacklers, keep the ball protected, and make all the right maneuvers to "run to daylight" is an extraordinary feat in attention-selecting skills.

How do athletes learn to do this? Almost entirely by trial and error; it is through countless repetitions that the decisions are made by the much faster "supercomputer" right brain. But it takes years to program this supercomputer by trial and error. We can now shorten the time necessary to learn attentional skills because sport psychologists are learning how some of these complex attentional programs work. Although simple recipes do not exist, you can teach athletes some very useful basics, thereby reducing the time they need to learn.

Orienting Response

The attentional mechanisms that control what you attend to are much like the autonomic nervous system that controls your heart rate, blood pressure, respiration, and other physiological responses. If you do not direct your attention to the autonomic nervous system, it carries out its functions automatically. But as you learned in chapter 7, you can control these factors if you choose to, and if you direct your attention toward them.

If you put your attentional mechanisms into automatic mode, then the nervous system regulates what you will attend to according to certain rules. The mechanism that serves as a regulator is called the *orienting response*. Its basic rule is to let you know if there is anything unusual or different in your environment. It's a terrifically ingenious response for the survival of our species because it alerts you to potential danger. Without the orienting response, you would need to avoid danger by constantly scanning your senses to see what you should attend to. The orienting response particularly commands your attention when the following external events occur:

- The stimulus is very intense, such as sudden, loud noise or a flash of light.
- The stimulus is large or unusual in size.
- The stimulus is novel or is in contrast to the prevailing stimuli in the environment. For example, you have the television on while you're reading, but suddenly there is a long silence. You are likely to look up to see why the television isn't making its usual noise.
- The stimulus moves. Even slight movements detected in our peripheral vision are quick to attract our attention.

Although it is not true that advertisers discovered the orienting response principles, they certainly utilize them as well as anyone. But you also have learned most of these and use them to get your athletes' attention. You blow a whistle or shout to get your athletes' attention when you wish to give instructions. When you are talking and you observe an athlete not paying attention, you may pause a moment to capture his or her attention. The athlete's orienting response notices the silence, and he or she quickly comes to attention.

While the orienting response has helped our species survive and is very useful in sport, it also must be overridden at times. In the competitive environment, if attention is not directed to the specifics of the task, then the orienting response would keep the athlete constantly distracted by crowd noise, movements on the sidelines, and so on.

In addition to these external factors influencing what athletes attend to through the orienting response, three internal factors greatly influence attention. They are

- interest,
- mind set, and
- ability to screen out irrelevant stimuli.

Athletes' Interests

Your attention follows your interests. You hear a lecture on the mating habits of loons and it is unlikely to keep your attention unless you have an interest in mating, loons, or both.

As a coach you can capture the attention of your athletes by utilizing this principle. When giving instructions to your athletes, always explain *why* as well as how to do something. Explain why you are teaching them a certain skill so they know where it fits into the total game plan and how it will benefit them. Explain why they are performing certain physical conditioning exercises. Explain why a certain strategy will be used. Explaining why increases interest and thus improves attention.

An athlete's interest in sport is, of course, to play the sport. If your practices consist only of instruction, drills, and conditioning, you are likely to have problems keeping athletes' attention. Make the practices appeal to their interests—make them fun—and you will have their attention.

You can also enhance attention in practice by letting athletes select what skills they would like to practice. This gives them a feeling of responsibility and control, which, as you know, increases their motivation. The increased motivation directs attention to the source of the motivation—practice.

Mind Set

The second internal factor influencing attention is the athletes' mind set. Through experience, or from coaching, athletes can develop a mind set to be alert to certain cues in the environment or within themselves. The technique of Thought Stopping is based on developing a mind set. It is, in a sense, programming athletes' minds to detect negative thoughts and quickly stop them.

When a football coach instructs the linebacker to observe when the quarterback drops back, and then to drop back to the short middle zone to cover for a pass, the coach is developing a mind set. Mothers seem to develop mind sets that alert them, even when they are sleeping quite deeply, to their infants' crying.

Mind sets can be positive or negative. Athletes can learn to attend to appropriate stimuli in the environment and to positive internal thoughts, or they can develop mind sets that focus on distractions and on their own negative thoughts. Helping athletes develop constructive and positive mind sets is a very important task for you.

The Soviets have ingeniously applied the principle of mind set to helping athletes prepare for dealing with distractions and uncertainty. Most Soviet teams prepare for significant international competition by studying models, movies, and photos of the playing fields, training facilities, and living quarters of the competitive site. Then, through imagery routines and role-playing techniques, they place themselves in this environment and go through their practice and competitive routines. Thus, when they actually arrive at the site, nothing is new; it is *déjà vu*—they have been there before, at least in their minds.

When athletes have excellent knowledge of the correct cues to attend to, and what potential distractors to avoid attending to, they are able to anticipate events and therefore respond more quickly. Such anticipatory skills as reading the movements of the opponent or the flight of the ball are essential in highly skilled performances. For example, by watching a batter's feet, a defensive player has some idea where the ball is likely to be hit. By watching a player's eyes, the target of a pass in basketball can be anticipated.

Attending to the cues from the opponent or ball in order to make anticipatory responses has costs and benefits. For example, a batter increases his odds of hitting by anticipating what type of pitch will be thrown. Consequently, many players will go to the plate with a mind set of looking for a fastball. However, if a curve comes, the player is less likely to hit it when expecting a fastball than if no expectation had existed at all. Consequently, some hitters will anticipate a particular pitch for the first two strikes, and then not anticipate for the third strike.

Another cost/benefit factor to consider is that skilled athletes learn that their opponents are observing them for cues to guide their responses. Thus they may choose to deceive and to disguise such cues. A basketball player looks to the left and the defensive player moves to the left in anticipation of the pass; the offensive player then moves to the right.

If the sport you coach involves anticipation, do you teach your athletes what cues to look for and how to respond appropriately to the anticipated event? Have you thought about the cost/benefit ratio of making certain anticipatory responses? Excellent coaches analyze their sport to identify these cues and teach anticipatory responses.

Screeners Versus Nonscreeners

Individuals differ in their abilities to screen out various stimuli in their environment and can be either screeners or nonscreeners (Mehrabian, 1976). Screeners are less anxious, lower in empathy, and more selective in what they respond to than nonscreeners. They also tend to rank automatically the parts of a complex situation. Nonscreeners, on the other hand, are more anxious and higher in empathy. Their attention is often diffuse, and they have difficulty selecting the appropriate stimuli in their environments and shifting their attention in the right sequence from one stimulus to another. Nonscreeners are much more easily distracted and upset by events compared to screeners. Thus athletes who are nonscreeners will need more help in identifying what stimuli to select and the priority that each stimulus should receive when attention is shifted from one to the other.

You have now learned some of the factors that influence athletes' attention when they are passive about its direction. However, the single most important factor determining what athletes attend to is their own willpower. This power—the power to direct their attention where they want—needs to be developed because the orienting response and other factors can exert substantial influence on the direction of an athlete's attention. Thus the next step is to examine what athletes should direct their attention to. Then you will learn *how* to help your athletes direct their attention to these cues.

Dimensions of Attention

Every sport has unique cues that need to be attended to, but all sports have some common denominators for analyzing attentional demands. Robert Nideffer (1976) identified two very useful dimensions to help you and your athletes understand the attentional demands of your sport. As shown in Figure 9.2, these dimensions are the *width* of attention, whether attention is narrowly focused or more broadly focused, and the *direction* of attention, whether attention is directed toward the external environment or internally to the self.

The width dimension refers to how many stimuli the athlete should attend to. For certain sport skills, a very broad focus of attention is desirable, such as when the quarterback is reading a defense and looking for receivers or a basketball player is trying to inbound a pass. A narrow focus is better for hitting a baseball, golf ball, or tennis ball.

The direction dimension refers to whether attention is focused inwardly on the athletes' thoughts and feelings or outwardly on the events happening in the environment. As you know, there is a time to turn attention inwardly and analyze what is happening, plan strategy, and monitor bodily responses. And there is a time not to attend to these things.

To analyze the attentional demands of any skill or activity in sports, you need to consider both of these dimensions together. While Nideffer's (1976) model as shown in Figure 9.2 suggests that both of these dimensions fall on two continuums, in fact, only the narrow-broad dimension is actually a continuum. With the internal-external dimension, an athlete is either one or the other, not a little more or a little less. The model is more correctly illustrated in Figure 9.3.

Take a moment to select a few skills from your sport and analyze them according to

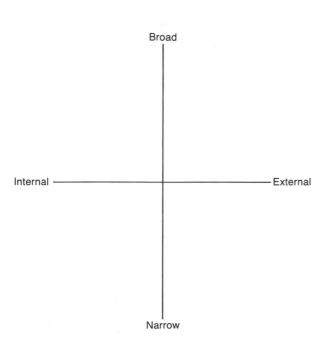

Figure 9.2 Nideffer's (1976) two-dimensional model for understanding the attentional demands in sport.

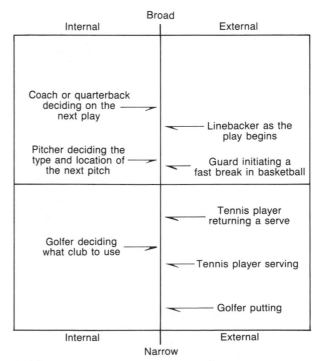

Figure 9.3 Nideffer's model reformulated to show internal and external attentional focuses as dichotomous rather than continuous.

Nideffer's model. Break each skill down specifically enough to clearly assign it a place. In the *Study Guide* you will be given more opportunity to do a thorough analysis of your sport. This is an important activity for every coach. The results of your analysis should be discussed with all of your athletes. It is an excellent way to teach the attentional demands of your sport.

Attention in Endurance Events

Let's take a look at what athletes attend to in long-distance events such as running a marathon, bicycling 100 miles, or skiing 50 kilometers. Research by William Morgan (1978) has provided some useful information about the unique attentional demands of these endurance events.

Morgan found that many participants in these events would dissociate their minds from the activity and from their bodies in order to deal with the monotony and pain of these grueling sports. For example, in their minds athletes would build a house while they ran, perform complex mathematical computations while bicycling, or sing to themselves while they cross-country skied. Thus their attention was internal as they focused on their thoughts, but their thoughts were intentionally directed away from analyzing the race or the feelings of their bodies. This is a unique coping strategy that some athletes have learned. Of course, it is possible only in sports where the activity itself is highly automated and where

attention to the external environment is not required.

However, when Morgan studied this phenomenon, he discovered that the very best athletes did not dissociate. Instead, they made a conscious effort to keep from dissociating. World-class long-distance competitors keep their attention focused externally on the other competitors and the course, and internally on their bodily responses and techniques. Outstanding athletes constantly shift their attention between external events and their own internal responses so that they can adjust pace and technique to optimize performance.

The attending strategy is the preferred strategy when athletes are in superior condition and are seeking to finish as high as possible in the standings. On the other hand, for those who are in less superior condition, and who may be competing not so much against others as simply against themselves to finish, dissociation can be an effective means to deal with the pain or boredom.

Guidelines for Improving Attention Selectivity

- The attentional demands for each specific skill in your sport should be analyzed by you and your athletes. You should identify whether the attention should be internal or external, and how broad or narrow it should be.
- When attention is focused externally, teach your athletes what cues should be attended to in what order. Keep the cues as few and as discernible as possible.
- When attention is focused internally, attend to positive and constructive thoughts, and leave negative thoughts unattended.
- When actually performing the skill, attend to the present and immediate forthcoming action, not to the past or future.
- Focus on task factors such as form and execution rather than on the score or the pending outcome. Athletes cannot concentrate on two different things at the same time. If athletes are focusing on the goal, they cannot concentrate on the means. In other words, if athletes are

thinking about winning, they cannot be thinking about hitting the next pitch, shooting the ball into the hoop, blocking the punt, or hitting an ace serve.

- Help athletes develop mind sets or expectations about which cues to attend to and which ones to filter out. Then teach them the appropriate responses to these cues.

- In conjunction with developing mind sets, teach your athletes the cues that help them to anticipate certain responses, and then analyze when it is appropriate to make anticipatory responses.

- When learning skills, direct athletes' attention to the feelings and sensations in their muscles as they execute them. Attending to these kinesthetic cues increases the rate at which athletes learn skills, and imagery is an excellent means of teaching kinesthetic awareness.

- When practicing, do attention-demanding instructional activity early in the practice period when psychic energy levels are high.

- Minimize distractions during practice when athletes are first learning skills, but then later introduce contest-simulated distractions so that athletes can practice their attentional skills.

- When the environment contains a great deal of uncertainty, especially uncertainty that athletes may perceive as a threat to their self-worth, the situation stresses them and increases the tendency to be distracted. Therefore, it is helpful to decrease uncertainty by following the suggestions in chapter 8.

  A special note: Athletes who are uncertain about their goals and their own self-worth are especially vulnerable to distractions. Comments from spectators, other players, or you about their quality of play can easily distract them, causing them to engage in unwanted self-analysis. Thus, as has been emphasized throughout, it is paramount in the development of all psychological skills that athletes develop stable, positive perceptions of themselves.

- Although uncertainty about athletes' self-worth is undesirable, uncertainty that introduces variety and novelty in practices can keep interest, and therefore attention, high.

SHIFTING ATTENTION

Athletes typically must deal with constantly changing external and internal environments. This requires them to effectively deploy, control, and shift the width and direction of their attention. The factors that influence athletes' abilities to shift effectively are discussed in this section.

Attentional Style

Nideffer's (1976) research indicates that many athletes have dominant attentional styles that are represented by one of the four quadrants in his model. These dominant styles develop because athletes experience success with a particular style and become comfortable using it. Thus it is likely that it is more difficult to shift attention to one of the other quadrants, especially if the athlete is weak in a particular attentional style. Let's look at Nideffer's four attentional styles, examining their strengths and weaknesses.

Broad-Internal Style

These athletes are thinking players; they plan the game well in their heads, are quick to make tactical adjustments in the game, and are skillful at analyzing the movements of their opponents and making anticipatory responses. On the other hand, these athletes can get caught up in analyzing, especially when the game is not going well. They also tend to outguess themselves and miss important cues in the game.

Broad-External Style

Athletes with this style are able to attend well to rapidly changing situations, taking in a lot of information. However, broad-external athletes are susceptible to information overload, which can result in their not being able to decide how to respond to rapidly changing events that they readily perceive.

Narrow-External Style

Athletes who golf and bowl, or perform any task in which the focus must be pinpointed, perform better with this type of attentional style. This style presents problems, though, when the environment changes and decisions need to be made about how to respond to the changes.

Narrow-Internal Style

This style is conclusive for diagnosing performance or strategy errors, but such diagnostic tendencies carry the risk of becoming highly critical self-analysis. Athletes with a narrow-internal style perform better in sports in which change takes place slowly and in obvious ways. Athletes who can benefit from dissociation are aided by a narrow-internal style.

Selecting a Style

Which is the preferred style for your sport? I can't think of a single sport for which it would be desirable to be dominant in only one of these styles and weak in the others. The ideal athlete is strong in all four styles and is able to shift readily from one type of attentional focus to another.

Nideffer (1976) developed a test for measuring these attentional styles, and an abbreviated form is in the *Study Guide*. With this test you can get a rough idea if an athlete is particularly weak in one or more of these attentional focuses. Then, by examining the attentional analysis you completed for the skills of your sport, you can identify any problems. For example, a quarterback clearly needs to be strong in all four attentional styles and be able to shift rapidly. A pass receiver who has a dominant broad-external focus and a weak narrow-external focus will be good at reading the defense, but when the ball is thrown, is likely to be distracted by the sound of footsteps or by some other competing stimulus and have difficulty concentrating on the ball. The pole vaulter who has a dominant narrow-external focus and a weak broad-internal focus will be good at concentrating when actually vaulting but will have considerable difficulty analyzing what may be going wrong and how to make adjustments. Once you have identified the problem, you can help the athlete improve a particular attentional deficiency by following the recommendations given later in this section and at the end of the chapter.

Timing the Shift

Another problem that has not been considered is that athletes not only have to learn *how* to change the width and direction of their attention, they have to learn *when* to change it. Many errors of attention occur because the athlete shifts too slowly or too rapidly from one focus to another. One example of shifting too slowly from an internal to an external focus might be a shortstop who, analyzing why he missed a groundball, fails to cover second base on the next hit to the second baseman for a possible double play. What the shortstop discovers, though, from his analysis is that he missed the ball because, just before catching it, he looked up to see where to throw. This error is an example of shifting his attention from one stimulus (the ball) to another stimulus (the base to throw to) too quickly. Only through careful observation, and discussion with your athletes who are making these types of errors, will you be able to identify problems.

Stress

The width and direction of attention is substantially affected by changes in the psychic energy level of the athletes. The width of athletes' attention narrows as psychic energy increases, first eliminating irrelevant stimuli and later, under high negative psychic energy or stress, eliminating task-relevant stimuli. This is a complex relationship, so let's look at it more closely.

Think of your width of attention as a beam of light, as shown in Figure 9.4. When you are low in psychic energy the beam is quite broad and you can readily attend to many stimuli. If you are playing a sport, you would attend to stimuli that are relevant to the game but you would also attend to some stimuli that are irrelevant to the game, such as the crowd or a conversation with a teammate (focus A in Figure 9.4). In that situation you clearly are not psyched up for the game, and your performance would not likely be optimal.

You realize you are stinking up the field with your lackadaisical play, so you have a stern but positive talk with yourself to get fired up. Now your psychic energy increases to the optimal energy zone, and your beam of light

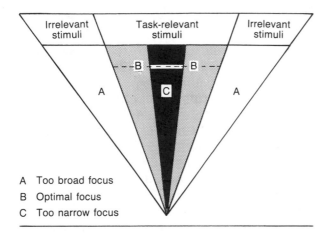

A Too broad focus
B Optimal focus
C Too narrow focus

Figure 9.4 The width of attention is influenced by stress.

narrows so that it focuses totally on the task and on no other irrelevant stimuli (focus *B* in Figure 9.4). Your performance is now optimal.

But just when you are in flow and playing brilliantly, your opponent throws a temper tantrum at the official and makes disparaging remarks about how you are playing over your head. You are angry and stressed by his actions. Your psychic energy is now high and negative, and the beam of light narrows further (focus *C* in Figure 9.4). Now some of the important cues to which you should be attending are missed, which causes you to make errors that you were not making moments ago.

Not only does the high negative psychic energy in the form of stress result in narrowing your attention too much, the stress causes you to focus your attention internally. You are caught up with your negative thoughts and the analysis of the events, thus not focusing fully on the task at hand. When you recognize that you are stressed and the beam of light is too narrow for you to see your way, you begin scanning the environment with the narrow beam of light looking for the relevant cues. It's like playing basketball with a pen light in a totally darkened gymnasium.

Scanning not only makes it much harder to find the right cues, but you are also more susceptible to distractions. Your light may fall on the bench where a teammate is yelling instructions, or on an attractive cheerleader on the sideline, or on an opposing player taunting you, or even on yourself, as you give yourself a verbal thrashing for making a dumb error.

Athletes high in trait anxiety and non-screeners are even more susceptible to these problems. While low trait anxious athletes and screeners focus more on task-relevant cues, high trait anxious athletes and nonscreeners focus more internally on self-evaluation and negative thoughts.

Thus stress makes it impossible to shift attention effectively. Both the width and direction of attention are impaired. Hence stress management skills are essential to maintain the ability to shift attention effectively. In turn, managing stress involves the skill of redirecting attention away from negative thoughts and muscle tension to task-specific stimuli. Thus deficiencies in managing stress impair attentional skills, and poor attentional skills impair the ability to manage stress. Improvement in either, therefore, helps the other.

Pain

Another factor decreasing athletes' ability to shift attention is when some stimulus is overwhelmingly strong and difficult to push aside. This may be some type of life crisis, creating a great deal of stress, grief, or excitement. When these types of events prevail in the minds of athletes, they will have difficulty shifting attention effectively to the appropriate stimuli in the sport.

One powerful stimulus that affects athletes frequently in some sports is pain. Without strong attentional skills the pain of continuing in an endurance event or the pain of an injury will preoccupy the athlete. Athletes with low pain thresholds are especially susceptible to this problem.

The skill of redirecting attention away from the pain has been shown to be a highly effective way to manage pain. Thus, if a person can learn not to attend to the Sensation → Perception link, as shown in Figure 9.1, pain will not be experienced. A stern warning though: Pain is a useful signal to the body that something is wrong, and teaching athletes to ignore pain indiscriminately is dangerous. Athletes, though, with low pain thresholds can learn to become less pain-sensitive in endurance events when they can redirect their attention elsewhere. Once an athlete is injured and medical personnel approve of the athlete continuing to play, the ability to redirect attention will be useful.

Guidelines for Improving Flexibility of Attention

Here are some recommendations for helping athletes shift attention more effectively.

- Athletes should be educated about the factors that influence their ability to shift attention, as has been discussed in this section.
- Athletes differ in their attentional styles and these styles can be measured to identify weaknesses in those attentional skills specifically needed for your sport. Wherever weaknesses exist, have athletes practice attentional exercises that will strengthen their deficiencies. Some exercises are found in the *Study Guide* and you can develop others that are specific to your sport.
- Managing stress is essential in helping athletes shift attention effectively. The ability to redirect attention is, in turn, very helpful in managing stress. Improvement of one of these skills will help improve the other skill.
- Attention may be redirected from pain and other powerful stimuli to the right cues when performing the skill.
- Psychic fatigue impairs the ability to shift attention effectively. Thus the mind must be conditioned to sustain the attention demanded by the sport, just as the body needs to be conditioned to meet the physical demands.
- Athletes can learn how to shift attention by observing and talking with athletes who have excellent skills in this area.

INTENSIVE ASPECTS OF ATTENTION

In addition to selecting the correct stimuli to attend to and having the skill to shift attention to these stimuli, athletes also must be able to attend with great intensity at times. The intensive aspects of attention involve concentration and mental alertness, each of which is considered next.

Concentration

Concentration and attention are often synonymous in the language of sport, but they should not be. *Concentration* has been defined as the narrowing of attention, a fixation of attention to certain stimuli, and sustaining attention on selected stimuli. To improve the precision of our language in talking about attentional skills, concentration should be limited to the latter meaning—*the ability to sustain attention on selected stimuli for a period of time*. We commonly call this *attention span*.

Developing concentration is a paradoxical effort. We know that intense concentration requires a great deal of psychic energy because when we concentrate for any length of time we feel mentally fatigued and less alert. Thus, when seeking to improve concentration skills, we confront the task with fierce mental effort—but this very effort causes concentration to elude us. Bobby Nichols, the superb golf professional, observed: "If you've got to remind yourself to concentrate during competition, you've got no chance to concentrate."

Concentration is not staring hard at something. It is not trying to concentrate directly. Concentration is effortless effort; it is fascination of the mind for the object upon which we focus. Adam Smith lauds Jack Nicklaus' great powers of concentration:

> Nicklaus plays in a trance. He and the club and the ball are all the same thing, and there isn't anything else. He can lock right in, real one-pointedness. I think he can influence the flight of the ball after it's hit, even. (1975, p. 184)

Concentration requires stilling or parking the mind. When I mentioned this in one of my classes, one bright student asked, "And where should the athlete park it?" Good question. Where should the mind be parked to concentrate? It should be parked in the present, so that wherever the athlete is, he or she should be all there. The athlete should park it squarely on the task and nothing else.

The ability to concentrate varies among athletes, some having greater capacity to concentrate than others. Also, some athletes are more susceptible to distraction, such as nonscreeners, because their attention-selection and attention-shifting skills are weak. Improve these attentional skills, as suggested earlier, and manage stress, and athletes are well on their way to developing this skill. Only one additional thing is needed—practice. Concentration can be developed by exercising the mind with tasks that require concentration.

My concentration skill changes rapidly with exercise. Writing, for me, requires intense concentration. Without practice, I cannot concentrate on my writing for longer than an hour or two. But after a few weeks of regular writing, I can readily concentrate for four to six hours before mental exhaustion chases me to the handball court or for a jog around the golf course.

Because concentration requires so much mental effort, or because athletes are unaware of the need to practice this skill, many athletes never practice concentrating for the length of time their event takes in competition. Their concentration exercise is limited to competitive events. Athletes would not dream of confining their physical skill development or conditioning to competitive events. And so athletes should also not go without practicing this essential psychological skill outside of competition.

You should teach your athletes that concentration is not practiced by gritting their teeth, tensing their muscles, and forcing their minds on the task. All this action results in not concentrating on the task at hand but concentrating on *concentration*. Concentration is letting yourself become absorbed in the here and now. It is achieving flow, and the procedures for enhancing flow will help develop concentration.

Alertness

The degree of alertness refers to a person's awareness to the stimuli impinging on the senses, or a person's responsiveness to the environment. Being alert, or paying attention, requires mental effort and thus is often measured by psychic energy indicators.

The degree to which people respond to their environment is dependent upon their mental capacity, which is the ability to process the incoming information from their senses. As the environment becomes increasingly complex, which it often is in sports, capacity may be approached, resulting in a deterioration in performance. Thus athletes need to narrow their attentional focus, shift attention correctly in the rapidly changing environment, and sustain the attention for the duration required.

When the mind becomes tired, it is difficult to continue the psychic-energy-demanding work involved in executing attention-selection, attention-shifting, and concentration skills. When working with the U.S. Olympic Cross-Country Ski Team, I often reminded the skiers not only to train their bodies during practice, but to practice their concentration so they would not experience psychic fatigue in a thirty- or fifty-kilometer race. These events, which last up to 2½ hours, require enormous psychic energy to perform optimally, and if athletes do not practice concentrating for these extended periods, they are unlikely to maintain the attentional focus they need throughout the race.

Because concentration consumes so much psychic energy, energy management skills are needed. Athletes need to know when to turn on the concentration and when to turn it off. Coaches should help inexperienced athletes know when to make these changes. In endurance events, you learned that highly skilled athletes keep concentration turned on throughout the race, but the capacity to do this must be developed through training. In events such as the decathlon or tournament sports—where athletes play, then wait, then play again—concentration must be managed more prudently.

When concentration is not managed prudently athletes are likely to experience psychic fatigue more than physical fatigue. Psychic fatigue causes all the attentional mechanisms to collapse: The correct stimuli are no longer selected efficiently, the shifts in width and direction of attention become sluggish, and concentration is elusive. Physical errors increase, less efficient skill execution requires more physical energy, athletes become more susceptible to powerful distractors such as pain, and insidious negative thoughts slither into the mind. Only when athletes' minds are adequately conditioned through Psychological Skills Training will they be able to avoid the many problems of psychic fatigue. Conditioning the body and not the mind is like baking your favorite cake and not eating it.

Guidelines for Improving Concentration

- Because concentration is a more passive process, this skill is improved in part by preparing the mind to concentrate. This involves getting rid of stress and becoming fascinated with the target of attention. The guidelines given for managing psychic energy and stress, especially the recommendations for achieving flow, will greatly help to improve concentration.

- Another useful way to develop concentration is through the use of pre-event routines, which, as mentioned earlier, help reduce uncertainty and decrease the potential for distraction. "Yes, I have a preparatory checklist of things to do and items to set out on my shooting position," says Linda Thom, the psychologically skilled Canadian Olympic gold medalist in pistol shooting.

> Also I have a checklist of cue words which make up my shot plan. These checklists and preparatory steps help me accomplish several things with economy of time and effort: they give me a physical and mental warm up, they focus my attention on exactly what I want to do, and they get me mentally into the match before it starts. (1986, p. 23)

- Concentration can be improved through the use of triggers—words or actions that remind athletes to concentrate. For example, fielders tend to lose concentration because of the slow, inactive nature of baseball and softball. It is too demanding to expect fielders to maintain intense concentration for the duration of the time they are in the field. A useful concentration strategy prior to each pitch is to repeat in their minds where they will throw the ball given various situations, and then use a trigger, such as touching the ground with their glove, to remind them to concentrate. Prior to the trigger the fielders can check out the crowd, adjust clothing, or whatever, but after the trigger, they know they must concentrate only on the ball and the batter.
- Concentration is quickly developed through practice. Athletes should spend time in practice sessions sustaining their attention in exactly the same way they must sustain attention when competing.
- Staying mentally alert and managing psychic energy during practices and competition will help produce not only razor-sharp concentration, but better attentional selection and shifting skills.

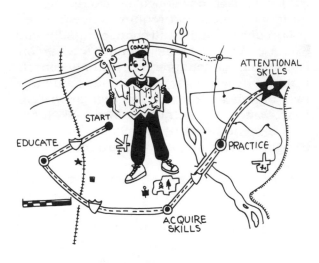

IMPLEMENTING AN ATTENTION TRAINING PROGRAM

In this last section, a map for following an attentional training program is presented. The steps are by now familiar: Educate, acquire the skills, and practice. The learning of attentional skills begins with you educating your athletes about the content of this chapter, and about the analysis you make (probably in conjunction with your athletes) of the attentional demands of the various skills and activities in your sport.

The purpose of the educational phase of attentional skill training is (a) to teach athletes how the attentional mechanisms work, (b) to identify the specific attentional demands of each skill to be performed, (c) to understand what factors cause attentional problems, and (d) to know that selection, shifting, and concentration skills can be developed to overcome these problems.

From my experience, the most important part of attentional skill training is education, and especially helping athletes identify attentional problems. Problem solution begins in problem identification, and attentional problems in sports have largely been unidentified. Coaches have always known athletes sometimes fail to perform well because of attentional problems, but coaches typically never go much beyond hoping that more practice and more experience, or yelling to "concentrate," will bring improvement. You can now do more, yet this chapter is unable to provide you with a cookbook solution. The value of this chapter, more than anything else, is to provide you with a framework for identifying the attentional demands and potential problems in your sport.

If you and your athletes know that (a) the athlete's attention involves three basic skills of selecting the right stimuli to focus on, which involves both the direction and width of attention, (b) the athlete must be able to shift attention as the sport environment changes, and (c) the athlete must be able to sustain attention or concentrate as the task requires, then you can begin to analyze the many skills in your sport for their attentional demands. The *Study Guide* provides you with a series of exercises for making these analyses. An excellent book written for athletes to help them develop their attentional skills is Robert Nideffer's *Athletes' Guide to Mental Training* (1985). It is not a substitute for your educating your team, but it is a helpful supplement.

The steps in summary form, then, for attentional skills training are as follows:

1. Educate your athletes about the attentional process and the attentional demands of your sport.
2. Determine your athletes' current attentional skills using the attentional skills test in the *Study Guide*.
3. Compare the athletes' strengths and weaknesses to the attentional demands of the sport skills to be performed. Given that other factors are equal, and attentional problems are serious, you may want to consider changing a player's position to make a better match between the player's attentional strengths and the attentional demands of certain positions.
4. Plan a training program to help each athlete develop attention selection, shifting, and concentration skills. The *Study Guide* contains some exercises to help you, but it is better if the skills are developed to be specific to your sport. Hence, you need to think of ways to help your athletes select the right cues to attend to, shift attention at the right time, and concentrate appropriately.
5. Next you are ready to have athletes practice those skills they need to develop. In the *Study Guide* you will find a series of basic exercises for helping to develop each of these skills. Many of the exercises use imagery techniques. Imagery is a vital tool for attentional skill development because imagery requires some attentional skill to begin with, so through imagery athletes are practicing their ability to direct and sustain their attention on the objects or activities of their mind's choice.

Imagery is especially useful for re-creating the competitive situation in order to identify the cues to attend to and to practice shifting the direction and width of attention as the situation changes. In imagery the rate at which the situation changes can be slowed down and speeded up as the mind wills it. Imagery also provides opportunities to attend fully to the environmental stimuli without worrying about making the appropriate response.

Attentional skills, of course, should also be practiced in practice sessions. As attentional skills develop, game-type distractions ought to be introduced into the environment so athletes have an opportunity to practice these attentional skills simulating the competitive environment as closely as possible.

It is also vital to remember that attentional skills cannot be developed in isolation from the other psychological skills. As has been pointed out, imagery and stress management skills are especially necessary to improve attentional skills. And as attentional skills improve, they permit the further development of stress management and imagery skills.

SUMMARY

1. Attention is the mental process whereby athletes direct and maintain awareness of stimuli detected by their senses.
2. The three major attentional skills are selecting the correct stimuli to attend to, shifting attention from one set of stimuli to another, and sustaining attention or concentration.
3. The orienting response is our automatic attention regulator, but can be over-

ridden by directing our attention toward what we choose.

4. People's attention follows their interest. Coaches can improve athletes' attention by keeping practices and competition interesting.

5. Athletes can develop a mind set to be alert to certain cues in the environment or within themselves. Coaches can improve athletes' attention by developing the right mind set.

6. Screeners are more selective in what they respond to in the environment than are nonscreeners. Coaches can help athletes who are nonscreeners attend better by reducing anxiety through the removal of unnecessary uncertainty.

7. The attention demands of all sports may be analyzed by considering the breadth (narrow to broad) and the direction (internal and external) dimensions for each particular skill.

8. Athletes in endurance events may dissociate by directing their attention to imaginary thoughts in order to endure the pain and boredom. Elite athletes in these events, however, prefer to attend to the events in the race and their bodily functions.

9. Numerous guidelines for improving attention selectivity were offered in this chapter.

10. The ability to shift attention is influenced by athletes' attentional style, which may be broad-internal, broad-external, narrow-external, or narrow-internal.

11. Athletes must learn when to shift their attention from one stimulus to another.

Failure to shift at the correct time is the source of many errors.

12. Stress has adverse effects on athletes because it narrows their attentional focus to the point where relevant stimuli are not attended to, thus causing them to scan more and to become more easily distracted. Stress also causes the attention to shift from external to internal, with the athlete focusing on nonproductive self-evaluations of whether he or she is meeting the demands of the task.

13. It is difficult to shift attention away from powerful stimuli, such as pain, in order to focus on task-relevant stimuli.

14. Several guidelines were offered for improving the ability to shift attention to the appropriate stimuli when playing sports.

15. The intensive aspects of attention refer to concentration and mental alertness, concentration being the ability to sustain attention on selected stimuli for a period of time.

16. Concentration is not improved by forcing the mind to attend, but by clearing the mind of distractors and becoming absorbed in the here and now. It is also improved by practicing to sustain the attentional focus required for the particular sport.

17. Psychic fatigue causes all the attentional mechanisms to collapse, but can be avoided through PST.

18. The attentional training program outlined in this chapter places emphasis on educating athletes about the attentional demands of their sport and practicing attentional skills.

Chapter 10
Self-Confidence and Goal-Setting Skills

I have yet to meet a coach or athlete who does not believe that self-confidence is vital to successful athletic participation. Champion athletes invariably say a key to success is believing in themselves, and they back it up by exuding self-confidence in their play.

While athletes know the importance of self-confidence, many lack the skill to manage this essential psychological quality. They see it in other athletes, but find it so elusive in themselves. Coaches recognize that athletes need self-confidence to win, but also know that athletes need to win to develop self-confidence. The puzzle is how to get on the winning/increased self-confidence/winning spiral, which breeds success, and get off the losing/increased diffidence/losing spiral, which yields failure.

In this chapter you will learn the answer to this problem. The key is effective goal-setting skills—essential psychological skills that both you and your athletes need to develop. While the other psychological skills discussed in this book are also important in helping to develop optimal self-confidence, goal-setting skills influence self-confidence more directly. The first part of this chapter explains what self-confidence is, and then you will learn the ingredients for a comprehensive goal-setting program.

UNDERSTANDING SELF-CONFIDENCE

In this section you will learn what self-confidence is, and the distinction between optimal self-confidence, diffidence, and false confidence. Self-confidence, you will see, is an expression of a person's self-worth and the ultimate self-confidence is the confidence in one's ability to become competent.

Self-Confidence Defined

Many athletes think self-confidence is believing they will win. One of the tenets of the American sport creed is that athletes should always think they will win. To think otherwise is sacrilegious. Athletes are told that if they don't feel positive about defeating the other team, then they are thinking like losers, which makes them losers.

It is this mistaken belief about what self-confidence is that often leads to a lack of self-confidence or to overconfidence. True self-confidence is an athlete's *realistic* expectation about achieving success. Self-confidence is an accumulation of the athlete's unique experiences in achieving many different things, which results in the specific expectations he or she has about achieving success in a future activity. It is a vital part of an athlete's personality, and is something others quickly recognize about him or her.

Self-confidence is not involved with what athletes hope to do, but with what they realistically expect to do. It's not always what they say they will do to others, but their innermost thoughts about what they are capable of doing. It's not pride in what they have done, but their considered judgment of what they will be able to do.

Some athletes have too little confidence; we say they are *diffident*. Other athletes have too much confidence or false confidence; we say they are *overconfident* or "cocky." And some athletes have an optimal amount of self-confidence; we refer to them as being simply self-confident. So self-confidence falls on a continuum; this continuum of confidence is from diffidence to overconfidence with optimal self-confidence somewhere in between. It is a continuum that is thought to be related to performance in the same way that psychic energy is related to performance (see Figure 10.1).

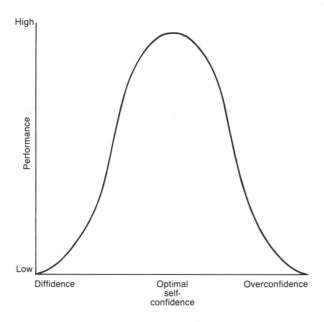

Figure 10.1 The relationship between self-confidence and performance.

As self-confidence increases up to some optimal level, performance improves, but when self-confidence increases beyond this optimal level, performance begins to deteriorate. It deteriorates because overconfidence deludes athletes into believing they are so gifted that they need not prepare diligently nor put forth as much effort as may be required.

Optimal Self-Confidence

Athletes with optimal self-confidence set realistic goals based upon their own abilities. Self-confident athletes "play within themselves"; that is, they understand themselves well enough to feel successful when they reach the upper limits of their ability and don't attempt to achieve goals that are unrealistic for them.

Possessing optimal self-confidence is a nec-essary and vital personal quality for athletes, but it alone does not guarantee they will perform well. Athletes must also possess the physical skills to perform well. All the self-confidence in the world will not replace having the physical skills and knowledge essential for the particular sport. Self-confidence and competence must develop together, each nurturing the other. To possess self-confidence without competence is to have false confidence.

Some athletes believe self-confidence gives them an immunity against making errors. It does not, but a healthy self-confidence gives an athlete a powerful weapon in deaing with errors. When athletes' self-worth is not in doubt, they feel free to pursue the correction of these errors. They are not afraid to try. Coaches who chastise athletes for making errors are likely to deny athletes the use of this powerful weapon.

Diffidence

A mistake does not shatter the self-confident athlete. A loss does not become a tragedy. Self-confident athletes know mistakes and losing are part of sports. Diffident athletes, on the other hand, fear failure so much that they are easily intimidated and act with trepidation. Consequently, diffident athletes become psychological prisoners of their own negative self-images. They see themselves as losers and they become losers. Alexandre Dumas (cited by Walker, 1980) captures such psychological incarceration with these words: "A person who doubts himself is like a man who would enlist in the ranks of his enemies and bear arms against himself. He makes his failure certain by himself being the first person to be convinced of it" (p. 160).

Self-doubts become devastating self-fulfilling prophecies. A self-fulfilling prophecy means that the sheer fact that you expect something to happen causes it to happen. Self-doubts cause athletes to fall from the ladder of success because they begin to behave in accordance with those doubts. It's a vicious cycle out of which many athletes cannot break. They expect to fail, which in turn leads to actual failure, which confirms their negative self-image, which increases their expectation of failure (see Figure 10.2).

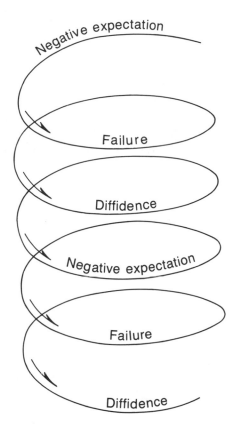

Figure 10.2 The negative spiral originating from negative expectations.

The self-doubts and negative expectations of diffident athletes undermine their performance by creating anxiety, loss of concentration, and uncertainty of purpose. Diffident athletes frequently focus so intensely on their shortcomings that it distracts them from attending to the things essential to good performance. Diffident athletes may conclude they are so inadequate that no matter how much more they practice, they will not be able to do better, so they quit trying. Diffident athletes become tentative in their actions and place blame inwardly when it should be placed elsewhere or not at all. Self-doubt insidiously forestalls their growth and enjoyment in participation.

But self-fulfilling prophecies need not be negative. Positive expectations are the psychological fuel that energizes athletes; positive expectations are the rudder steering athletes toward their goals. Positive, yet realistic, expectations can also be potent self-fulfilling prophecies, just as negative expectations can.

The power of positive self-fulfilling prophecies can be seen in Wendy, who, at the age of ten, was given a newly developed test that claimed 99 percent accuracy in predicting future success in sports. As it happened, Wendy possessed only ordinary athletic talents, but when the computer processed her test, an electrical storm caused an undetected glitch. It switched Wendy's score with Sally's, who was in reality an exceptionally gifted athlete.

When those in charge saw Wendy's score, which identified her as an unquestionable future superstar, they convinced her parents to place her in a special school of the motorically gifted. In this school Wendy received the finest instruction, was given ample opportunity to practice with the best equipment and facilities and often highly talented young people, and was provided with every incentive. Even when Wendy initially played with her ordinary ability, coaches expressed confidently to her that her supertalent would surface; it was only a matter of dedicated practice and time, for the computer was never wrong.

And the computer was not wrong. With practice and time, and absolute self-confidence, Wendy fulfilled what the computer prophesied for her. She became a superstar athlete. And Sally was never heard of in the sport world, which was exactly what the computer had predicted for her.

Do you recognize how powerful self-fulfilling prophecies can be? Are you effective in communicating positive expectations to your athletes so that they are more likely to approach their potential? Do you ever make the same mistake that the computer did and incorrectly label the ability of a young person? That's fine if you're Wendy, but it's devastating if you're Sally!

False Confidence

Let's now look at the overconfident athlete. Actually, overconfidence is a misnomer. Athletes cannot be overconfident if the confidence is well-founded in their abilities. When we refer to someone being overconfident, we really mean they are falsely confident; their confidence is greater than their competencies warrant.

False confidence comes in two forms. Some players honestly believe they are better than they really are. Pampering from parents or coaches may have caused this overconfident attitude, but whatever the reason, these athletes are headed for disappointment.

The second type of false confidence is seen among athletes who act confident on the outside, yet underneath are actually diffident and worried about failing in sport. Falsely confident athletes are often regarded as brash, haughty, uppity, presumptuous, arrogant, and pretentious. Mistakenly, some athletes believe this is the way they should act to show others they have confidence. Behavior of this type only makes it more difficult for them when their skills eventually reveal their false confidence.

Self-confident athletes differ from overconfident athletes in that they distinguish reality from fantasy by accurately judging their abilities and efforts. Overconfident athletes misrepresent reality, confusing what *is* with what they *wish would be* or what *ought* to be. Self-confident athletes see hope in their personal efforts to achieve their goals; overconfident athletes hope for a break.

Athletes who do not possess self-confidence often fake it because they know how important self-confidence is. When they do so, they actually are less likely to deceive others than they are to deceive themselves. False confidence is psychological fraud, the perpetrator often also being the victim. The consequence of this self-hoax is that athletes evade the real cause of their diffidence. They avoid situations that threaten their self-confidence or find behaviors to protect their fragile egos—such as faking injury when they perform poorly. The falsely confident find it difficult to admit to their errors, abound with excuses, and often are difficult to coach because they will not accept responsibility for their mistakes.

Not only do athletes perpetrate this hoax on themselves, they are encouraged to do so by coaches and drugstore sport psychologists. The encouragement comes in the form of advice to "think positive"—that any goal you truly set your sights on can be achieved. I have already commented on the fallacy of simplistic positive thinking. Positive thinking alone will not give athletes confidence. Confidence is gained when it is earned, not stolen on false hope. And confidence is earned by working to become competent. Confidence is obtained through improvement in performance, and improved performance comes about by setting realistic goals and doing the work necessary to obtain those goals.

Steve Combs, former Olympic wrestler and executive director of U.S.A. Wrestling, says his source of self-confidence when he wrestled was not in thinking he was more skilled than others but that he was better prepared. Combs was confident he was in better condition and had done all he could do to prepare himself for the match. If his opponent was more skilled, so be it; that was beyond his power to do anything about.

Yes, of course athletes should think positively, but within realistic terms. They should appraise themselves as favorably as possible, but check against wishful thinking. Too many athletes are misguided into believing that fallacious sport credo: "You must believe you will win; otherwise you are a loser." When winning is unrealistic, programmed failure increases diffidence and impairs performance. When athletes believe they should win every time, the inevitable failure to fulfill excessive expectations results in more adverse psychological effects than the supposed positive effects of believing they will win. Do you encourage this type of false confidence?

Self-Worth

Throughout this book I have emphasized the significance of an athlete's self-worth. It is a fundamental psychological concept that must have preeminence in your mind in order for you to coach your athletes successfully. Nothing is more important to each of us than our own self-worth, and we go to great effort to protect it. Great coaches enhance athletes' self-worth; poor coaches destroy it. Self-worth is the key to motivation, and the key to the coaching philosophy espoused in chapter 1.

Self-confidence is an expression of a person's self-worth. Early sport experiences are vital in shaping a youngster's self-confidence. Those who experience initial success become more self-confident, feel more worthy, and are more motivated to pursue excellence. Those who experience initial failure become more diffident and feel less worthy.

Optimal self-confidence cannot be developed in athletes who have negative perceptions of their self-worth. When you encounter athletes who think poorly of themselves, you will have to help them develop positive perceptions of their own worth as beings in order to help them develop optimal self-confidence. You can do three things to help athletes develop and maintain wholesome perceptions of their self-worth:

- Teach the techniques and tactics of sport effectively so that athletes develop the competencies needed to be successful.
- Communicate your positive perceptions about your athletes' self-worth independently of their performance in the sport.
- Help athletes recognize that the most important source of self-confidence is not winning but their own abilities to become competent.

The Ultimate Self-Confidence

The most important self-confidence that athletes can possess is not the conviction they will always win or they will never err, but that they can correct their errors by working to become the best they can be. The most significant self-confidence for athletes is *confidence in their ability to acquire competencies*—both physical and psychological.

Armed with confidence in the ability to become competent, athletes will not be intimidated by opponents' successes nor disturbed by their own temporary failures. The significance of an immediate win or loss is given appropriate weight in view of their long-term objectives. Athletes will more likely view a particular contest and its outcome as a test to measure their progress as they pursue their objectives. Winning the game no longer becomes the most important objective; becoming better does.

UNDERSTANDING GOAL SETTING

A systematic program of setting goals and working to achieve these goals is a highly effective means of improving self-confidence—and becoming more competent. Goal setting has been repeatedly shown in research and practice to help athletes develop both physical and psychological skills.

Benefits of Setting Goals

Setting goals is not new to coaches and athletes; since the first contests of ancient times athletes have set goals for themselves. Sports readily lend themselves to setting goals, whether they be individual or team sports, objectively or subjectively scored. So why do you keep hearing about the value of goal setting? Because coaches and athletes often do not know how to set goals effectively, nor do they pursue goal setting systematically. Too often goals are vague, conflicting, unchallenging, misdirected, and sporadically set. Also, some coaches advocate early-season goal setting, but then do nothing to focus on and facilitate striving for those goals.

Calvin Peete, an outstanding professional golfer, learned about goal setting through experience.

> When I first got interested in golf, my goal was to break 80. Then 75. Then scratch. Then to improve my short game. Then to go on tour. Then to qualify on Mondays. Then to make cuts. Then to make the top 25 in a tournament. Then the top 10. Then, finally to think of winning. The reason I probably didn't play well at first was that I got ahead of what was possible. I just felt everything would come together and I'd go from 94th to first. I didn't. (Moore, 1983, p. 43)

In this section you will learn how to help your athletes and yourself keep from getting ahead of yourselves. Sport psychologists have learned a great deal about how to set goals more effectively. When the principles of goal setting are properly followed, the benefits are many, as shown in Table 10.1.

Table 10.1
Benefits of Goal Setting

- Goals improve performance.
- Goals improve the quality of practices.
- Goals clarify expectations.
- Goals help relieve boredom by making training more challenging.
- Goals increase intrinsic motivation to achieve.
- Goals increase pride, satisfaction, and self-confidence.

A well-planned goal-setting program improves performance in four ways: Goals direct athletes' attention and action to the tasks needing practice. Goals mobilize athletes' energy and effort. Goals increase the persistence of athletes when progress is painfully slow. And goals motivate athletes (and coaches) to search for the most appropriate strategies for achieving them.

In the final two sections of this chapter you will learn the principles and methods of the *Goal-Setting Training* (GST) program, which were put to a critical test in a doctoral dissertation completed by Damon Burton (1983). Burton took the position of assistant coach with the University of Illinois swim team for an entire season to carry out the study. From the first day of practice in the fall to the last day of competition, Burton systematically taught both the men and women as well as the other coaches the principles of goal setting.

Two comparisons were made in Burton's study: One was between those on the Illinois swim team who became good at setting accurate goals (defined as a small discrepancy between the swimmer's prerace goal and the actual time span) and those who were not so accurate at setting goals. The other comparison was made between the Illinois team and Indiana University's swim team, a perennial power in the Big Ten and nationally. Indiana University's team did not receive the GST program.

From both comparisons, the results showed that those swimmers who were excellent at setting realistic goals

- were less anxious,
- concentrated better,
- were more self-confident,
- performed better, and
- were more satisfied with their participation.

These findings are the most impressive scientific results for the use of goal setting yet reported in sport. They are proof of the value of *systematic* goal setting—and systematic is the key.

Burton worked hard daily to teach the goal-setting skills of the program. Yet some athletes simply never showed much interest (even though they were encouraged to participate by the head coach), nor did they show the ability to set realistic goals. Other swimmers showed

dramatic improvements in goal-setting skills and corresponding improvements in their performance. From this work, Burton learned much about how to help athletes set goals more effectively, and this information is included in the GST program described shortly.

Types of Goals

It will be valuable in the development of your GST program to distinguish between goals and objectives. An *objective* is something to be maximized or continuously improved; it is a continuum dimension. A *goal* is a point on the objective continuum; it is a specific target behavior that is either achieved or not. An objective for an athlete is to develop his or her athletic abilities to the fullest. A goal is to hit .300 and field .900 on the Babe Ruth team next year. The Olympic creed, "citius, altius, fortius" (faster, higher, stronger), is an objective; running a 9.5-second 100-meter race, high jumping 7'6", and lifting 425 pounds are goals.

Goals are concrete and specific. Thus they are more immediate because they take into account the impending situation and the athlete's state or qualities. Objectives are vague because they look much further into the future and therefore cannot consider specific situational factors. The difference between objectives and goals is not a mere semantic distinction; it is important in applying goal-setting principles correctly.

Goals have two important properties. First a goal has *direction*; athletes set their goals toward something. A goal also has some *intensity* to it; the goal can be the most important in an athlete's life or it can be of only mild importance.

Athletes and coaches often set goals to win—to win the next game, or to win so many games during the season, or to win the league championship. These goals are called *outcome goals*; they are the outcomes of competition. Athletes and coaches may also set performance goals. *Performance goals* are restricted to the specific behaviors of an athlete. For example, a performance goal in basketball would be to make 90 percent of a player's free throws, or to make five assists per game, or to reduce individual turnovers by 30 percent.

Goals also may be set with regard to acquiring certain knowledge and strategies about the sport, and about attaining certain fitness or training levels. And, certainly, goals can and should be set for acquiring psychological skills.

GOAL-SETTING PRINCIPLES

The principles of goal setting are few in number and simple to state, as shown in Table 10.2.

Table 10.2
Principles of Goal Setting

- Set performance goals, not outcome goals.
- Set challenging, not easy, goals.
- Set realistic, not unrealistic, goals.
- Set specific, not general, goals.
- Set short-term, not long-term, goals.
- Emphasize individual goals over team goals.

Understanding these principles thoroughly and applying them systematically, however, is not so simple. Let's examine each of these principles closely.

Performance Versus Outcome Goals

Performance and outcome goals differ in some very significant ways. Consider the goals you encourage as you read the following sections.

Control of Goals

Performance goals are greatly superior to outcome goals because athletes have greater control over their performances than they do the outcome of a contest. It makes little sense for athletes to evaluate their achievements on the basis of attaining or not attaining goals that are not fully controlled by them.

Performance goals, you will recall, are specific behaviors to be achieved and are not dependent on the actions of others for someone to attain them. Outcome goals, especially winning, are only partially under the control of any one individual. The outcome of a competitive event is dependent not only on the player in question, but on teammates (if it is a team sport) and on the other competitors, as well as officials and coaches. The outcome is also determined by many situational factors, such as the condition of the equipment and playing fields, the weather, and luck. I am amazed by how coaches and athletes discount the importance of luck in determining the outcome of a sports contest. Coaches especially appear to believe they exert greater control over the outcome than is really possible.

In chapter 7 I told you about the study by Randy Lowe (1971) that looked at the inverted-U relationship between psychic energy and performance. In his study Lowe measured batting performance by how solidly the ball was hit, not by the outcome of the hit—that is, whether or not it was a base hit. An observer in the stands assigned point values from 1 to 5 for how solid the contact was. A very solid line drive that was snared by a diving third baseman received a high performance score, but the outcome was negative. When a little squibbler was hit in front of the plate and was picked up by the catcher, who overthrew first base with the hitter advancing to third base, a low performance score was given, but the outcome was positive. The relationship between performance and outcome in this study was zero, indicating that at this level of baseball, the winner of the game is determined mostly by luck, not by the skill of the players.

As the skill of players increases, performance surely influences the outcome more directly, yet the outcomes of all sports contests are determined in part by factors other than the performance of one player or team. The next time you go to a football, baseball, or basketball game, or any other sports contest, think about how much of the game is really determined by the performance of a player or team, and how much is determined by other factors, especially luck. You might also think about how much the outcome is influenced by your coaching.

Why is this a problem? Let me present a little more background because this first principle is the most important of the six, and in fact, is among the most important principles I have learned in sport psychology.

The setting of outcome goals causes many psychological problems for athletes. Yet it is very difficult to convince athletes not to set outcome goals. Athletes know that society rewards winners, regardless of whether they perform well or not. Society equates winning with good performance.

Also many coaches are highly resistant to accepting this goal-setting principle. They tend to interpret it to mean that athletes should not try to win. They don't focus their attention on the message that athletes will perform better by striving to achieve performance goals. And how do you increase the likelihood of winning? By performing better, of course! Advocating performance goals is not recommending that athletes should not try to win. Rather it is suggesting that to optimize athletes' chances of being the best they can be, you should avoid focusing on the outcome of winning, which impairs the ability of an athlete to perform as well as possible.

Coaches encourage athletes to evaluate themselves based on the outcome by attempting to convince their athletes they alone are totally responsible for the outcome. How I recall the pregame oratories of some of my coaches telling me that if I or the team would only take charge, we could determine the outcome of the game.

Coaches want athletes to feel control and responsibility for the outcome in hopes that it will motivate them and assure victory. And, of course, such control is sometimes seen. Individuals or teams sometimes totally dominate other teams, but does that mean one athlete or team is totally responsible for the outcome? No, not at all. Just as much as the outcome is determined by one team being strong, it is equally determined by the other team being weak. No athlete is totally responsible for the outcome of any sports contest. Athletes are responsible only for their own performances.

Degree of Control

Ideally athletes should set performance goals that are 100 percent under their control, but typically many performance goals cannot be 100 percent under an athlete's control. Hence athletes should set goals that are as much under their control as possible.

The goal that an athlete will run twenty miles this week to train for the upcoming contest is certainly much more under the athlete's control than a goal of winning the contest. Think of all the variables that will determine this athlete's achievement of the winning goal compared to the achievement of the training goal. Yet the training goal is not 100 percent under the control of the athlete either. He or she could become sick during the week, sprain an ankle, or get hit by a car. But this training goal, by any reasonable subjective estimate, is more under the control of the athlete than winning.

Consider the comparison between the following pairs of goals.

Pair One:

- My goal is for our team to win this game.
- My goal is to make twenty points in the game.

Pair Two:

- My goal is to make twenty points in the game.
- My goal is to take high percentage shots, where I'm in the open and within twenty feet of the basket, 90 percent of the time.

Which goal of each pair offers greater control? The second one of each pair does. As we have discussed, winning is influenced by many, many things. An athlete certainly has more control over how many points he or she makes than over whether or not the team wins. Yet how many points a player makes is still determined, in part, by chance opportunities and the opponent's defense.

Thus, in the second pair, an athlete has greater control over the second goal because it is less influenced by what the opponents and the player's teammates do. The point here is that no goal is 100 percent under a person's control, but performance goals are more under personal control than outcome goals are. In the *Study Guide* you will have an opportunity to practice developing goals that are more under personal control than are some of the traditional goals in sport.

Self-Worth and Achievement

In our society those who achieve more are considered to be more worthy individuals. In sports, achievement is usually measured by one simple criterion—winning. Winning is seen as success, and losing as failure. Winners, therefore, are more worthy and losers are less worthy. And even the youngest of athletes quickly learns this standard of achievement in our society.

When athletes base their self-worth, and therefore their self-confidence, on whether or not they win, their self-confidence rests precariously on the actions of others. When athletes make the mistake of basing their self-confidence on the goal of winning rather than on attaining a performance goal, then self-confidence is likely to be highly unstable.

You probably have seen athletes who quickly become overconfident after a win or two, only to lose and then become desperately diffident. The instability of self-confidence for such athletes becomes a source of uncertainty, anxiety, and frustration.

Athletes who base their self-confidence on winning, and who are among the vast majority who do not win all the time, usually feel helpless in doing anything about their unstable self-confidence. They have become so convinced that the only criterion for evaluating their worth is whether or not they win that they are unable to separate their performances from the outcome.

Why Performance Goals?

So how do you help athletes achieve stable self-confidence and feel worthy regardless of whether they win or lose? The answer is to replace the pervasive and infectious goal of winning with realistic performance goals. *Success must be redefined to mean athletes exceeding their own performance goals rather than surpassing the performance of others.*

I asked Phil Niekro, the ageless knuckle-baller, how he explains those days when he is "on" and when he is "off." He answered,

> I don't try to explain it. Some days I feel like I have great stuff and I get knocked out in the third inning. Other days I feel lousy before the game and when I'm pitching, I will throw the ball right into the batter's power zone, but the batter pops it up rather than hits a home run. I don't try to work out the problems of winning and losing. I don't have any control over it.

To implement an effective goal-setting program, you must understand the insanity of athletes basing their evaluations of themselves on factors beyond their control. It makes no sense to have athletes perform well, to reach realistic performance goals, but to consider themselves failures because they lost the contest; nor does it make sense for them to perform poorly, win because of a weak opponent or luck, and still consider themselves successful.

The great athletes inevitably avoid getting caught up in constantly evaluating themselves on the basis of every win or loss. (I believe this is prerequisite to becoming a great athlete.) They set long-term objectives for themselves, measuring their progress toward these objectives by evaluating their own performances in light of the quality of the competition, without regard to whether they win or lose. Carl Lewis, the great sprinter, states:

> I'm the type of athlete who doesn't worry about winning or losing. I only worry about being on a level where I can perform. I won't step on a track unless I can perform on a quality level . . . I'm running a preset race, dealing with a preset meet situation, and I know exactly how I want to do it, and I just do it that particular way. I'm not worried about winning or losing, because as long as I compete at the level I know I can, that's going to take care of itself. (Runner's World, 1984, p. 22)

Great athletes often evaluate their play to a considerable extent on how much effort they put into their performance. In short, they judge themselves not on winning or losing but on having tried their best. The now trite cliché,

"It's not whether you win or lose, but how you play the game," contains such wisdom that even its overuse does not diminish the significance of its message.

Great athletes make a critical distinction between having confidence in themselves and having confidence that they will win. True self-confidence is the belief that one can successfully execute the skills that one possesses. Confidence in winning is the expectation or belief that the performance of one's skills will result in winning. Great athletes focus on the former, not the latter.

When coaches and athletes fully embrace this cardinal principle of goal setting, the positive results reported in Burton's study (1983) are consistently obtained. When athletes can unload the burdensome goal of winning, they perform better, are more self-confident, are less anxious, and enjoy sports more. What a bountiful harvest from planting the performance goal seed. Performance goals rather than outcome goals are the cornerstone principle of the GST program.

Challenging Versus Easy Goals

It seems obvious that athletes should set challenging goals rather than easy goals. Research shows that challenging goals yield better performance than moderate or easy goals. But just how challenging goals should be is not so easy to determine. Goals should not be so difficult that athletes will fail to take them seriously, or fail to reach them after repeated effort, because they will lose their motivation. Goals that are too difficult lead athletes to conclude they are failures and threaten athletes' self-worth.

The relationship between goal difficulty and motivation is shown in Figure 10.3. Like the rabbit in a dog race, goals should be kept just outside the reach of the athlete's grasp—but now and then the rabbit must be caught. The reward of attaining the goal will reinforce athletes to pursue the next, slightly more difficult goal. One of the arts of coaching is helping athletes set difficult goals that elicit maximum motivation, as shown in Figure 10.3—but not so difficult that they give up.

How do you know how challenging goals should be? I have found it best to use athletes' most recent performances, preferably within

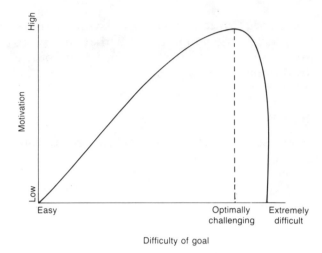

Figure 10.3 The relationship between the difficulty of a goal and motivation, showing that when goals become too difficult, motivation dramatically drops.

the past week or two, as a baseline. Longer baseline periods allow too many factors to interfere, making it more difficult to set accurate goals.

It is not uncommon to find athletes who set their goals based on an outstanding performance one, two, or three years earlier. Athletes often resist adjusting goals to take into account changes in their health or the conditions under which they must play. Failure to make adjustments in goals based on situational and personal factors is often the cause of goals being too challenging, and athletes concluding they are failures when their goals are not achieved.

To keep goals challenging, but not too difficult, I highly recommend the staircase approach to goal setting (see Figure 10.4). The immediate goal is set only slightly above the athlete's previous performance or average of the past several performances (the present baseline). Then a series of steps are planned, each progressively more difficult than the previous. This staircase approach to goal setting provides coaches with frequent opportunities to reward achievement, which builds motivation and self-confidence. You will need to caution your athletes that few progress directly up the staircase. Sometimes they will take a step back, but with continued commitment they will most likely find their way up. It is also wise, and consistent with the other goal-setting principles, to avoid projecting goals too far into the future. Three or four

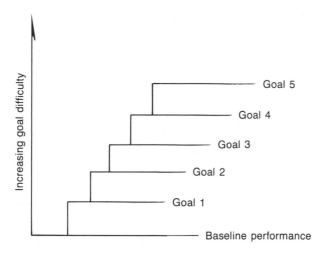

Figure 10.4 The staircase approach to goal setting.

steps, covering a time span of no more than a month, are recommended.

Lack of commitment is not an uncommon problem when goals are exceptionally high. Diffident athletes will see difficult goals as threatening while self-confident athletes will see them as challenging. Thus it is important for you to build different staircases, depending on the level of self-confidence of your athletes. The staircase for self-confident athletes can be considerably steeper than the staircase for diffident athletes.

When an athlete has difficulty achieving the next step in a staircase, you should consider two possibilities. The first is that the step is too big and thus should be divided into two or more smaller steps. The second is that perhaps your athlete has not been properly instructed on how to do the skill that is blocking the attainment of the next step. If this is the case, then you need to assist the athlete in learning the skill.

Realistic Versus Unrealistic Goals

This is another obvious principle, but it is not so easy to put into practice. It is obvious to me that athletes should set performance goals, not outcome goals, but in the midst of a heated softball game with archrivals I sometimes find myself focusing on winning, not performing. Athletes tend to set unrealistic goals for several reasons and it is important to recognize and deal with these factors.

- Athletes desire to obtain the rewards given to winners. This desire pushes them to set goals that will insure they win, even when these goals are well beyond their present capabilities.
- Parents, friends, and coaches often advocate setting goals that are beyond the athletes' current skill levels.
- Sometimes athletes set goals to be unrealistically low because they fear failure.
- Goals may be unrealistic because athletes lack sufficient information about their abilities or those of their fellow competitors, or the conditions under which the contest will be played.
- Athletes who experience initial success may begin to believe the overzealous expectations that emerge from the media or fans. When athletes advance into college or professional sports they often are compared to the greats of the game. "He'll be another Red Grange." "She plays with the same tenacity as Billie Jean King." "This kid will be the next Mickey Mantle." All too often these comparisons become a "kiss of death" because the athlete aspires for too much too soon.
- Athletes may have one great performance, their own Bob Beamon long jump, and then expect themselves to perform at the same level or even better every time thereafter. Excessive self-expectations have destroyed many an athlete. When goals are unrealistically high, athletes may attempt to play beyond their capabilities, impairing their performance by pushing too hard, suffering injury, or burning out.

The key to setting realistic goals is for athletes to know who they are, and not confuse who they are with what they wish to be. Just as you need to know who you are in order to be an effective coach, athletes need to know who they are to set realistic goals. Veteran athletes frequently comment on how important it was (and what an ordeal it became in some cases) to come to know themselves. Athletes can easily live under delusions, especially when experiencing early success in their communities. I have seen high school state champions or all-stars come to a university and be shattered when they realize that every other athlete on the team holds similar credentials.

While it is not easy to set realistic goals, it is easier to set them realistically at the outset than to adjust them based on changing circumstances or changes within the athlete. For many athletes, once they focus on a goal, it is difficult to let go. This is another one of those values that we inculcate into athletes: Adjusting goals downward is one step short of admitting defeat. Yet goals need to be adjusted if they are to remain realistic. Consider the story of Bill Koch who, in 1976, was the only American ever to win a silver medal in Olympic cross-country skiing.

After a disappointing 1980 Olympics, Bill bounced back to win the 1982 Nordic World Cup Championship, a more coveted title among skiers because it is earned by points based on finishes in a series of races. Because Bill was back, there were great expectations for him to win another medal, maybe even a gold medal, in the 1984 Winter Olympic games.

But Bill had been ill much of the 1984 season, which had limited his training. Weeks before the games he seemed to be getting back into form, only to be hit with another heavy cold during the games. Also, the heavy snowfalls in Sarajevo created track conditions not well suited to Bill's style of skiing. America did not alter its expectations of Bill Koch, but Bill did.

Bill tied for twenty-first; the nation was disappointed and television coverage of the event was immediately curtailed to a brief clip. Americans, you know, want to see the struggle only when it leads to triumph.

When Bill was asked about his performance, he responded by saying, "I feel like a winner. I know a lot of people will be disappointed I didn't get a medal. But the effort is really what counts. I gave it all I had. To me, that's what makes a winner." Bill had adjusted his goals based on his previous training and his current health. In working with

our Olympic cross-country team that season, and in watching Bill ski that race, I can tell you it was an accomplishment. Bill was successful that day, but it took extraordinary perspective for him to keep his goals realistic in face of the tremendous pressure to win a medal.

At those same games, the U.S. ice hockey team had been programmed by ABC Sports to pull another "miracle" on ice as they did in 1980. Yet in pre-Olympic competition that year the U.S. team was ranked seventh. Despite this, ABC Sports hyped the team endlessly and planned extensive coverage of the team's play. The pressure on coach Lou Vairo, and on the young team assembled only months earlier, was enormous. The team lost the first two games, and in the eyes of many was a dismal failure—but only because of unrealistic expectations. The team finished seventh in the games, exactly where they were ranked in world standings.

A caution about adjusting goals downward, though: It is tempting for athletes, especially diffident athletes, to look at every little circumstance or condition as a possible excuse for failing to reach a goal. Excuses are especially likely when coaches use goal setting only to motivate athletes to achieve outcome goals or as a punitive measure when goals are not achieved. Effective goal setting requires making adjustments to goals within the context of a trusting relationship between coach and athlete, with both working jointly to achieve the athlete's long-term objective.

Specific Versus General Goals

I used to recommend the goal of "do the best you can." It seemed like an excellent goal. Athletes could never exceed it, because no one ever knew exactly what their best was. It also was a safe goal. Athletes need not fail because they can always say they did their best, which is difficult to define and thus difficult to deny. But it is precisely this vagueness that is the goal's shortcoming. Actually, it is not a goal at all, but an objective—something for which athletes can continuously strive.

Specific goals are more effective because they direct behavior more precisely by specifying the criterion for success. Consequently, they communicate clear expectations to athletes. Specific goals should be quantifiable and specify a time period or precise event. The following are examples of specific goals for various sports.

- To run the 1,500-meter race on Saturday in 3:57.
- To keep the man I'm guarding from having more than three open shots in tomorrow night's game.
- To shoot at least five takedowns in the first period against Wally Davis.
- To make solid contact with the ball 80 percent of the time in batting practice this week.
- To block the correct person every time in today's scrimmage.
- To score a 72 in the championship round on Tuesday.
- To read the defense correctly 90 percent of the time, and to call the correct audible when the defense is loaded against the play called in the huddle in this week's game.
- To pitch the ball to the spot called for by the catcher 80 percent of the time in tomorrow's game.
- To extend my concentration practice today from five to six minutes.
- To record at least 50 percent of my negative thoughts today and then to spend twenty minutes this evening practicing the substitution of positive but realistic thoughts in their place.

You will have the opportunity in the *Study Guide* to develop specific goals for your sport. Depending on the sport, you may find this a more difficult task than you think. One of the reasons systematic goal setting is still applied so infrequently is that it involves considerable work on your part, and requires the ability to develop creative means to quantify specific behaviors of athletes. Give your sport some thought for a moment: How can you help your athletes set realistic, specific, challenging performance goals? Initially it is not easy, but once you put your mind to it you can find many ways.

Short-Term Versus Long-Term Goals

Setting short-term goals rather than long-term goals is part and parcel of setting challenging, realistic, and specific performance goals.

Long-term goals simply cannot be very challenging, realistic, or specific because too many conditions and events are unknown that will inevitably have a bearing on whether or not the goals are achieved.

Through a series of short-term *goals*, long-term *objectives* can be pursued. While it is valuable for athletes to have long-term objectives that may extend one, two, or more years into the future, goals should not be set further ahead than a month. Goals that are projected much longer than this tend to be unrealistic, vague, and either too challenging or too easy. Illness, injury, life crises, rates of learning, availability of facilities and equipment, weather, and many other factors result in long-term goals being vague and ineffective.

Short-term goals are more effective because they are more motivating and provide immediate direction to actions the athlete should take. Long-term goals are likely to be too distant in time to have much effect, especially when athletes have many other factors competing for their time.

Short-term goals, as with specific and challenging goals, provide greater opportunity for you to reward success in moving toward long-term objectives. Also, they help you identify specific problems athletes may have in acquiring the skills needed to attain the goals. This will permit you to adjust your coaching plans to meet the exact needs of each athlete.

Individual Versus Team Goals

The emphasis in your goal-setting program should be on individual goals rather than on team goals. Team goals tend to be vague, to diffuse responsibility, and often are outcome goals that are not fully under the control of the team or its individual players. In fact, in many cases they are not goals at all but long-term objectives. More importantly, research has shown that team goals simply are not effective unless they are accompanied by individual goals that conform to the principles of good goal setting.

Yet team goals have value when the sport requires a high level of cooperation and coordination. Sports such as volleyball, football, basketball, and soccer will benefit from team goal setting because the group goals help motivate individuals to work together. Team goals, however, are effective only when individual goals also are clearly set. Without individual goals, athletes are more inclined to loaf.

It is not useful to set a goal for the team to bat .300 in the next tournament without having each player set a realistic but challenging goal for his or her own hitting. It is not helpful to set a goal of keeping the opposing team from scoring more than two touchdowns without developing specific goals for each individual on the defensive unit with regard to his assignment. This type of team goal is also poor because it is an outcome goal not fully under the control of your team. The scoring of points is partly influenced by the opposing team, and in football the ball can take some crazy bounces that can best be attributed to luck.

In setting team goals you must watch so that individual and team goals do not conflict with each other. For example, you might have a team goal to always pass until the team finds the open person for the shot; but if an individual has a goal to score thirty points, passing to a teammate with a slightly better shot may jeopardize achieving this individual goal. Also note that, in this particular example, the number of points scored by any one player is very much dependent upon the circumstances within the game; therefore, a goal to score a certain number of points is really more of an outcome goal than a performance goal. In basketball it would be better to set individual goals about making a certain percentage of shots when open from various zones on the court.

In summary, team goals can help motivate athletes to work more effectively together, but they must be accompanied by individual goals that hold the athlete responsible and that are within his or her control. You should be alert to, and take action to prevent, the possibility of individual goals conflicting with team goals.

Guidelines for Setting Goals

1. Set performance goals, not outcome goals, because athletes have control over performance goals. Thus they can rightfully accept responsiblity for their success or failure to achieve these goals.
2. Set challenging goals rather than easy goals because challenging goals are more motivating. However, if goals are too difficult athletes may not commit themselves to attaining them. Using the staircase approach to goal setting is a safe method of keeping goals challenging.
3. Set realistic goals. That task requires you to help your athletes resist the powerful forces that influence them to set unrealistic goals. A key to keeping goals realistic is to help athletes come to know who they really are.
4. Set specific rather than general goals because they direct the behavior of athletes more precisely and communicate clear expectations.
5. Set short-term goals because long-term goals cannot be very realistic, challenging, or specific. Too many conditions and events are unknown that will cause long-term goals to be ineffective.
6. Give emphasis to individual goals, but use team goals when you want to motivate the group to work better together. Caution: Avoid team outcome goals.

THE GOAL-SETTING TRAINING PROGRAM

In this final section of the chapter you will learn the steps to implement the Goal-Setting Training program.

Setting Goals

You have learned the six principles of goal setting. Now you need to put them into action.

Step 1: Task Analysis

To begin, you need to look at your sport in what may be a very new way. You need to consider the specific actions that each player must perform to accomplish the task successfully. For each position on the team and for each skill for that position, you need to describe the task to be successfully accomplished in *performance*, not outcome, terms.

For example, you might specify that the player must hit the serve with high velocity into the opponent's receiving court. Or the wrestler must retain control over his opponent when down on the mat by keeping the opponent continuously off balance. Or the athlete must try to recognize when he or she is becoming angry and redirect the anger into positive motivation and more intense concentration to perform the task.

A comprehensive task analysis for a sport such as football requires considerable time, yet it is an essential part of effective coaching, whether or not it be used for goal setting. So if you haven't done such an analysis, you should. Also, you may find it useful to consult some books on your sport that have performed these types of task analyses.

Step 2: Measuring Performance

This is another challenging task. Find a way to measure the performance of the task specified in Step 1. If possible, use objective measurement techniques such as time, distance, or weight, as long as these measures reflect the athletes' performances, not outcomes. The use of time in track and swimming, distance in shot putting or high jumping, or weight in weight lifting makes quantification easier than in sports such as football, wrestling, or gymnastics.

These latter sports all must rely on more subjective means to measure performance, although some objective methods can also be employed. Some football coaches quantify the performance of every position by reviewing videotapes of games while subjectively rating the performance of each player on each play. Some wrestling coaches use similar subjective rating systems to analyze each offensive and defensive action in a match. Gymnastics, because of the nature of the sport, has developed a highly refined subjective method of measuring performance.

Too often coaches rely on the inherent structure of the game to provide the only measurement of performance. A player either makes the basket, scores the goal, or gets a hit. Yet innovative coaches find means to measure performance more accurately in order to quantify specific performance goals. For example, soccer coaches will use streamers to identify various sections of the goal area, awarding more points for kicking the ball into certain zones under certain conditions. In basketball coaches may change the scoring system by awarding one point for the ball hitting the rim,

two points for hitting the rim and going through the net, and three points for ripping the net without touching the rim. In addition, they may multiply this score by the number assigned to various zones on the court that represent increasing distances from the basket.

The challenge is for *you* to find appropriate ways to measure the specific performances that are identified in Step 1. Coaches have not given this task sufficient attention and there is much need for innovation here. Increased use of video and electronics offers some useful possibilities, but the greatest prospects lie in the inventiveness of coaches who see the value in quantifying performance to an even greater extent.

Step 3: Set the Goal

Apply the principles reviewed in the last section to set realistic, challenging, specific performance goals. Be sure to specify the time span involved for achieving each goal. A goal cannot be sufficiently specific if athletes do not know when they are expected to attain it.

A question of considerable importance is how involved you should become in helping your athletes set the specific standards to be attained. That question will be addressed when I discuss the issue of gaining commitment to a goal.

Step 4: Ranking goals

When there are multiple goals, the athlete should rank them in order of importance. Or when there are a series of skills to be learned, and they are learned optimally in a particular sequence, then they should be structured into a staircase goal program. Coaches often can be of great assistance to their athletes in ordering the goals to be achieved.

Step 5: Coordination Requirements

Especially in team sports, certain goals can be achieved only by coordinating the specific tasks of each team member with those of other team members. Football players must know their assignments, have the skills to perform the tasks of blocking, tackling, and so on, and then know precisely *when* to execute these skills. Thus an important individual goal in team sports is timing the execution of a specific skill that interacts with the execution of teammates' skills.

Gaining Commitment

Now you have helped your athletes set specific, realistic, challenging, performance goals that will be measured. Next you want to make certain they are committed to these goals. Without commitment, these goals obviously will not affect their performances. Remember, as goals become more difficult, athletes tend to make less commitment to them because there is greater risk of failing.

You can do a number of things to increase athletes' commitments to their goals. Most importantly make sure that they are *their* goals, not yours. Athletes should participate actively in setting their own goals. This increases their feeling of responsiblity for their own actions, which helps to develop perceptions of internal control. Athletes not only commit greater effort to goals they set, they work harder to find methods to achieve these goals. If one strategy blocks their progress, they will look for another strategy. Coach-imposed goals simply are not owned by athletes, and if athletes do not own their goals, goal setting backfires.

This is not to say, however, that you should not be involved in the goal-setting process. Obviously you need to provide guidance, the degree depending a great deal on each athlete. When first learning the skills of the sport, players will prefer, and benefit from, greater guidance because they do not know the sport or their own abilities well enough to set appropriate goals. But as they learn the sport, you should then let them have greater say in setting their goals. The more mature, experienced, and confident an athlete, the less you should direct his or her setting of goals.

Another important tool for improving commitment to goals is the use of imagery. Maxwell Maltz's (1969) psychocybernetics places great significance on individuals imaging their goals, which he says will guide them automatically to attaining these goals. While I don't believe that goals are automatically pursued just because they are imaged, I do believe imagery is very helpful in achieving greater commitment to goals.

Imaging goals permits athletes to try out goals in their minds, and possibly even adjust them to a realistic level. Imaging goals will help them focus on the strategy or method for achieving a goal. Imaging the goal regularly, and visualizing its attainment, keeps the goal prominent in athletes' minds and develops anticipatory motivation for its eventual attainment. The use of imagery in goal setting is outlined in greater detail in the *Study Guide*.

Listed in Table 10.3 are some additional things you can do to increase commitment to achieving goals.

Table 10.3
Ways to Increase Commitment
to Achieving Goals

- Explain to your athletes the benefits of setting goals and pursuing them systematically. Also explain the principles of goal setting described in the last section in language your athletes can understand. Finally, help them understand the nature of the goals you jointly set with them (if they are not obvious) and the reasons a certain standard should be selected.

- Do not use threats or intimidation in urging players to set goals at a certain level.

- Be highly supportive of your athletes. The process of identifying specific goals and selecting a standard to be achieved should be done in such a way that it communicates you care about the athlete and respect his or her self-worth. Research shows that when coaches are supportive it gives athletes the confidence to set higher goals because they have less fear of failure or fear of punitive actions on the part of the coach.

- Give rewards for progress and attainment of goals. The use of praise, recognition, and tangible rewards can all increase commitment when they are correctly administered.

- Providing regular feedback about progress is essential to commitment and goal attainment. I will discuss this issue in greater detail shortly.

- When athletes see that you will help them with a plan of action that will develop the skills and knowledge they need to achieve their goals, they will have much greater commitment. The ingredients of this plan of action are discussed next.

Plan of Action

Setting goals and then expecting athletes to achieve them magically is unrealistic. Motivation of the highest degree is of little value if athletes do not have the basic skills and knowledge to play the game. Thus the next step in the GST program is to incorporate all the goals your athletes have set into your daily practice plans and competitive schedule.

It will be a challenge for you to find ways to accommodate the practice needs for what inevitably will be diverse goals. However, by your planning practices to meet the individual and team goals, your athletes will know that you are seeking to help them achieve their goals.

In individual sports it is easier to design unique practice plans to accommodate each athlete. In team sports it is more difficult, but can be done by devoting a portion of each practice to working on individual goals through drills or special activities and then by spending the remaining time practicing the coordination of these skills as a group.

Achieving certain goals may also require the planning of a series of competitive events to acquire the experience and training necessary. Other goals, such as acquiring psychological skills, may require either bringing in a sport psychologist to implement a program or implementing a program yourself based on what you have learned by reading this book.

Providing Feedback

Goal setting works only if there is timely feedback showing progress toward the goal. In one study (Bandura & Cervone, 1983), eighty cyclists were assigned to one of four different coaching conditions. Twenty cyclists set specific performance goals, twenty received feedback about their performances but were not instructed to set goals, twenty set goals and received feedback, and twenty did not set goals or receive feedback (control group). The results of the study, shown in Figure 10.5 in terms of percent of improvement, clearly reveal the importance of feedback in conjunction with goal setting.

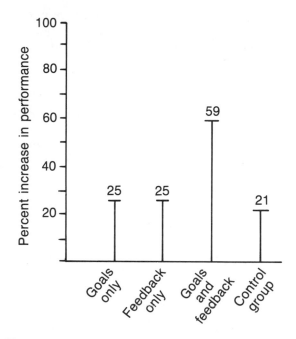

Figure 10.5 The results of Bandura and Cervone's (1983) study showing that using goals accompanied by feedback is more effective in improving performance.

Feedback directs behavior and motivates your athletes, but can be given only when performance is measured. It is my opinion that far too many coaches who know their sports very well fail to help their athletes as much as they could because they don't bother to measure their athletes' performances regularly and as accurately as possible. Thus the quality of the feedback is based on guesswork, or on outcomes rather than performances.

Coaches often defend their failure to provide detailed performance feedback by citing a litany of other tasks that must be completed and that leave them little time for anything else. Yet performance feedback seems to be at the heart of coaching—what could be more important?

Some coaches also believe that the most important feedback is whether or not their athletes win when competing, and they rely on this single criterion to judge the achievement of all athletes' goals. This clearly is an abrogation of responsibility in the performance of coaching duties.

When coaches devise accurate means of measuring performance, athletes often set spontaneous goals because of their competitive natures. Also the fact that you have gone to the trouble of measuring performance to give feedback is a signal to your athletes that you consider a skill to be important and that you care about their reaching this goal.

One very effective means of providing feedback is the use of a chart that shows the goals and the performances of the athletes. This feedback chart should contain three valuable sources of information: how well the athletes are performing now, what progress they have made, and how far away they are from reaching their goal.

Such charts are frequently kept in athletes' training logs, but sometimes are posted in the locker room. Generally, I recommend that they be kept private so that those who are progressing more slowly are not threatened or embarrassed. When the goal is a common one for all members of the team, and you believe some friendly competition would be helpful, then the posting of the feedback chart is recommended.

Some Final Points

Remember, success in achieving goals is not guaranteed, even with a good goal-setting program and well-executed action plans (although these certainly increase the chances of success). Goals may be harder than expected and obstacles may arise that could not be foreseen. The setting of specific, challenging goals in fact increases the chance of failure for some athletes and may increase diffidence, anxiety, or apathy.

But here is where you can make another tremendous contribution to your athletes. You can help them learn the lessons associated with losing in sports and failing to achieve their goals. The ability to recover from losing and failure is an important psychological quality that you can help athletes acquire as you implement the goal-setting program.

It has been my experience that the problems associated with failure can be minimized by your clearly communicating that the goal-setting program is a tool to help each athlete develop to his or her fullest. Never, never use failure to reach a goal as a means to chastise

or punish an athlete. Treat today's failure as a problem to be solved tomorrow by setting new goals and developing a better action plan.

A final point: In the midst of setting all these goals, it is important for you to keep one *objective* (not goal) in mind. Keep the sport fun for the athletes and you.

SUMMARY

1. Self-confidence is an accumulation of the athlete's unique experiences in many different achievement activities that results in the specific expectations he or she has about achieving success in a future activity.
2. Self-confidence falls on a continuum, diffidence on one end and overconfidence on the other, with optimal self-confidence in between.
3. False confidence comes in two forms: true overconfidence in those players who honestly believe they are better than they are, and affected confidence in athletes who are actually diffident.
4. Self-confidence is an expression of a person's self-worth, and cannot be developed optimally in athletes who have low self-worth.
5. The most significant self-confidence for athletes is confidence in their ability to acquire competencies.
6. The benefits of goal setting are numerous. It helps athletes perform better, reduces anxiety, builds self-confidence, and increases satisfaction.
7. The six key goal-setting principles are as follows: set performance goals, not outcome goals; set challenging rather than easy goals; set realistic rather than unrealistic goals; set specific rather than general goals; set short-term rather than long-term goals; and give emphasis to individual goals over team goals.
8. The GST program involves a task analysis that helps to identify specific performance goals, develop ways to

measure performance more specifically, set goals according to the six principles just mentioned, rank the goals when appropriate, and plan the coordination requirements to achieve the goals.

9. The best way to gain athletes' commitments to their goals is to let them set the goals while you provide guidance.

10. Coaches must develop plans of action that incorporate all the goals of their athletes into daily practice plans and the competitive schedule.

11. Goal setting works only if there is timely feedback showing progress toward reaching the goal.

Chapter 11
Implementing Psychological Skills Training

You have learned a great deal about the psychology of sport, and now it is time to launch your own Psychological Skills Training (PST) program. You could, of course, offer many reasons why you won't be able to do so. You could claim to be too busy with all the other regular duties of a coach. But you know that while the other things you do are important, helping your athletes develop psychological skills is at least equally important.

You could say you are not comfortable yet with the material presented in this book. But you recognize that it is quite normal to feel uncomfortable with all this new material. You realize that dedicated coaches will get comfortable with PST by first improving their own psychological skills and by working through the *Study Guide* exercises. Then, if still uncomfortable, they will begin by teaching one or two of the basic skills, and expand the program later.

You could easily claim that psychological skills training is not the function of a coach; it should be conducted by a sport psychologist. And unfortunately you can't find one or don't have the money to pay one. While it may be preferable to have a highly competent sport psychologist initiate the program, you know the reality of that prospect. Anyway, you know *coaching* is more than just teaching the physical skills of the sport and training the body. Excellent coaches take responsibility for their athletes' psychological preparation as well.

You could even conjure up such a weak reason as you are not convinced it is all worthwhile. But you know better. You recognize that coaches who don't help their athletes prepare psychologically will be at a significant disadvantage. Because you want to be the best you can be, and because you want the same for your athletes, you know the time has arrived for you to take responsibility for their psychological preparation.

This book is full of reasons why you should offer the PST program. It's simply beyond my realm of understanding why a coach would choose not to be a student of sport psychology. A knowledge of sport psychology is vital to successful coaching, whether success is defined as winning games or helping athletes develop into better human beings.

In this chapter you will learn how to launch your own PST program, incorporating all of the psychological skills you have learned in part III. Next we will look at precompetition preparation—how PST is used to prepare your athletes for competition. Then we will consider the important responsibilities you have after the contest—what I call *postcompetition debriefing*.

LAUNCHING THE PROGRAM

To get your program started, you first need to determine what specific goals you wish to accomplish with PST. Then I will outline the steps to launching your PST program. Finally, I will answer some commonly asked questions about starting a program.

Your Goals

The specific goals you establish for the use of PST will be determined ostensibly by your coaching philosophy, especially by your coaching objectives. The first issue you need to address is whether you embrace the philosophical tenets upon which the PST program is based as I have espoused them throughout this book. These tenets are as follows:

- Athletes need to become responsible for themselves.
- Enhancing an individual's self-worth is of key importance.
- People become more worthy by becoming more competent.
- The essential psychological qualities for being successful are skills that can be learned.
- Self-awareness is the first step to developing these psychological skills.
- These skills are developed through *systematic* training.

If you agree with these principles, then the PST program will add a powerful and exciting new dimension to your coaching endeavors.

Next you need to decide how you will use PST. Will you use the program just to increase the team's chances to win, or will you also emphasize helping your athletes to become better individuals? You will then need to determine whether you will launch the full program in a comprehensive way, or begin more slowly, selecting certain skills and then building on them later. Set your specific goals and use the principles of goal setting in the last chapter as you do so. If at all possible, I highly encourage you to initiate the entire program, but if you cannot, begin with at least a part of the program.

Basic Steps to Starting PST

OK, you have decided to initiate the PST program. That's the first step. Now what do you do?

Initial PST Orientation

You should begin the basic steps of initiating a PST program by introducing the entire program to the team during the off-season or early in the preseason training program. This is best done during a one- to two-hour meeting in which you present the key concepts of the program. Those concepts will include the content of chapter 5, which introduced you to PST.

When presenting these concepts, I like to use examples of athletes who have succeeded because they were psychologically skilled, and athletes who have failed because they lacked these skills. The most important idea I try to get across is that these psychological qualities that help athletes achieve their best performances are not inherited abilities but *skills* that can be learned through *systematic* practice. I then review briefly how important each of the psychological skills is, again using examples of how they influence performance.

When presenting this information, I find it best to let the athletes ask questions as I proceed. I try to keep the presentation informal and very upbeat. At the close of the session you should give athletes the questionnaires you decide to use to evaluate their psychological skills. In the *Study Guide* that accompanies this book you will find the questionnaires needed to evaluate each psychological skill.

Initial Evaluation

At this second session you should have all members of the team bring with them their completed questionnaires. In the session, explain how to score each questionnaire and discuss how to interpret the results.

The key to interpreting these questionnaires is to emphasize that they are not validated tests—athletes do not pass or fail. Their only purpose is to help athletes become more *aware* of their present skill levels for a particular psychological quality. That Bill scores twice as high as Frank does not mean Bill is twice as skilled as Frank is psychologically.

The important comparison to be made is not between athletes, but within one athlete over time. You want your athletes to determine their present skill levels, and then after practicing PST for a while, see if they perceive any improvement.

I recommend that the athletes not share the results with other members of the team, but that they do share them with you. A caution though: It is easy to make an offhand comment or joke about an athlete's score on one of these questionnaires, but don't do it. The results of these questionnaires will come close to the heart of your athlete's feelings of self-worth, and although you may be most innocent in your meaning, you will find your athletes very, very sensitive about their psychological skills.

In this same session, you want to introduce athletes to the *PST Journal*. This journal is one you will prepare for them and is a vital part of the PST program. The athletes will record the results of their periodical self-evaluations and the record of their psychological training in these journals. I have found from teaching psychological skills that these journals are essential in monitoring progress and recording other pertinent observations. The format for a *PST Journal* is provided in the *Study Guide*.

I also highly recommend that you provide athletes with a copy of one of the books listed below. The investment will be worth it, and will take a little pressure off you in delivering all the vital information during the educational phase.

- *In Pursuit of Excellence*, Orlick (1980)
- *Athlete's Guide to Mental Training*, Nideffer (1985)
- *Psyching for Sport*, Orlick (1986b)

PST Team Sessions

Now you are ready to introduce all members of the team to a specific psychological skill, each skill requiring a one- to two-hour session. Have your athletes take notes on the key concepts that you present, recording them in the *PST Journal*. After completing the education phase, and answering any questions your athletes have, you should offer periodic sessions for acquiring each psychological skill. The number of sessions will depend a great deal on which skill is being taught and on the skill levels of your athletes. You will need to use your judgment about how frequent these sessions should be.

If you have decided to teach all the skills that comprise the PST program, I recommend they be taught in the order presented in part III. I teach imagery first because it is the psychological skill used to practice all the other psychological skills. After this skill, I do not have any good justification for the order other than it has worked well for me. As you will recall, all the skills are interrelated, and the development of any one helps the development of others.

If you decide to teach less than the full program, my recommendation is that, if nothing else, you teach imagery and goal-setting skills. I recommend imagery because it is a building block for further psychological skill development; and I recommend goal-setting skills because, from my experience, the setting of outcome goals is the single biggest cause of psychological problems for athletes. When athletes learn to let go of winning as an immediate concern and focus on performance goals instead, then anxiety, concentration, and self-confidence problems often disappear.

Individual Counseling

Now you will want to meet with each athlete to discuss his or her level of skill for each psychological quality. Discuss with the athlete how to personalize the program so that it can meet his or her objectives. This is the time to help set goals as discussed in chapter 10, both performance goals and goals for psychological training.

This type of individual session is a terrific opportunity for you to get to know your athletes better. You can discover those things that are important to them, which becomes helpful to you in motivating them in the future. Furthermore, this is one good opportunity to individualize both the physical and psychological training of athletes—an important objective for you as coach, as I have emphasized throughout this book.

In this session you want to work with the athlete to outline his or her PST practice schedule. Much of the practice of PST can be done on the athlete's own time, but a schedule needs to be established and recorded in the *PST Journal*. Then the actual work done also needs to be recorded by the athlete along with any observations about the training. This individual session should close with you reinforcing how important you believe the PST program is and encouraging the athlete to accept responsibility for developing these skills.

Incorporating PST Into Practice and Game Plans

Learning to manage psychic energy and stress, improving concentration, and setting effective goals must be worked on in practice if they are to be functional skills when competing. You will need to plan practices with time given to allow athletes to get into flow and to work on integrating rather than always analyzing. You will want to structure drills and emphasize in your instructions the attentional demands of the task at hand. You will want to find ways in practice for athletes to measure the achievement of their new performance goals rather than the traditional outcome goals. This will all require substantial work on your part, but will make you a far more effective coach.

One of the most helpful things you can do in practice is simulate competition so that athletes can work on their psychological skills. Coaches often simulate the day of competition with physical preparation, but rarely do they emphasize psychological preparation. I recommend three levels of simulation. The first level is the practice of psychological skills by using imagery to simulate the competitive environment. The second level is for you to make practices simulate the day of competition as realistically as possible. The third level is for athletes to regard the competitive event itself as a simulation in which they can practice their psychological skills for future, more important competitive events.

Monitoring Progress

As the PST program progresses, you will want to consult periodically with each of your athletes to see how they are progressing. I highly recommend that you schedule individual meetings to review their *PST Journals*. Quite frankly, one reason for doing this is to increase their commitment to the program. As I mentioned, the biggest problem with PST is getting athletes to practice as systematically as they should. The *PST Journal*, and your monitoring of their progress, are very helpful in increasing commitment. Also, as you become more experienced with PST, you will be able to help athletes try alternative techniques if they are having difficulty with certain skills.

Season-End Evaluation

It is very helpful to have all athletes evaluate their psychological skills at the end of the season and determine what progress they have made. Based on this evaluation, it is a good time to plan additional psychological training that can be practiced during the off-season. You should also request that the athletes evaluate the PST program. You can develop a short questionnaire for that purpose or you can use the questionnaire developed by Orlick in *Coaches Training Manual to Psyching for Sport* (1986a).

You should also evaluate the psychological skills of each member of your team individually, involving your assistant coaches if you have assistants. You should then evaluate the entire PST program and consider how you can improve it the next year.

Questions About Getting Started

In the following section, I have responded to many of the questions coaches ask as they consider implementing a psychological skills training program. I hope that you will find this discussion valuable in your efforts to launch your own program.

Should PST Be Used With All Athletes?

PST can be beneficial to any athlete who has reached the "age of reason," which is usually about age seven. It has been my experience that postpubescent athletes are much more receptive to the program because through their sport experiences they have realized how important psychological factors are in their own performances. Young children are often so occupied with learning the physical skills of the sport they do not yet recognize the role of psychological skills. Younger children, however, can certainly benefit from PST, and I encourage you to introduce young athletes to this training. Imagery and physical relaxation skills generally are easier to teach to young athletes. Remember when teaching PST to children that it is essential to adjust the program to their level of reasoning and language comprehension.

Is PST Just for the More Skilled Athletes?

No, not at all. PST can be beneficial to every athlete. And, who knows, perhaps the development of these psychological skills will release hidden physical skills.

Should Athletes Be Required to Participate in PST?

Your coaching philosophy will be the source of the answer to this question. My view is that all members of a team should be required to attend the team meetings that introduce the program and explain the basics. Thereafter, each athlete should be given the freedom to choose whether or not he or she utilizes the program.

When Should I Initiate the PST Program?

It is best to do the basic training during the off-season or as early as possible during preseason training. It will take a long time to learn the psychological skills well; this is not a program where athletes practice for a few weeks to master the skills. Psychological skills are no different from physical skills. Full mastery takes years. Once the program is initiated, then it must become a regular part of your training program. You must include it in your practice plans and in your preparation for competition.

How Much Time Will It Take to Implement the PST Program?

The answer depends on how much of the program you decide to implement. You should plan on spending one to two hours to introduce the program initially and one to two hours to teach the educational phase for each psychological skill. Once the basics have been introduced to the team, you will need to spend considerable time helping each athlete structure the program to his or her specific needs. Finally, I recommend you give about fifteen minutes of time in each formal practice to work on one psychological skill. Gradually PST should become such an integral part of your practice and competitive routine that there is no separation between this program and your physical training.

What Are Some of the Obstacles to Implementing the Program?

The coach who decides not to do it, or to make only a token effort to implement PST, is the biggest problem. When coaches aren't committed to the program, when their philosophies are at odds with the philosophical tenets of PST, then the program usually fails, even when a highly competent sport psychologist implements it.

Are There Other Obstacles?

Yes. If the program is not presented correctly, athletes may not take it seriously. When the program is presented in a structured, organized form as suggested throughout part III, athletes are more likely to receive the program enthusiastically. It also is important that PST is presented in such a way as to encourage athletes to support each other's practice of these skills. If some of the team members joke about or ridicule athletes who are practicing PST, the program may be undermined. When athletes work in small, supportive groups to practice the skills, the group becomes a source of powerful rewards for making progress.

Where Can I Learn More About Psychological Skills Training?

You are in luck because more and more information is becoming available. I especially recommend Terry Orlick's *Psyching for Sport* (1986b) as a book your athletes should read, and Orlick's *Coaches Training Manual to Psyching for Sport* (1986a) is an excellent resource for your own use. Orlick has also written another book titled *In Pursuit of Excellence* (1980), which athletes and coaches alike have praised highly. I also recommend Robert Nideffer's *Athlete's Guide to Mental Training* (1985), especially for helping you with developing attentional skills. All these books are published by Human Kinetics Publishers. For more resources, review the references cited at the end of this book.

PRECOMPETITION PREPARATION

Precompetition preparation involves getting ready physically and psychologically. The physical preparation includes such things as the logistics of getting athletes and their equipment to the competitive site, arranging for meals and lodging, dressing at the competitive site, and warming up properly. The psychological preparation involves preparing the Integrator, setting realistic goals, mentally rehearsing the physical skills and strategies to be used, and preparing the mind for the psychological demands of the competition. Let's look more closely at what you need to consider in helping your athletes prepare for a competitive event.

General Psychological Preparation

Your objective should be clear. You want your athletes in the best physical and psychological condition possible. You want to optimize their chances of experiencing flow, of reaching that optimal energy zone. You want your athletes to be high in positive psychic energy and to have little or no negative psychic energy. Your athletes should feel in control. They should be so prepared for the unexpected that the unexpected can never occur.

The psychological preparation for a specific event should begin several days before the contest and involve the following activities.

Integration of Psychological Skills

When working on complex motor skills, you practice the components with various drills, and then work on integrating these components into the total game plan. As the contest nears, you tend to emphasize the integration of all these components because you know this is essential for optimum physical performance. Few coaches realize it, but you need to do exactly the same thing psychologically. Early in the week you can let the Analyzer be dominant, working to improve both physical and psychological skills, but as competition nears you want to let the Integrator be the driver and put the Analyzer in the back seat.

To put the Integrator in the driver's seat, have your athletes take a rest from their nor-mal routine of developing any one of the psychological skills for two days preceding competition. During this time they should shift from learning these skills to using these skills. Therefore, have them use their imagery skills to image the entire contest, seeing themselves executing the physical skills and strategies to the best of their abilities. Also encourage them to image their psychological preparation for the contest. This involves imaging the attainment of the optimal energy zone, seeing themselves manage any stress, selecting and shifting their attention effectively, and keeping focused on their *performance* goals. I suggest that your athletes practice this type of imagery at least three times per day for the two days prior to the competitive event, and one more time several hours before the event.

Next help athletes integrate their psychological skills by simulating the contest. I suggest a simulation practice not the day before the contest, but two days before the contest, just in case the simulation may be psychologically fatiguing. Make this simulation as real as you possibly can.

Setting Performance Goals

The day before the contest, if adequate information is available, have athletes record their goals in their *PST Journals*. These goals should be set by your athletes, but in consultation with you if necessary, using the goal-setting principles of chapter 10. For your athletes to evaluate these performance goals, you will need to have in place the systems you have designed to measure them properly. Remember—no longer are you measuring just the outcome of the contest.

Engineer the Environment

Both you and your athletes should be prepared to engineer the environment as much as possible to accommodate your athletes' preferences. Your mutual objective is to eliminate any hassles that may cause athletes to experience unnecessary distractions or stress. You or the athletes need to make certain that wake-up calls are promptly made, meals are eaten on schedule, transportation is properly planned, equipment is in proper condition, and room assignments are made. You can also engineer to some extent who communicates with whom, looking to bring athletes together who provide each other with social support. At the higher levels of competition, you will need to engineer the media too. You should set rules about when the media can visit with athletes and when they are off limits.

There are countless other factors that could be mentioned, but I think you get the idea. The objective is to minimize disruption, to create a hassle-free environment that lets athletes focus on the positive side of competition. Some of this engineering is your responsibility, and some is the responsibility of your athletes. Don't coddle them too much in trying to make the environment perfect; let them arrange the environment to suit their preferences as much as possible, but they should also have the psychological skills to cope with environments that are *not* perfect—that is what psychological skills are all about.

On-Site Preparation

Your athletes' first objective when they arrive at the site of the contest is to become thoroughly familiar with it, if they are not already. Also, they should begin to consider any other environmental factors, such as the weather, that might influence the competition. If they find factors in the environment that cause them concern, you or they should have them changed if possible. If it is not possible to change them, then plan a strategy for dealing with them. Remember—you want to eliminate the unexpected.

Within one hour of competition, your athletes should reexamine their goals and make any appropriate adjustments. Weather or playing conditions, an athlete's physical health, and changes in the opponents all may be good reasons for adjusting goals. Some coaches may see these last-minute changes in goals as a potential source of excuses, and they may be, but if the goal-setting training program has been properly learned, this won't be the case. Athletes will not need excuses when they know their worth is not being judged on the basis of the outcome.

Next athletes need to begin moving toward their optimal energy zones. Based on previous competitions, athletes begin psyching up to increase positive psychic energy, or psyching down using stress management techniques, to find their optimal energy zones. Finding the optimal energy zone is a vague, subjective process, but through the PST program athletes can become much better at finding it more consistently. As part of the effort to get in the right frame of mind, to be high in positive psychic energy, I highly recommend the pre-event routine.

Pre-Event Routine

The pre-event routine can be used prior to the start of a game such as football, basketball, or baseball, or it can be used prior to an event within a game, or series of trials within a contest, such as batting in baseball, or high jumping, or shooting free throws. Many athletes have developed their own routines prior to a contest. They eat the same food before each game, they put their clothing on a certain way, and they go through a specific routine for warming up. Why do they do this? Typically, when having played very well, they go back and look at what they did to find something in their preparation to explain their superior performance. Because performing well consistently is so difficult in sports, athletes look for any type of reason to discover a cause, even if it's the wearing of an orange sock or a blue sweater. Most routines therefore emerge from superstititious beliefs that have developed over the years about what may have caused an excellent performance.

I used to think superstitions were dumb and discouraged such beliefs in athletes, but not any more. I've learned that whether they are bizarre superstitions or rational pre-event routines, they are distinctly beneficial. Remember, I emphasized earlier that athletes benefit by trying to control their environment, and routines are a way of implementing control over some aspects of the sports environment. They provide a stable element in an environment that may be highly unstable. The pre-event routine can be a trigger to begin concentrating and using other psychological skills, and is especially helpful to highly anxious athletes because it keeps them occupied with the routine, denying their analytical minds the opportunity to engage in negative self-talk.

Pre-event routines can begin several days before the contest, but let's consider the extended routines as part of the general precompetition preparation and restrict the use of the term *pre-event routines* to those activities performed immediately before an event. I believe these actions, moments before performing, play an especially important part in the total psychological preparation of the athlete.

There is no one ideal pre-event routine; whatever the athlete is most satisfied with is certainly best. However, we know some of the elements that constitute a better routine than others. These elements are as follows:

- The routine should begin with some *cue* that signals the athlete to begin the routine. This may be a certain time, such as five minutes before game time, or some event in the contest, or some activity that athletes always do, such as remove their warm-ups or take a golf club from the bag.
- After the cue, I suggest athletes engage in a very short *imagery* session where they image themselves doing the task, seeing, and especially kinesthetically feeling themselves executing the skills very well.
- As athletes complete the imagery, they should focus on the positive feeling of having performed well. This type of *affirmation* is a useful positive self-reinforcement, something many of us do not do often enough.
- Next the athlete should have a *checklist* of activities to perform, almost like a pilot going through a preflight check of the instruments. This list of activities can include checking equipment, clothing, position of the opponents, the score, almost anything that seems useful in preparing to execute the skill. The purpose of this checklist is to help athletes focus their attention on the task at hand.
- As athletes complete the checklist, *attention* should be focused fully on the appropriate cues for performing the task as they have learned through their attention control training.

This entire routine of cuing in, imaging, affirming oneself, reviewing the checklist, and focusing attention may take as little as fifteen seconds or as long as five minutes, depending on the athlete and the sport event. It is, of course, a highly individualized activity, something each athlete has to develop for him- or herself. However, you can be helpful by providing guidance to developing a useful routine.

Some Common Questions About Pre-Event Preparation

When Coaching a Team Sport, Should the Coach Establish the Pre-Event Routine?

For those activities where the team needs to coordinate its practice, such as the running of plays in football or basketball, then of course you will need to schedule these. However, for the psychological preparation, you should permit each athlete to prepare in his or her own way. Some athletes will want quiet so they can contemplate; others want to be active and talking. Both can be ideal ways for certain individuals to prepare. You should try to find ways to accommodate both styles. I think it is an error to ask the entire team to spend five or ten minutes in quiet meditation to think about the game. That may help some, but for highly anxious athletes who engage in a lot of negative self-talk, this quiet time may only lead to more negative self-talk. Perhaps these anxious athletes have found that if they keep busy talking with others they don't have time to talk to themselves.

What Do I Do to Get the Team Psyched Up?

You should know the answer to this by now. If you have done a good job with PST, you should need to do little. The responsibility for being optimally psyched lies with each of your athletes. You certainly don't want to give the traditional pep talk. What you want to do, rather, is be available so that any athlete who wishes can consult with you, and be observant for anyone who appears to be needing assistance.

Is the Pre-Event Routine Different for Different Sports and Different Events Within Sports?

Yes. Team sports will be different from individual sports. Long-distance events will be different from short-distance events and continuous performing events will be different from intermittent performing events, such as putting the shot. Help your athletes design a routine that best fits them and the event.

Intermittent Performing Events Seem to Present Unique Demands on the Athlete to Avoid Engaging in Negative Self-Talk. What Can Be Done to Help Athletes in These Events?

I have found imagery to be especially helpful for athletes who tend to engage in considerable negative self-talk when a performance is below their expectations in intermittent performing events. For several weeks prior to the competition I have athletes mentally rehearse an ideal performance, and if film or tape of such a performance is available, I have them view it and then practice imaging it. This is repeated many times while in a physically relaxed state. Then, between trials during the contest, the athletes rehearse this ideal performance rather than focus on the possible errors made in the previous trial. I also find that the pre-event routine itself, with the positive imagery emphasized in the pre-event routine, is especially helpful in keeping them occupied with constructive thinking.

What Do Athletes Do if Their Pre-Event Routines Are Disrupted by Something?

First, they should expect this to happen sometimes and be prepared to deal with it in one of two ways. If time permits, simply repeat the entire routine. If time does not permit, they should have an abbreviated routine planned that consists primarily of focusing attention on the correct cues before proceeding to perform.

POSTCOMPETITION DEBRIEFING

The contest is over. The athletes rush to the locker room either elated with victory or sullen in defeat. They dress and quickly depart with friends until the next practice. That is a fairly typical scenario of events with many teams. But it is not the best one for helping athletes develop better psychological skills, and thus better physical skills.

Sport psychologists have learned a great deal about the importance of how athletes attribute causes to the results of a contest, what the Analyzer says to them about how they played. As you can appreciate, how athletes interpret the outcome of one contest is likely to have substantial influence on how they perceive the next contest. Consequently, you do not want to leave these interpretations, or what psychologists call *attributions*, to chance. An important part of your continued psychological preparation of athletes is to assist them in making the most effective attributions possible.

Your objective is to help athletes make attributions about their performances that will enhance their self-worth by taking credit for when they performed well and responsibility for when they performed poorly. You want them to keep the importance of the contest in proper perspective. And you also want to provide direction for future development of both physical and psychological skills.

When do you do all this? You want to provide a general debriefing shortly after the contest. Then you want to go into greater detail at the next practice when you have had more time to evaluate the contest. To help your athletes develop constructive attributions immediately after the contest requires that you have the psychological skills we have been studying. If you cannot control your emotions, if you preach performance goals but evaluate yourself and your players on the basis of the outcome, then your postcompetition debriefing is likely to undo much of the work you devoted to launching the PST program.

The Four Basic Debriefings

The results of any contest for any athlete can be placed into one of four categories, as shown in Figure 11.1. Your athlete or team can have won or lost the game, and they can have played well or poorly. Based on what we have learned from attribution psychology, I will suggest some appropriate comments for your debriefing remarks based on these four categories.

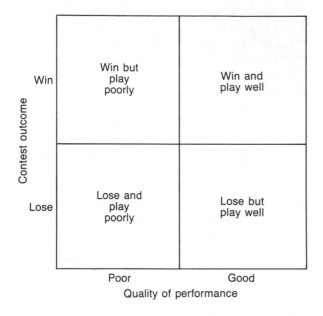

Figure 11.1 The four categories used in debriefing athletes based on the outcome of the contest and the quality of performance.

Win and Play Well

When athletes win and have played well, you want to have them attribute their success to their abilities—both their physical and psychological skills. This will increase their self-worth and self-confidence. You want to emphasize being satisfied, not so much from winning (although that is nice), but from a solid effort and from their performance. If this is a major win, you will want to try to keep the athletes from believing that now they are so superior they need not continue to put forth so much effort. On the other hand, you do not want to diminish the significance of the accomplishment. Thus you may need to reduce the importance somewhat. For a less significant win, you may need to increase the importance a bit.

After you have had adequate opportunity to evaluate everyone's play, you should reward those players who displayed solid effort and who achieved their performance goals rather than simply recognize those who scored the most points or perhaps were placed in the

spotlight by the media. In other words, recognize those who performed well, not those who happened to have good outcomes.

Then you will want to focus attention on those aspects of the team and individual play that need improvement. This needs to be constructive feedback, not highly critical feedback that attacks athletes' self-worth. It needs to be feedback that is specific enough that the correct skill can be practiced and that time can be made available in practice to work on it. It also is helpful in practice to review those skills that were performed well and keep vivid what athletes did correctly.

Win But Play Poorly

When the team and individual players have won the game but performed poorly you want them to attribute success to a weak opponent rather than to their ability. If their effort was also inadequate, they should be asked to examine why. The reason for making these comments in your debriefing is that you do not want athletes rewarding themselves for achieving outcome goals and crediting their ability and effort when the reason for victory was a weak opponent, or possibly luck.

You should make the same comments regarding the importance of the game when the athletes win and play well. Reward individuals who play well and make good effort, and focus attention on improvement. At the next practice you will want to discuss the need for better psychological preparation and effort. Encourage athletes to identify and work on the skills that they did not perform well. The approach here should not be punitive, but positive and constructive.

Lose But Play Well

When your team loses but plays well, you will want to attribute the loss to the superior play of the opponent and focus on the need to improve skills in order to win in the future. For many coaches this is a very difficult debriefing, for they are reluctant ever to admit that another team is actually superior. Remember, though, being superior in play one day does not mean being superior from that time on. When the team loses but plays well, coaches are inclined not to see the good play, or they may focus on the luck of the opponent or officials' bad calls. Focusing on these reasons for losing, unless they clearly are the causes, is not as helpful in the long-term psychological preparation of your athletes as attributing the loss to the opponent being superior *that day*. Remember, you want your athletes to take credit for when they perform well and responsibility for when they perform poorly. Through these attributions, they will be intrinsically motivated to perform better in the future.

When your team loses but plays well you should emphasize your pleasure from a solid effort and performance despite the loss. This is a good time to emphasize the achievement of the performance goals. You should also decrease the importance of the outcome if this was a contest of major importance in order to reduce damage to the athletes' perceptions of their own self-worth or perceived ability. In turn, you will want to increase the importance of a minor loss to increase motivation to improve skills in future practices.

Lose and Play Poorly

When your team loses and the individuals play poorly you will want to attribute failure to inferior effort, to the need to improve physical skills, and possibly to the need to improve psychological skills. You should express your dissatisfaction with the poor effort and performance, but not with the loss.

You will want to decrease the importance of a major loss to reduce the damage to your athletes' perceptions of their ability and increase the importance of a minor loss to increase motivation to improve skills. Reward only those players who displayed solid effort and who achieved their performance goals.

You will also want to focus attention on the instability of performance and the possibility that the team just had a bad game, which will inevitably occur from time to time. The athletes should be encouraged to learn from the game, but not to dwell on the loss. This is a terrible time to offer constructive criticism. Wait until the next practice to work on improving both physical and psychological skills.

For all four categories, you should repeatedly remind your athletes to look at any one contest as a test of achieving their long-term objectives. A contest is a check of their progress toward the objectives they have established. If they achieve their goals, they should thoroughly reward themselves for their accomplishments and look forward to taking the next step toward their objectives. If they did not achieve their goals, then they should look for the reason and return to practice with the conviction that they will improve. This is a highly constructive way to look at each contest, to keep a proper perspective about winning and losing.

Two Other Postcompetition Activities

As part of your PST program for your athletes, you should ask them to do several things after each game. First, have them image those things that were performed well. Athletes have the tendency to focus on those skills that were performed poorly. They can have played brilliantly 99 percent of the time, but will focus only on the 1 percent when they did not. While it is helpful to strive for perfection, it is equally helpful to strengthen the right mental blueprint of a well-performed skill by recalling it vividly in imagery. Encourage athletes to let go of their mistakes until the next practice and then work on them.

Finally, athletes should record their observations about the contest in their *PST Journals*. They should evaluate their psychological skills for the contest. They should note any unusual feelings or perceptions that affected their play. They should especially try to determine where they were on the psychic energy continuum and what they might do next time to come closer to achieving the optimal energy zone if it was not achieved. They should record anything they did differently that had a positive or negative effect on their play.

The *PST Journal* is vital for helping athletes see trends over a long period of time. Without it the changes in psychological skills and the deficiencies in psychological preparation just aren't observed. This journal should be completed within twenty-four hours after the contest so the perceptions are as fresh as possible. Replaying the contest through imagery is an excellent way for athletes to recall their emotions and psychological skills when preparing to record their observations in their journals.

SUMMARY

1. The first step to starting a PST program is for you to determine your specific

goals for this program, and especially to consider whether the philosophical tenets of PST are compatible with your coaching philosophy.

2. The basic steps for starting the PST are (a) an initial orientation, (b) athletes' initial evaluation, (c) team sessions to learn the basic skills, (d) individual counseling, (e) incorporation of PST into practice and game plans, (f) monitoring progress, and (g) a season-end evaluation.

3. The *PST Journal* is an essential tool for athletes to monitor their progress in developing and using PST.

4. The general steps for precompetition psychological preparation include preparing the Integrator, setting performance goals, and engineering the environment to the extent possible.

5. An important part of the athlete's on-site psychological preparation is the pre-event routine. A good routine consists of cueing, imaging, affirming, checking, and attending.

6. Coaches have tended to neglect or haphazardly approach postcompetition debriefings. These debriefings are important because they help athletes make appropriate attributions about the contest that affect their psychological preparation for future competition.

7. Recommendations are made in this chapter for coaches' debriefings based on whether the team or individual won or lost, and played well or poorly.

8. After each contest athletes should review their successes using imagery and should record their observations about their psychological responses in the *PST Journal*.

References

Arnold, M.B. (1946). On the mechanisms of suggestion and hypnosis. *Journal of Abnormal and Social Psychology, 41*, 107-128.

Bandura, A., & Cervone, D. (1983). Self-evaluative and self-efficacy mechanisms governing the motivational effects of goal systems. *Journal of Personality and Social Psychology, 45*, 1017-1028.

Barber, T.X., & Wilson, S.C. (1979). Guided imagining and hypnosis: Theoretical and empirical overlap and convergence in a new creative imagination scale. In A.A. Sheikh & J.T. Shaffer (Eds.), *The potential of fantasy and imagination* (pp. 214-271). New York: Brandon House.

Bennis, W., & Nanus, B. (1985). *Leaders: The strategies for taking charge.* New York: Harper & Row.

Blake, R., & Mouton, J. (1969). *Building a dynamic corporation through grid organization development.* Reading, MA: Addison Wesley.

Blakeslee, T.R. (1980). *The right brain.* Garden City, NY: Doubleday.

Brandon, N. (1983). *Honoring the self: The psychology of confidence and respect.* New York: Bantam.

Brodie, J., & Houston, J.D. (1974). *Open field.* Boston: Houghton Mifflin.

Burton, D. (1983). *Evaluation of goal setting, training on selected cognitions and performance of collegiate swimmers.* Unpublished doctoral dissertation, University of Illinois, Urbana.

Cautela, J.R., & McCullough, L. (1978). Covert conditioning: A learning-theory perspective on imagery. In J.L. Singer & K.S. Pope (Eds.), *The power of human imagination* (pp. 227-278). New York: Plenum.

Christina, R.W., & Corcos, D.M. (1988). *Coaches guide to teaching sport skills.* Champaign, IL: Human Kinetics.

Corbin, C. (1972). Mental practice. In W.P. Morgan (Ed.), *Ergogenic aids and muscular performance* (pp. 94-118). New York: Academic Press.

Csikszentmihalyi, M. (1975). *Beyond boredom and anxiety.* San Francisco: Jossey-Boss.

de Charms, R. (1976). *Enhancing motivation.* New York: Irvington Publishers.

De Mille, R. (1973). *Put your mother on the ceiling: Children's imagination games.* New York: Viking Press.

DeVore, S., & DeVore, G. (1981). *Sybervision: Muscle memory programming for every sport.* Chicago: Chicago Review Press.

Dowling, T. (1970). *Coach: A season with Lombardi.* New York: Norton.

Dyer, W.G. (1976). *Insight to impact.* Provo, UT: Brigham Young University Press.

Eccles, J. (1958). The physiology of imagination. *Scientific American, 199*(3), 135.

Ellis, A., & Grieger, R. (1977). *Handbook of rational-emotive therapy.* New York: Springer.

Ellis, A., & Harper, R.A. (1975). *A new guide to rational living.* North Hollywood, CA: Wilshire.

Fabun, D. (1970). *Three roads to awareness.* Beverly Hills, CA: Glencoe Press.

Feltz, D.L., & Landers, D.M. (1983). The effects of mental practice on motor skill learning and performance: A meta-analysis. *Journal of Sport Psychology, 5*, 25-57.

Fenz, W.D., & Epstein, S. (1967). Gradients of physiological arousal of experienced and novice parachutists as a function of an approaching jump. *Psychosomatic Medicine, 29*, 33-51.

Frank, J. (1961). *Persuasion and healing.* Baltimore: Johns Hopkins Press.

Gallwey, W.T. (1974). *The inner game of tennis.* New York: Random House.

Gazes, P.C., Sovell, B.F., & Dellastatious, J.W. (1969). Continuous radioelectrocardiographic monitoring of football and basketball coaches during games. *American Heart Journal, 78*, 509-515.

Goleman, D. (Narrator). (1976). *Flow and mindfulness: An instructional cassette.* New York: Psychology Today.

Gordon, T. (1974). *Teacher effectiveness training.* New York: David McKay.

Griffith, C.R. (1930). *Psychology of football.* Unpublished manuscript.

Hall, E.T. (1966). *The hidden dimension.* New York: Doubleday.

Harris, D.V., & Harris, B.L. (1984). *The athlete's guide to sports psychology*. Champaign, IL: Leisure Press.

Harris, T.A. (1967). *I'm OK—you're OK*. New York: Avon.

Hickman, C.R., & Silva, M.A. (1984). *Creating excellence*. New York: New American Library.

Jacobson, E. (1932). Electrophysiology of mental activities. *American Journal of Psychology, 44*, 677-694.

Johnson, D.W. (1981). *Reaching out: Interpersonal effectiveness and self-actualization* (2nd ed.). Englewood Cliffs, NJ: Prentice-Hall.

Kerr, J.H. (1985). The experience of arousal: A new basis for studying arousal effects in sport. *Journal of Sport Science, 3*, 169-179.

Killy, J.C. (1977, September). Skiing is all in your head. *Ski*, pp. 100-102, 104, 106.

Knapp, M.L. (1978). *Nonverbal communication in human interaction* (2nd ed.). New York: Holt, Rinehart & Winston.

Kolbenschlag, M. (1976). Tranquilizers, towel drawing, tantrums: All part of work stress. *The Physician and Sportsmedicine, 4*(1), 97, 99, 101.

Kolonay, B.J. (1977). *The effects of visuo-motor behavior rehearsal on athletic performance*. Unpublished master's thesis, Hunter College, City University of New York.

Kroll, W. (1982). Competitive athletic stress factors in athletes and coaches. In L.P. Zaichkowsky & W.E. Sime (Eds.), *Stress management for sport* (pp. 1-10). Reston, VA: American Alliance for Health, Physical Education, Recreation and Dance.

Landers, D.M. (1985). Psychophysiological assessment and biofeedback: Application for athletes in closed skilled sports. In J.H. Sandweiss & S.L. Wolf (Eds.), *Biofeedback and sport science* (pp. 63-105). New York: Plenum Press.

Lane, J.F. (1980). Improving athletic performance through visuo-motor behavior rehearsal. In R.M. Suinn (Ed.), *Psychology in sports: Methods and applications* (pp. 316-320). Minneapolis: Burgess.

Lang, P.J. (1970, October). Autonomic control: Or learning to play the internal organs. *Psychology Today*, pp. 38-41, 98, 100, 102.

Levinson, H. (1968). *The exceptional executive*. Cambridge, MA: Howard University Press.

Libby, B. (1982). *The coaches*. New York: Dutton.

Lindemann, R. (1973). *Relieve tension the autogenic way*. New York: Wyden.

Loehr, J.E. (1978). *Athletic excellence training*. Denver: Athletic Excellence.

Lowe, R. (1971). *Stress, arousal, and task performance of Little League baseball players*. Unpublished doctoral disseration, University of Illinois, Urbana.

Luria, A.R. (1968). *The mind of a mnemonist*. New York: Basic Books.

Maltz, M. (1969). *Psychocybernetics*. Englewood Cliffs, NJ: Prentice Hall.

Marks, D. (1977). Imagery and consciousness: A theoretical review from an individual difference perspective. *Journal of Mental Imagery, 2*, 285-347.

Martens, R. (1982, September). *Imagery in sport*. Paper presented at the Medical and Scientific Aspects of Elitism in Sport Conference, Brisbane, Australia.

Martens, R., Christina, R.W., Harvey, J.S., Jr., & Sharkey, B.J. (1981). *Coaching young athletes*. Champaign, IL: Human Kinetics.

Maslow, A.H. (1962). *Toward a psychology of being*. New York: Van Nostrand.

Mechikoff, R.A., & Kozar, B. (1983). *Sport psychology: The coach's perspective*. Springfield, IL: C.C. Thomas.

Mehrabian, A. (1968, September). Communication without words. *Psychology Today*, pp. 52-55.

Mehrabian, A. (1976, August). The three dimensions of emotional reaction. *Psychology Today*, pp. 57, 59-60, 114.

Meichenbaum, D. (1977). *Cognitive-behavior modification*. New York: Plenum Press.

McKay, M., Davis, M., & Fanning, P. (1981). *Thoughts and feelings: The art of cognitive stress intervention*. Richmond, CA: New Harbinger.

McKay, M., Davis, M., & Fanning, P. (1983). *Messages: The communication book*. Oakland, CA: New Harbinger.

Moore, K. (1983, April). His was a great act of faith. *Sports Illustrated*, pp. 36-45.

Morgan, P. (1978, April). The mind of the marathoner. *Psychology Today*, pp. 38-49.

Nicklaus, J. (1976). *Play better golf*. New York: King Features Syndicate.

Nideffer, R.M. (1976). *The inner athletes*. New York: Crowell.

Nideffer, R.M. (1985). *Athletes' guide to mental training*. Champaign, IL: Human Kinetics.

Orlick, T. (1980). *In pursuit of excellence*. Champaign, IL: Human Kinetics.

Orlick, T. (1986a). *Coaches training manual to psyching for sport*. Champaign, IL: Human Kinetics.

Orlick, T. (1986b). *Psyching for sport*. Champaign, IL: Human Kinetics.

Peters, T.J., & Austin, N. (1985). *A passion for excellence*. New York: Random House.

Powell, G.E. (1973). Negative and positive mental practice in motor skill acquisition. *Perceptual and Motor Skills, 37*, 312-316.

Powell, J. (1969). *Why am I afraid to tell you who I am?* Niles, IL: Argus.

Pryor, K. (1984). *Don't shoot the dog!* New York: Simon & Schuster.

Richardson, A. (1967a). Mental practice: A review and discussion (Part 1). *Research Quarterly, 38*, 95-107.

Richardson, A. (1967b). Mental practice: A review and discussion (Part 2). *Research Quarterly, 38*, 263-273.

Rogers, C.R. (1983). *Freedom to learn for the 80s*. Columbus, OH: Charles E. Merrill.

Runner's World Gold Medal Exclusive. (1984, January). [Interview with Carl Lewis]. *Runner's World*, pp. 21-30.

Ryan, E.D. (1979, May). *Athletic scholarships and intrinsic motivation*. Paper presented at the North American Society for the Psychology of Sport and Physical Activity Conference, Trois-Rivieres, Quebec, Canada.

Ryan, E.D., & Simons, J. (1983). What is learned in mental practice of motor skills: A test of the cognitive-motor hypothesis. *Journal of Sport Psychology, 5*, 419-426.

Sabock, R.J. (1985). *The coach* (3rd ed.). Champaign, IL: Human Kinetics.

Samuels, M., & Samuels, N. (1975). *Seeing with the mind's eye*. New York: Random House.

Sathre, S., Olson, R.W., & Whitney, C.I. (1973). *Let's talk*. Glenview, IL: Scott, Foresman.

Selye, H. (1956). *The stress of life*. New York: McGraw-Hill.

Simonton, O.C., Matthews-Simonton, S., & Creighton, J. (1978). *Getting well again: A step-by-step self-help guide to overcoming cancer for patients and their families*. Los Angeles: Tarchers.

Singer, J.L., & Pope, K.S. (1978). *The power of human imagination*. New York: Plenum Press.

Smith, A. (1975). *Powers of mind*. New York: Ballantine.

Suinn, R.M. (1976, July). Body thinking: Psychology for Olympic champs. *Psychology Today*, pp. 38-43.

Suinn, R.M. (1980). *Psychology in sports: Methods and applications*. Minneapolis: Burgess.

Thom, L. (1986, January/February). [Untitled article]. *Coaching Review*, p. 23-27.

Walker, S.H. (1980). *Winning: The psychology of competition*. New York: Norton.

Wallace, R.K., & Benson, H. (1972). The physiology of mediation. *Scientific American, 226*, 84-91.

Warren, W.E. (1983). *Coaching and motivation: A practical guide to maximum athletic performance*. Englewood Cliffs, NJ: Prentice-Hall.

Weinberg, R.S., Seabourne, T.G., & Jackson, A. (1981). Effects of visuomotor behavior rehearsal, relaxation and imagery on karate performance. *Journal of Sport Psychology, 3*, 228-238.

Index